SELECTED WRITINGS

OF

MAHAMAHOPADHYAYA

GOPINATH KAVIRAJ

INDICA

Cover illustration: Photo of M.M. Gopinath Kaviraj by Richard Lannoy, 1957

First published in 1990

Published in 2006 by

Indica Books
D 40 / 18 Godowlia
Varanasi - 221 001 (U.P.)
India

indicabooksindia@gmail.com
www.indicabooks.com

ISBN: 81-86569-60-X

Printed in India : *First Impression*, New Delhi
011-22481754, 09811224048

Photo by Richard Lannoy, 1957

Contents

*

~1~

The Doctrine of Pratibha in Indian Philosophy

In the history of philosophical thought in India one very often meets with the problem which starts from a sense of the inadequacy of intellectual powers and points to the necessity of recognising a distinct faculty for the explanation of phenomena beyond the range of these powers. It was in attempting to offer a solution to this problem that the doctrine of *Pratibhā*, or as it is somewhere called, *Prajñā*, had its origin.

The word *Pratibhā*, which literally means a flash of light, a revelation, is usually found in literature in the sense of wisdom, characterised by immediacy and freshness. It might be called the super-sensuous and supra-rational apperception, grasping truth directly, and would, therefore, seem to have the same value, both as a faculty and as an act in Indian philosophy, as Intuition has in some of the Western systems. From a general survey of the literature concerned and a careful analysis of its contents, it would appear that the word is used in two distinct but allied senses:

1) To indicate any kind of knowledge, which is not sense-born nor of the nature of an inference. But as such knowledge may range over a wide variety of subjects, it is possible to distinguish it again as lower and higher. The phenomena of ordinary clairvoyance and telepathy are instances of the former, while the latter kind is represented in the supreme wisdom of the saint.

2) In the latter sense, however, the use of the term is restricted to the Āgamic literature, where it stands for the Highest Divinity, understood as Principle of Intelligence and conceived as female. In other words, *Pratibhā*, otherwise known as *Parā Saṁvit* or *Citi Śakti*, means in the Āgama, especially in the Tripurā and Trika sections of it, the power of self-revelation or self-illumination of the Supreme Spirit, with which it is essentially and eternally iden-

tical. The employment of the word in the sense of 'guru' (as in Abhinavagupta, *Tantrasāra*, p. 120) comes under this second head.

The prime characteristic of this super-sensuous knowledge is, as we have observed, its immediacy and intense clarity. According to all the systems, such knowledge is considered transcendental, being held to be free from the time and space limitations, which are imposed as a matter of necessity on all inferior knowledge and from the indispensable conditions which govern the origin or manifestation of the latter. Consequently we find in every respect a strongly marked contrast between the two. This higher knowledge dispenses, in its rise, with the need of sense-organs and, unlike reflective judgement, with that of the rational faculty. It reveals the past and the future as in a single flash, and also the absent and the remote. Nothing escapes its searching light. It is aptly described as simultaneously illuminating everything in every aspect and as eternal (*Yoga Sūtra*, III, 84).

In Nyāya-Vaiśeṣika, and occasionally in Vedānta, the term *Pratibhā* and sometimes *Ārṣa jñāna* is employed to express this supreme knowledge, a term which has the sanction of usage in Yoga literature. The word *Prajñā* too is sometimes used in Yoga works as a synonym of *Pratibhā*. In Vyākaraṇa both *Prajñā* and *Pratibhā* are to be found, and these are declared identical in sense with the Paśyanti stage of the four-fold *Vāk*. The Āgamas retain all these terms and add *Saṁveda* to the list of synonyms. The Buddhist are familiar with the name *Prajñā* even in their oldest canonical literature, but do not seem to know anything of *Pratibhā* or the other terms. But the Jainas have, curiously enough, not a single one of these words in their philosophical vocabulary, though they have fully treated of the subject in their works. They have discussed the question in their own way and under their own technical appellation e.g., *avadhijñāna*, *kevalajñāna* and so forth. From a survey of the entire field it will be evident that the problem has recurred everywhere and has everywhere, to all appearances, been similarly dealt with.

-I-

NYĀYA VAIŚEṢIKA

In early Vaiśeṣika and Nyāya literature we find not only indication of the existence of the doctrine, but even the very term *Pratibhā*, used in its technical sense. But since these systems busied themselves particularly with the empirical forms of reality and more or less with dialectic, they could not give the subject the same fullness and precision in its treatment as its nature demanded. The little, however, that has been left on record by these philosophers is highly interesting and would enable us, following along their lines, to have an idea of what they really meant.

While mentioning the various kinds of knowledge derived from ordinary sources, Kaṇāda confines himself to sense-perception, inference and verbal cognition, of which the first two he conceives as really independent and the last one as only a form of the second. This shows that according to Kaṇāda, the senses, aided by the natural light of reason, constitute for the average man the only valid source of knowledge. The testimony of the senses is sometimes deceptive, and so, when a doubt arises as to its correctness, it has to be verified either by an appeal to Reason or by *pravṛttisāmarthya* and the certitude which the verification thus result in establishing must be regarded for all practical purposes as sufficient and final. And consequently the Reality which such a certitude discloses is only empirical. Further the scope of the natural faculties is very limited; they cannot operate except under definite physical and physiological conditions. Absolute knowledge, in every sense unlimited and revealing the heart of Reality, is therefore not within the reach of ordinary humanity.

But such knowledge is declared to exist and is said to be attainable by every man who develops within himself, by continued effort, the faculty of immediate vision and becomes in this way a *Ṛṣi* or Seer. And for this reason it is known as *Ārṣa*. The *Vaiśeṣika Sūtra* (9.2.13) mentions this, in association with what it calls *Siddhadarśana*, and explains its supersensuous character.[1]

The process of the genesis of this knowledge may be easily explained. It is assumed in this system that no knowledge can arise except through the contact of the *manas*, the atomic intra-organic faculty of attention, with the self, this contact being an invariable causal antecedent to the phenomena of conscious life in general. The character of the resulting knowledge is determined by the state of the *manas*, viz, whether it is at rest or in motion. If it is moving — and all movement it ultimately due to the action of prior dispositions (traces etc.) and of *adṛṣṭa* — it comes of necessity into relation with the senses which may (as in waking) or may not as in dream (somnambulism etc.) be in touch with the objects, and the ensuing consciousness is either *jāgrat* or *svapna*. But if the *manas* be absolutely motionless, two states may follow according as this motionlessness is consequent merely upon Nature's demand for rest or on intense concentration. In the former case, consciousness will be in total abeyance until it emerges again, along with the renewal of motion in *manas*, under a Vital Impulse (*Jīvanayoni-prayatna*) acting from beyond. This is the state known as *suṣupti* (dreamless sleep). The second state is called *Yoga* or *Samādhi*, in which consciousness, far from subsiding, is exalted into an extraordinary clarity of Immediate Intuition. Time, space and other limitations having vanished, the *manas* stands face to face, as it were, not only with the pure self but, with the realities of all things.

---

[1] Śaṅkara Miśra points out that both this *Ārṣajñāna* and *Siddhadarśana* reffered to in the *sūtra*, have for their objects things which are not accessible to the ordinary means of knowledge, but while the former reveals the past and the future, the latter, which is artificially induced clairvoyance, makes known what is hidden or distant (spatially) from the senses. This distinction is evidently unfounded. For if *Ārṣajñāna* is held to be identical with *Pratibhā*, as certainly it is (cf. the statement of *Padārthapraveśa* quoted by Śaṅkara Miśra), there is no reason for setting limits to its power. It illuminates the distant in *space* with as much perspecuity as it does the distant in *time*, and moreover it is not restricted by the conditions which are found to be indispensable for the origin of ordinary knowledge. Pañcānana Tarkaratna, in his commentary on the *Upaskāra*, takes *Ārṣa* (as an alternate explanation) as equivalent to the unobstructed illumination of *Yuktayogin* and *Siddhadarśana* as the reflected omniscience of *Yuñjānayogin* (Bangabasi edition of *Vaiśeṣika Darśana*, p. 462).

This vision is *Pratibhā* or *Ārṣajñāna.*[2]

This is *Yogipratyakṣa*, pure and simple,[3] but Jayanta, in his *Nyāyamañjarī*, does not seem to be inclined to accept it as identical with *Pratibhā*. He distinguishes between two kinds of intuition, viz, the one which arises in the manner of a sudden flash even in the life of an ordinary individual (usually female) at some rare lucid moment, and the other which appears when the mind has gone through a process of regular discipline and Yoga. Jayanta would restrict the use of the term *Pratibhā* to the former kind of intuition alone.

But this restriction is apparently arbitrary. The term being really a coinage of the Yoga system, it is unreasonable why it should be narrowed down so as to exclude the vision of the *yogins* and to signify merely the sporadic intuitions of average humanity. It would be simpler therefore and more consistent with the general laws of argumentation to maintain that *Prātibhājñāna* is one in its essence but differing in kind according as it is developed by a steady and continuous effort or produced automatically by virtue of bare *adṛṣṭa*.

In both cases, however, the essential characteristics of *Pratibhā* are to be observed and it is these which differentiate it from sense-perception and other forms of inferior knowledge. What Jayanta says of *Yogipratyakṣa* holds good for *Pratibhā* in all its aspect, of course with varying degrees of applicability. Though simple and indivisible in its unity, it comprehends the entire objective world in a single moment, i.e., simultaneously.[4]

The usual conditions of knowledge which preclude the possibility of two cognitions rising simultaneously in the field do not avail in the case of *Pratibhā*, for the simple reason that it is a single act, and does not consist of a series of separate states. So long as it endures it is a continuum, and it endures till there is no break

[2] One to whom such a vision reveals itself is called a *Ṛṣi*, the word *Ṛṣi* etymologically meaning a 'seer'.

[3] Cf. Kālvivara Vedāntanāgiśa, *Sāṁkhya Darśana*, p. 147.

[4] *Yugapad ekyaiva buddhyā drakṣyanti sarvatra sarvān arthān yoginaḥ* (*Nyāyamañjarī*, p. 107).

in its unity. But as soon as this unity is dissolved *Pratibhā* also disappears, being superseded by the ordinary life with its chain of successive and mutually exclusive mental states.

Thus understood, *Pratibhā* would seem to be an approximation to the wisdom of the Supreme Being. It is distinguished from the Divine wisdom only in this that it is a product which the *manas* brings occasionally into existence through a certain process of self-immobilisation, whereas the latter is eternal and stands eternally adjoined to Him, in which the necessity of an organ is out of question (cf. *Nyāyamañjarī*, p. 178).

In the *Bhāṣāpariccheda* (verse 66) Viśvanātha Nyāya Pañcānana describes the Yoga intuition as of a two-fold character, viz, that of the *yogin en rapport* (*Yukta yogī*) and the other of one just a degree below (*Yuñjana yogī*). The former is the mirror of Eternal Light in which the totality of things remains perpetually in manifestation (*yuktas ya sarvadā bhānam*), but the latter requires the aid of reflection and contemplation for such manifestation.

-II-

YOGA

In the Yoga system, especially in that represented by Patañjali, *Pratibhā* is synonymous with an aspect of *Prajñā*. It is said to be the supreme faculty of omniscience which is evolved through a continued practice of concentration on the self, not in its absolute and transcendent nature, but as appearing in the form of the phenomenal ego (*vyavahārika grahītā*). The Pure Self is not an object of contemplation. It is said that as practice continues, and before the glory of the final illumination yet breaks forth, there dawns on the zone, in the fashion of the effulgence of the morning sun before the actual rise of the orb above the horizon, an unspeakable splendour in which the entire universe stands fully revealed. It is a vision in Eternity, *sub specie aeternitatis* —

simultaneous (*akrama*), truthful, all comprehending and serene. It is, so to speak, the vision of the many as reflected in the mirror of the one, and although there is still predominance of multiplicity, it is at this stage so thoroughly infused with the unity that it is in a sense identical with it. In view of this multiplicity in the object of this vision it is held to be an impediment to *Kaivalya* and to the highest wisdom which leads through the cessation of all mental life to that supreme state. And when in course of *sādhanā* this multiplicity disappears from the field of vision and the One, the Pure Self begins to shine upon itself, there being nothing left external to it, the highest wisdom takes its rise as an Immediate Consciousness of Pure Being with reference to the self. To know itself as pure is, for the self, to know itself as distinct from the objective phenomena. Such knowledge is called *Vivekakhyāti* and is the immediate antecedent of *Kaivalya*. For to *know* oneself as pure is verily to *be* pure.

From the above it would follow that in Yoga, though a slight distinction is made between *Pratibhā* and the highest kind of *Prajñā* called *Tārakajñāna*, *Pratibhā* in its ultimate nature is nevertheless nothing but the Light of the *Prajñā* falling upon the many instead of the one. That it is an *anaupadeśika jñāna*, as much as the *Prajñā* itself and is, therefore, to be differentiated from the ordinary kinds of knowledge, more or less conceptual, is recognised; but how such a knowledge is gained and how it embraces as its object the entire universe (*sarvam*) on which the *citta* was not concentrated are questions which present themselves in this connection.

To answer the questions properly we must inquire into Patañjali's theory of intuitive knowledge and study the cognate notions of his school. It is assumed that the word (*śabda*), idea (*jñāna*) and object (*artha*) are really distinct entities, and that though in ordinary experience they are found to be interrelated they may be separated from one another by a process of abstraction. It is indeed true, the *yogin* would say, that thinking is impossible without some kind of language; in other words, it is admitted to be a fact that except through the use of a series of symbols with a certain conceptual value attached to them no mediate knowledge can possibly arise. But this does not imply that the symbol is in truth identical with the object for which it stands or with the idea to which it is correlated. The cow as an *idea* is certainly distinct from the cow as an external *object* visible to the eye and both from the cow as the *name*, which expresses this idea and this object. The very nature of discursive thought is based on the non-recognition of this distinction and on the consequent of a real identity among these three things. In the technical language of Yoga, such thought, thus confused and indiscriminate, is said to be dominated by *vikalpa*.

But a discrimination is possible. It is by the exigencies of our practical life founded on convention (*saṅketa*) that this identity of reference is established, so that the presence of one thing (e.g. the word) revives the memory of another (c.g. the object) and vice versa. Practice in meditating upon the object without any conscious verbal reference is, therefore, supposed in course of time to succeed in breaking this false notion of indentity (*smṛtisāṅkarya*) and illumining the object *qua* object, pure and simple. In this system an object is held to possess a two-fold aspect of reality, one universal (*sāmānya*) and the other individual (*viśeṣa*), of which the former is amenable particularly to those forms of knowledge in which the conceptual element (*śabdaja vikalpa*) predominates, viz, *āgama* and *anumāna*, but the latter aspect, i.e., the object as an individual with a nature of its own, and as such distinguished from other individuals belonging to the same or to a different class, cannot be made known except by direct perception. But in ordinary perception, which for practical purposes is equivalent to *savikalpa jñāna*, the conceptual element is not wholly removed. When, however, this element is eliminated and purity of the intention ensured, the *prajñā* becomes intensely clear and reveals the object wholly and faithfully until at last it sinks altogether and the object shines by itself. It sounds absurd to say that the object alone remains, without the *citta* or *jñāna* to take cognisance of it, but what is meant seems to be that the *citta*, through extreme purity, becomes at this stage so tenuous as to be in fact a luminous void; it does not exist and it must do so until *kaivalya* is reached,[5] though identified in a sense with the object. And when there is a falling off from this state of *ekstasis* and a subsequent recoil from the object, it remains a dim *saṁskāra* of that supreme experience which it formulates in terms already familiar to it. It is needless to add that this is an intellectual act in the making of which the concepts known to the mind play an important part. The freshness of the original intuition is then gone; and thought and language grope about in vain to seize and express a truth beyond their farthest reach.

It is then clear that as soon as the mind, by gradual training, is free from the invading influence of the concepts and the 'memory images of the past' (*vikalpas*), it acquires the power of merging itself in unity with any object (*dhyeya*) which may be presented to it — or indeed being filled with it and pervaded by it (*samādhi*). No matter what this object may be, it is then fully illumined and its real nature perfectly brought out. This illumination (the act and the power both) is called by the name of *Prajñā* and is characterised as *Ṛtambharā*, because it reveals the whole truth and is never falsified. But even at this stage it cannot make known everything — the All. It discloses that alone — whether a concrete whole (*avayavī*) as in *nirvitarka samādhi* or the infra-atomic particles (*tanmātrā*) as in *nirvicāra* — from the contemplation of which it arose. But with continued practice this limitation is transcended. It is explained in the *Yoga Sūtras* that when the aspirant steps beyond the first two stadia of ecstasy, viz, *grāhya* and *grahaṇa samāpatti* and concentrates his *citta* on its own self (i.e. *asmitā* or phenomenal ego, the subject of relative consciousness, as illumined by the light of the Spirit above), he becomes self-conscious. This is *grahītṛ samāpatti* (*sāsmitāsamādhi*) or what we might loosely describe as a subjective intuition, and the consciousness is self-consciousness in its utmost purity. But it must be remembered that this self-consciousness, which is the last term of our phenomenal

[5] I have elsewhere tried to show at some length what is meant by saying that in *kaivalya* the *citta* is non-existent. The whole question turns upon the admissibility and meaning of what is technically designated *śuddhasattva* i.e. *sattva* absolutely free from *rajas* and *tamas*.

life, consists in the relative unity of subject and object, and equivalent to the *so'ham jñāna* of Vedānta. It is the pointed apex of a broad-based pyramid-like edifice, beyond which is Eternity.

But how is it that concentration on *asmitā* (i.e., *grahītṛsamāpatti*) leads to omniscience? How does concentration on *one* thing result in knowledge of all? The question is rather perplexing, but it becomes very much simplified if we remember that the one here referred to is a composite unity — a unity holding in its bosom the germs of plurality, so that the vision of one is also, at this stage, the vision of all. The *asmitā* is the essence of *citta* and is the empirical subject. The *Yoga Bhāṣya* remarks that when the *yogin* succeeds in realising himself as *subject* by means of *grahītṛsamāpatti*, the objective phenomena, infinite as they are, and their knowledge become simultaneously present to his cosmic consciousness: *sarvātmano guṇā vyavasāyāvyavasāyātmakāḥ svāminam kṣ etrajñaṁ praty aśeṣadṛśyātmatveno'patiṣṭhante* (*Yoga Bhāṣya*, 3.49). The Self-consciousness, which is All-consciousness, is *Pratibhā* in the light of which all things are simultaneously (*akramam*) and in all their aspects (*sarvathāviṣayam*) revealed. It constitutes the highest mystic acquisition of the *yogin*, next only to his self-realisation.

A question may here be asked: what is the moral value of such a consciousness, however exalted? Does it serve any practical purpose in the way of restoring the soul to its lost glory? To this question it is replied by pointing out that it does; because *Pratibhā* merges ultimately in *Tāraka* or Saving Knowledge, which leads to deliverance. The soul on its way to liberation needs must pass through this stage of omniscience. For without the direct knowledge of all there can be no absolute detachment, i.e. detachment from *everything* alien or external to the Self (*paravairāgya*), which is a precondition of *Kaivalya*. In other words, detachment from everything presupposes a knowledge of everything. This detachment of *jñāna* or *citta* from everything is held to be its highest purity and is immediately followed by *Kaivalya*. It is called the *dharmamegha samādhi*, representing the highest form of *Prajñā*, in which the *citta* (*sattva*) attains in purity to the likeness (*śuddhisāmya*) of the Self, so that the subject and the object are now eternally and *absolutely* lost in unity, and the din of phenomenal existence is forever hushed in the calm of sweet repose.

But before the actualisation of *Kaivalya*, when the *citta* still stands at the crest of the universe, ready to sink, the *yogin* feels within him, as it were, a fresh emotional stir. For it is said that the rise of *Prajñā* is accompanied by the awakening of a deep compassion on suffering humanity. In the *Yogabhāṣya* the sage (*prājña*) is likened to one standing on the hilltop and looking down from his tower of glory on the toiling moiling multitude below.[6] This infinite compassion is the only justification of his abstention from a plunge into the *Kaivalya* which is immediately to follow. Under deep compassion he then builds up a new *citta*, the so-called *nirmāṇa citta*, from the stuff of *asmitā*, and a new body called *nirmāṇakāya*, from the *tanmātrās*, and having assumed these teaches wisdom to the world sunk in ignorance.[7] The only motive for him is philanthropy (*bhūtānugraha*). According to Yoga, as to Mahāyāna Buddhism, the sage owes it as a duty to his less fortunate brethren to inspire them with hope and courage and to point out to them the way to final release.

-III-

VYĀKARAṆA

Having given an outline of the views of the Yoga school in regard to *Pratibhā*, I now pass on to consider at some length what the Vaiyākaraṇas have to say on this question. I may take liberty to suggest here that the philosophy of grammar built upon the basis of Patañjali's *Mahābhāṣya* by the great savant Bhatṛhari was

[6] *Prajñāprāsadam āruhya aśocyaḥ śocato janān |*
bhūmiṣṭhān iva śailasthaḥ sarvān prājño'nupaśyti ||

[7] It was thus that Kapila is said to have taught Āsuri: *ādividvān nirmāṇacittam adhiṣṭhāya kāruṇyād bhagavān paramarṣir āsuraye jijñāsamānāya tantram provāca* (*Yogabhāṣya* under I, 25).

affiliated to the Āgama literature, akin to the Śaiva and Śākta Āgamas of Kashmir.[8] With this in our mind we shall be able to follow its conclusions without any difficulty.

The grammarian's doctrine of *Pratibhā* is intimately bound up with his view regarding the origin of knowledge and of the objective world, and as this subject has not yet been dealt with elsewhere it would be well to furnish a short account of it here.

It is the fundamental thesis of the Śābdika that the source of all phenomena is the Eternal Verbum, called Śabda Brahman or *Parā Vāk*. This is of the nature of simple unity, Pure Being (*mahāsattā*), Great Universal (*mahāsāmānya*). To it belongs an infinite number of Śaktis mutually exclusive, but in essence identical with it (*ekatvāvirodhinyaḥ, avibhaktāḥ, ātmabhūtāḥ*). Of these *Avidyā*, viz, the power not only of veiling the Essence but of exhibiting the many, and *Kāla*, viz, the power of projecting the eternal *kalās* of Śabda Brahman in succession,[9] may be regarded as the chief. These two *śaktis* are closely associated. But even of these two, *Kāla śakti* is held to be the Supreme Power (*svātantrya*) to which all other *śaktis* are subordinate and under the influence of which the eternal *kalās* within the *śabda* (*avyāhatāḥ kalāḥ*), though many, yet so long mysteriously identified with it, are apparently sundered from it and become the sources of the manifoldness of the phenomenal world (*bhāvabhedesya yonayaḥ*).

The world of the phenomena, when analysed, exhibits a perpetual flux, which may be said in some sense to be cyclic. Motion begins from the Unmanifest and ends in the Unmanifest— and the two moments of appearance and disappearance of a phenomenon

---

[8] Bhartṛhari complains that this Āgama had been practically lost for long ages when it was recovered and proclaimed by Candrācārya. Puṇyarāja, according to the tradition, attributes the original Vyākaraṇāgama to Rāvaṇa and ascribes its recovery through a Brahmarākṣasa to Candrācārya, Vasurāta (the teacher of Bhartṛhari) and others. For Candrācārya, see *Rājataraṅginī*, I. 176.

[9] The Śābdika, indeed every exponent of āgamic philosophy, rejects the Vaiśeṣika view of *Kāla* as an independent and supersentible substance, but conceives it as a power, really indivisible, but appearing as discrete (*pravibhakta*), i.e., prior and posterior, on account of what might be called movement particles or units of movement.

represent only the two opposite directions, *anuloma* and *pratiloma*, of the same wheel of movement (*pariṇāma*).

The Primal Being (*sattā*), though in itself one and immutable, yet appears as many and in motion by virtue of its own inalienable Power (*māhātmyāt*), as already pointed out. This appearance of one as many constitutes its division, by which what is comprehensible and un-nameable becomes subjective and objective, so that herein we have a distinction between *jñāna* (knowledge) and *jñeya* (knowable) on one hand and *vācaka* (name) and *vācya* (namable) on the other. The *Kālaśakti* being conceived as an eternal and innate power of the Pure Being, we may assume that to the Śābdika, as to the Tāntrika elsewhere, the Godhead has a two-fold aspect — as *Transcendent beyond Time* in which it is above all predication in thought and language, and as *Immanent in Time* in which it is the subject, as well as predicate, of all judgements.

Now it is assumed that knowledge as a mode [10] (*vṛttijñāna*) is never free from verbal association (*śabdānugama*), evidently for the reason that it originates from *Śabda*. Hence an object (*artha*) which is knowable (*jñeya*) is also nameable (*abhidheya*) and the relation between the name and the nameable, as between knowledge and knowable, is an eternal relation (*anādiyogyatā*), which the Supreme Being simply manifests in the beginning of each aeon. The manifestation of this relation is co-eval with the origin of the objective world. In other words, in the womb of the Supreme World or the Highest Universal, after its seeming self-division or self-multiplication, there appears an infinite number of eternal *kalās* (= *śaktis*, potencies) or Universals (*aparasāmānya*) — hierarchy of ideas — each of which has its appropriate name and thought through

[10] I say knowledge as a mode (*vṛtti*) only to exclude Eternal *jñāna* or Brahman, which is no other than the Supreme Word in the System. In the expression *na so'sti pratyayo loke* (*Vākyapad*, I. 124), the word *loke* implies modal consciousness. This consciousness is discursive and relative. It must be borne in mind that the grammarian does not admit what is ordinarily known as *nirvikalpaka vṛttijñāna;* cf. the Stoic view on the connection between language and thought (Janet and Sérailes. *History of the Problems of Philosophy*, Vol. I, p. 208).

which it is revealed. It is through this name [11] and this thought that the Universal is manifested, i.e. creation in time (= production of individuals) follows. Naming and thinking being virtually an identical process, this manifestation of the Universals is the same as the revelation of Veda, which is nothing but the body of the eternal names and thoughts in eternal relation to the Universals.

The Veda, as thus understood, is really synonymous with *Pratibhā*. It is the self-revelation of the supreme Śabda, which in revealing itself reveals everything within it at the same time. Puṇyarāja (under *Vākyapadīya* 2.493) describes it as the purest from of *Prajñā* (*bhagavatī vidyā viśuddhaprajñā pratibhākhyā*) and identifies it (1.14) with the *Paśyantī* stage of *Vāk* (*paśyantyākhyā pratibhā*). It is eternal (*anapāyinī*), undivided (*avibhāgā*) and devoid of succession (*akrama*), i.e., is of the nature of an intuition continuum. The supreme transcendent Śabda is as it were the dark back-ground of all manifestations and forms, the Absolute of the grammarians. But the *Paśyantī* stage, though also eternal like Parā, differs from it in being, as its name indicates, luminous. Having realized this light by mode of spiritual culture to which the grammarian applies the term Vāgyoga, the self attains peace and may be said to have fulfilled its highest destiny. There is nothing left for it to strive after.[12]

---

[11] The subject is as complicated as it is interesting. A detailed study of the issues involved will appear in the writer's forthcoming work on Yoga and ancient Indian mysticism. It may just be noted here that creation following from 'name' is a conception very old in India, cf. the Vyāhṛti theory of creation *Vedānta Sūtra* 1.3.28; *Manu-Saṁhita* 1.21. That it follows from 'thought' is illustrated in the operation of the so-called *icchā-śakti* of the *yogin*, in which an idea or thought-image, as soon as formed, may be externalised into a real material object; cf. in *Yoga Vāsiṣṭha* (*Nirvāṇa Prakaraṇa*, I. 82.24): *viditātmāno bhāvayanti yathaiva yat | tat tathaivāśu paśyanti dṛḍhabhāvanayā tayā* || To the grammarian the thought is the same as the object, with this difference that the former is an internal, while the latter is only an external aspect of one and the same Reality. The *thought* relates to the Universal in itself (abstract) as well as to the Universal revealed in the Individual (concrete). So with the *name*.

[12] *Avibhāgā tu paśyantī sarvataḥ saṁhṛtakramā | svarūpajyotire'vā'ntaḥ sai'ṣā vāg anapāyinī || sai'ṣā saṅkiryamāṇā'pi nityam āgantukairmalaiḥ | antya kale'va somasya nā'tyantam abhibhūyate || tasyām dṛṣṭasvarūpāyām adhikāro nivartate | puruṣe ṣodaśakale tāmā'hur amṛtāṁ kalām* || (Quoted from comm. on *Vākyopadīya* under I. 145).

Indeed *Paśyantī* or *Pratibhā* represents the very essence of the self — the Inner Light of its Nature (*svarūpajyotirevāntaḥ*). It is of an infinite variety according as it reveals the object as one with it or as distinct from but related to it or as it stands alone in its own glory.[13] In any way it is above the ceaseless flux of the phenomenal world, and whether conceived as the Pure One or as the One with the eternal and infinite *kalās* held within, it is the highest end of human aspirations.

Puṇyarāja quotes a passage, apparently from an old Trika Āgama in which the *Paśyantī* or the Divine *Pratibhā* is described as the sixteenth (*ṣoḍaśī*) or the Immortal (*Amṛtā*) Kalā of the Moon, i.e. the Self, *Puruṣa*. This Immortal *Kalā* is elsewhere known as *daivī vāk*.[14]

Helārāja in introducing his commentary on the third *kāṇḍa* of *Vākyapadīya*, gives a beautiful description of *Pratibhā*. He says there that as soon as this celestial light dawns on the soul, the heart begins to taste of an ineffable joy that is not born of the senses and knows no fading, and the consciousness of divine majesty wells up from within in ever never forms.[15] It is a state of beatitude in which the soul is wrapped in the veil of the supreme glory of the Highest.

This *Pratibhā*, viz, *Paśyantī*, which is Veda proper, is subtle, eternal and super-sensuous. On realisation of this, the *Ṛṣis*, desirous of communicating it to the world, are said to have expressed it in the form of the so-called 'Vedas' and 'Vedāṅgas' (*bilma*), that is of

---

[13] *Paśyantī tu sā calācalapratibaddhasamādhānā sanniviṣṭajñeyākārā pravilīnākārā nirākārā ca paricchinnārthapratyavabhāsā saṁsṛṣṭārtha-pratyavabhāṣā ca praśāntasarvāthapratyavabhāsā ce'ty aparimitabhedā* || (Comm. on *Vākyapadīya*, I. 145).

[14] Cf. Bhavabhūti's benedictory line at the beginning of his *Uttararāmacarita*: *vandema devatām vācam amṛtām ātmānaḥ kalām*. If this, the *Paśyantī* is the 16th or *Pūrṇa* (full) *kalā* as the extract cited by Puṇyarāja shows, the *Parā* of the grammarians would correspond to the 17th or *Amā* (void) *Kalā* of the Tāntrikas.

[15] *Yasmin sanmukhatāṁ prayāti ruciraṁ ko'pyantarujjṛmbhate nedīyan mahimā manasy abhinavaḥ puṁsaḥ prakāśātmanaḥ | tṛptiṁ yat paramāṁ tanoti viṣa-yāsvādaṁ vinā śāśvatiṁ dhāmānanda sudhāmayorjitavapus tat prātibhāṁ saṁstumaḥ* ||

articulate language.[16] Hence it is declared to be the source of all sciences and arts. It is clear, therefore, and so it is asserted, that to the grammarian the term *Pratibhā* has the same connotation as the mystic *Praṇava* which is the essence of revealed literature and of human sciences [17] (*pravādāḥ*), which is the creator (*vidhātā*) of the worlds, the fount of all *vidyās* and *mantras*, and the matrix of all names and forms.[18] But the *Pratibhā* and *Parā* are the two eternal aspects of the same *Vāk*; it is also intelligible why the *Praṇava* is sometimes, though rarely, used as synonym of the *Parā*.

It may be of interest to note there that the *Vāk* qua *vācaka* is the *sphoṭa* and qua *vācya* is the *Mahāsattā*. Bhartṛhari says plainly that there is only One Supreme Object (*artha*), viz, Universal Being which is the true *vācya* of all words and which though indivisible and undivided appears as many (*bahurūpaḥ prakāśate*) by reason of the differentiation of its power (*śaktivibhāgena*). It is on this object as the background that the *vikalpas* of seer, seen and light are being constantly manifested. And similarly, he points out, there is one indivisible *vācaka*, viz, the Eternal Light of *Sphoṭas* [19] which reveals every *vācya*. Just as inspite of multiplicity in appearance the object (*artha*) is ultimately one, viz, Brahman conceived as *Sattā*,[20] so the word (*śabda*) too is really one in the end, viz, Brahman as *Sphoṭa*, and thus the two are identical in essence.[21]

---

[16] *Yāṁ sūkṣmāṁ nityām atīndriyāṁ vācaṁ ṛṣayaḥ sākṣātkṛtadharmāṅo mantra-dṛṣāḥ paśyantī tām asākṣātkṛtadharmedbhyaḥ parebhyaḥ pratívedayiṣyamāṇāḥ bilmaṁ samāmananti* || (Comm. on *Vākyapadīya*, 1.5).

[17] The word *pravādāḥ* means systems of thought devised by human intellect on the basis of, or independently of revealed scriptures. These do not proceed from personal intuition on the part of their authors.

[18] *Sa* (i.e., *praṇavaḥ*) *he sarvaśabdārthaprakṛtiḥ* ||

[19] The *vācakatā* of individual letters is denied. The real *vācaka* is either *padā* (according to Kaiyyaṭa) or more properly *vākya*. *Sphoṭa* is essentially an indivisible *vākya* (*akhaṇḍavākya*) with a unity of its own.

[20] Cf. *Vācyā sā* (i.e. *sattā*) *sarvaśabdānāṁ śabdāc na pṛthaktvataḥ* |
apṛthaktve'pi saṁbandhas tayor nānātmanor iva ||
Also : *Ekasyaivā'tmano bhedo śabdārthāva'pṛthaksthitau* ||

[21] The word *sphoṭa* and *sattā* refer obviously to the *cit* and *sat* aspects of the Supreme Lord, and mean the same thing as applied to the Lord. But they appear

Although we are employing the terms *vācya* and *vācaka* in reference to one and the same Reality, they convey here no sense, except that there is only one Reality which reveals Itself by means of Itself (for Śakti too is nothing distinct from this Reality). This self-revelation is *Pratibhā*.

Besides this primary meaning of *Pratibhā*, viz, Intuition or Revelation (as used in the mystic sense), there is another, a secondary one, which is also found in this literature. In this sense *Pratibhā* may be supposed to agree in its main features with the conception of instinct. Thus it is said that when we come in contact with an object which is felt to be pleasurable or painful, something from within impels us to go out towards the object in search of it or else to withdraw from it. Now this impulse is said to be due to *Pratibhā*, which stands, therefore, at the bottom of all our activities (*pravṛtti* and *nivṛtti*) and is the mainspring of our practical life (*sarvavyavahārayoniḥ*). It is this flash from within which, revealing the truth (though perhaps subconsciously and in a dark mysterious way not analyzable by the intellect), spontaneously determines the *itikartavyatā* of all creatures, so that even the movements of the beasts (*tiraścām api samārambhāḥ*) are ultimately traceable to its guiding influence. The class-instincts of certain animals, which are so varied and so marvellous, are instances of the multifarious manifestations of *Pratibhā*. Being an innate unerring faculty, it does not require to be trained from outside. Though incommunicable and inexpressible in language, its existence and even its working is justified by the inner experience of every man (*pratyātmavṛttisiddhāḥ*). It rises spontaneously (*ayatnaja*) in the

---

as distinct to the eye of Ignorance, the one as *vācaka* (or *jñāna*) and the other as *vācya* (or *jñeya*). This *vācya-vācakabhāva* of the One constitutes its multiplication. But we must bear in mind that this Many is eternal and simultaneously shining on the One in *Paśyantī*, but it is successive and subject to appearance and disappearance in *saṁsāra* after its fall from the *Paśyantī* stage.

We should also remember that in the *Paśyantī* stage there is no *vibhāga* (actual split) or *krama* (succession) in *Vāk*. This stage is distinguished from the *Parā* in this only that It is aware of Itself — whereas the *Parā* is beyond such self-awareness. To put the matter a little differently we may say that it is the self-awareness of *Parā* which is known as *Paśyantī*.

mind and would appear to the superficial observer to be quite of an accident. But on closer examination it is found to be, so far as its manifestation in a definite manner is concerned, a result of continued effort (*abhyāsa*) in the past.

This explanation of our practical life by the principle of an innate sense named *Pratibhā* is opposed to the rationalistic view of Maṇḍana Miśra, who, in his *Vidhiviveka*, lays down the principle that the only impetus to all conscious action is the *upāyajñāna* (adaptation of means to ends), without which no action would be possible.

But this objection of the Mīmāṁsaka is brushed aside by the grammarian on the ground that the principle of *upāyajñāna* cannot be maintained in all the cases. Thus even when the right means to the accomplishment of an end are unknown and under circumstances unknowable even by the wise (*durjñānopāyeṣu ca prajñair api*), the end in question is observed to be successfully realized through the instincts of the animals. Even the learned man, for instance, with his accumulated experience, does not know the means whereby he may be able to modulate his voice exactly as the cuckoo does so easily and gracefully on the advent of spring. The wonderful instincts of bees and ants are well known. The Vaiyākaraṇa points these out as illustrations of his thesis that instinct and intuition are really far more potent faculties than the intellect or even the senses (*pramāṇebhyo 'pi sāmarthyātiśayaṁ pratibhāyāḥ*). Besides, these never err while the accredited means of right (?) knowledge are known to be deceptive on occasions. It is further addedd, in repudiation of the Mimāṁsaka's theory, that the *upāyajñāna*, which arises directly from repeated personal observation (*asakṛddarśana*) and indirectly from the testimony of other (*upadeśa*), is not capable of explaining what the instinct actually accomplish.

Regarding the origin, or rather the manifestation of instinct, the grammarian accepts the conclusion of the Yoga system and connects it with the question of antenatal dispositions. It is well-known that every *karma* or experience leaves behind it a definite *saṁskāra*, a trace which remains impressed in a subtle state on the *citta*. The *saṁsāra* being without beginning, these *saṁskāras* are numerically infinite and exist from eternity in the *citta*. Some of these are known as *vāsanās* and serve, when awakened by a stimulus, as psychological antecedents to memory and recognition. But there are others called *karmāśayas* which determine the formation of a particular kind of corporeal existence, i.e. rebirth, as a particular being fitted with a particular organic vehicle. Thus *karmāśaya*, as a bundle of similar *saṁskāras* grouped together, appears at the dying moment of the individual under the influence of his predominant thought of the moment; this is the so-called *prārabdha*, the seed which explains the nature of the next birth, with the joy and sorrows of that life and the term of its continuation. Instincts peculiar to the particular species are also evolved out of the stock from which *prārabdha* originates. Prior *karma* being the determinant of both birth and instincts, it is easy to see how certain *saṁskāras* are intimately associated with certain forms of existence.

-IV-

THE ĀGAMAS : ŚAIVA ŚĀKTA SCHOOLS

In the Tāntrika literature, however, the doctrine of *Pratibhā* finds a brilliant and elaborate treatment. The whole of *Mantraśāstra* is indeed full of interesting matter bearing upon this question. But as we cannot fully examine, within the narrow limits of this paper, the various currents and cross-currents of thought with which the history of the doctrine is closely interwoven, we consider it more expedient to attempt only a brief exposition of the salient features of the doctrine, avoiding the quicksands controversy as far as possible. And this we shall do on the basis of the Trika and Tripurā literatures. But as these two literatures are very intimately connected and present very few point of difference (except in rituals) we may take them together.

As in the Vyākaraṇa, so in Tantra proper, the doctrine of *Vāk* plays a very important part and the study of *Pratibhā* is really the study of this *Vāk*, so far as its place in this literature is concerned.

But we must bear in mind at the outset the fundamental distinction between the two rival systems of thought in order that no confusion may arise. The Supreme Reality is conceived in Vyākaraṇa in terms of *Śabda* or *Vāk* (cf. *anādinidhanaṁ brahma śabdatattvaṁ yad akṣaram*), so that to the Vaiyākaraṇa the difference between Śabda Brahman and Para Brahman is in reality a difference without any distinction. To him the two represent the two aspects of the same Supreme Śabda: accordingly, the so-called Śabda Brahman is synonymous with *Paśyantī* and Para Brahman with *Parā*. But in Āgama the *Parā Vāk* occupies a subordinate position, being conceived as the Power of the Supreme Reality or Parama Śiva, and would thus seem to correspond to Śabda Brahman while Parama Śiva and Para Brahman would be identical. Though there is admittedly no essential difference between *Paśyantī* and *Parā* in Vyākaraṇa or between *Parā Vāk* and Parama Śiva in Āgama, there is no denying the fact that there is some slight difference between the two systems regarding the character of *Vāk*, in so far as one holds it to be independent and self-subsistent, while the other makes it a power subordinate to the substance with which it is identical.

In other words, *Vāk*, according to Āgama, is the Supreme Power of Parama Śiva — the Power, ever in association with Him, of His eternal self-contemplation and self-revelation. Though identical in essence with the Godhead and not separable from it, it is nevertheless distinguishable and is real. It is the Power whereby the Divine Self knows Itself and enjoys Itself eternally, without restraints and without limitations. It is the will of the Absolute and the personality of the Impersonal, if we may use these expressions. The Āgamas speak of it under various aspects, viz, *Vimarśa* (Word, Logos), *Sphurattā* (Self-illumination), *Aiśvarya* (Lordship), *Svātantrya* (Freedom), and *Parāhantā* [22] (Supreme Personality).

This *Vāk* is said to be two-fold according as it relates to the primary object (*mukhya artha*), viz, the Pure Light of Cit or the

[22] Cf. *Virupākṣapañcāśśikā*: *īsvaratā kartṛtvaṁ svatantratā citsvarūptā ce'ti* | *ete cā'hantāyāḥ paryāyāḥ sadbhirucyante* ||
See also *Nāgānandasūtra* as cited by Bhāskararāya in the *Guptāvatī*.

Absolute Unity, free from all kinds of limitations, or to the contingent object, viz, the Universe (*viśva*), which is multiple and is limited by various conditions, such as universal, quality, action, name etc. The first is called *pratyavamarśa* or *vimarśa* proper and the second *vikalpa*.[23]

The usual classification of *Vāk* as fourfold is also recognized. The *Parā* seems to me stand really for that aspect of the *Vāk* when it is one with Parama Śiva and is transcendent. The *paśyantī* represents the *Vimarśa*, and the remaining two, viz, *madhyamā* and *vaikharī* are only cases of *vikalpa*.

As *Vimarśa* means the self-revelation of the Lord (*prakāśasyā'tmaviśrāntiḥ*) it is intelligible that it is another name of *Pratibhā*, with which, in the system of grammatical philosophy, *Paśyantī* has been shown to be synonymous. And this is borne out by the description of *Pratibhā* found in the literature.

Thus in the *Pratyabhijñāhṛdaya* (p. 52) Kṣemarāja quotes a verse [24] in which *Pratibhā* is identified with the supreme subject, whose nature is infinite intelligence (*anantacidrūpa*), indivisible and void of time-limitations (*akrama*). It is unalterably and everywhere One, being the one Light whose reflection shines through every state of modal consciousness. The *yogin* reaches this plane of Divine *Vāk* when he succeeds in shaking off the fetters of bondage. Omniscience and Omnipotency, among other divine attributes, are manifested in him as matters of course. His will becomes paramount and invincible. The *Spandakārikā* (4-7) says that everything, however remote in time and removed in space, presents itself to such a *yogin* any aspect in which he wants to see it present. During the period of *ekstasis*, and even afterwards (if the *yogin* happens to have reached perfection), the self loses its limitations and becomes unified with the entire universe, so that the mere rise of the will with reference to a particular object suffices to bring it into manifestation (cf. Rāmakaṇṭha, pp. 107-8).

---

[23] See Ramakaṇṭhācāryā's *Vivṛti* on the *Spandakārikā*, p. 141.

[24] *Yā ca'ṣā pratibhā tattatpadārthakramarūṣitā |*
akramānantacidrūpaḥ pramātā sa maheśvaraḥ ||

The state of the *yogin*, thus abiding in the Reality and pervading All, is technically known as *rahasyamudrā* — a state in which he enjoys rest, freedom and joy, with all his desires fulfilled; and the solitude in which he lives is the supreme solitude of union with Reality.

The *Tripura Rahasya*, the *magnum opus* of the Tripurā system of philosophical thought, speaks exactly in the same strain. It describes *Pratibhā* as the supreme form of the Ultimate Reality (*parā sā pratibhā devyāḥ param rūpaṁ mameritam*)[25] and says that it is on this, as on a mirror, that the Universe is shining like a reflection. It appears to the ignorant as the objective world and to the *yogin* it reveals itself in the form of the eternal and indeterminate consciousness of the pure Self. The lover turns to it as to his beloved and finds the inmost cravings of his heart satisfied.[26]

-V-

VEDĀNTA

The word *Pratibhā* seldom occurs in Vedāntic literature but the doctrine was certainly recognized. In the ninth *anuvāka* of his *Vārttika* on the *Taittirīya Upaniṣad* (the only instance in which the term *Pratibhā* is found in Vedānta), Sureśvara mentions it by name (*prātibhājñāna*) and calls it *ārṣa*, thereby implying that this knowledge, by nature transcendent, is the characteristic of *ṛṣis* or seers,[27] and it is further stated there that is comes into manifestation only to that seeking soul who, by means of constant repetition of *mantra* and of prolonged meditation, is able to throw off the veil of *Māyā* and enter into conscious communion with the Supreme

[25] *Tripura Rahasya*, *Jñānakhaṇḍa*, ch. XX, Verse 36.

[26] Ibid., ch. XX, 31-36.

[27] Acyutarāya Modaka, in his commentary on the *Jivanmuktiviveka* (p. 52), explains the word *ārṣa* as meaning 'procceeding from Veda, which is self-illumined' (*svayaṁprabhāta veda*). This meaning is derived from the equation *ṛṣi* = Veda.

Being.[28] By way of illustration it is pointed out that such an intuition dawned upon Triśaṅku (*triśaṅkor brahmabhūtasya hy'ārṣaṁ sandarśanaṁ param*) to whom the *mantra*, viz, *ahaṁ vṛkṣasya rerivā* (*Taittirīya Āraṇyaka*, 7-10-1, p. 732 of the Bib. Ind. edition) was revealed. And in consequence of this manifestation of *Pratibhā* Triśaṅku was converted into a *ṛṣi*.

A proper understanding of this conversion is not possible without consideration on the general theory of Divine Omniscience in this system. It is asserted that human omniscience is accidental, being the result of a *rapport* with the Divine substance which is all-knowing and all-powerful. But what is the nature of this Divine Wisdom?

Here we are confronted with a wide divergence of views among scholars. Even in the system of Śaṅkara there is hardly any unanimity; and the exponents of orthodox Vedānta who are presumed to represent Śaṅkara are very largely divided in their opinions. Thus in the *Siddhāntaleśa*, Appayadīkṣita quotes no less than five different theories on the question of divine Omniscience, viz, the theories associated with the names of the authors of *Prakaṭārtha*, *Tattva-Śuddhi* and *Kaumudī* and of Bhāratī Tīrtha and Vācaspati Miśra.[29]

Among these, the view of *Tattva-Śuddhi* is opposed to the traditional teaching of all the mystics and may be dismissed as untenable. The Divine knowledge being everywhere recognised

---

[28] Cf. also: *mumukṣos tatparasyai'va śrautasmārteṣu karmasu* |
api ca prātibham jñānaṁ āvirbhavti mokṣadam ||
(*Vārttika*, verse 160, *Anuvāka* IX)

[29] It is curious to find that even in scholastic Vedānta the eternity of divine omniscience is sometimes impugned. Advaitānanda, for instance, in the *Brahmavidyābharaṇā* (p. 148) explicitly affirms that during *pralaya* there is a total lapse of such omniscience, apparently for the reason that it is only a mode and therefore a product which is by nature occasional. But how are we to understand Śaṅkara's own lines: *Yatprasādād'hi yogināmapy atītānāgataviṣayaṁ pratyakṣaṁ jñānamicchanti yogaśāstravidaḥ kumu vakṭavyaṁ tasya nityasiddhasye'śvarasya sṛṣṭisthitisaṁhṛtiviṣayaṁ nityajñānaṁbhavatīti* (under *Ved. Sūt.*, 1.1.5)? If the *nityajñāna* be taken as *svarūpajñāna* why should it be characterized as *saviṣayaka*? It is only a *vṛtti* which can be *saviṣayaka*.

as immediate, the author of *Tattva-Śuddhi* stands by himself when he asserts it to be of the nature of memory in the case of the past and of *Uha* (as it is named in the *Vedāntāsiddhāntasūktimāñjarī*) in that of the future. He fails to see that the knowledge of a being which is *ex hypothesi* eternal and omnipresent can hardly be characterised as anything but immediate. But the view of *Praka-ṭ ārthavivaraṇa* is more plausible in this respect. It states that God's immediate knowledge of the multiple phenomena of all times is explicable through the reflection of Pure Consciousness received into the infinite modifications of *Māyā*. This *Māyā*, like the inner organ of *jīva*, is the limiting condition of Īśvara; in other words, it is through association with *Māyā* that Īśvara, himself identical with consciousness (*jñānātmaka*), is capable of becoming the subject of consciousness (*jñātā*). This view is alright, so far as immediacy is concerned. But it loses sight of the fact, as pointed out by the author of *Vedāntakaumudī*, that God's omniscience is *not* a case of relative and adventitious consciousness which ceases during *pralaya*. It is rather due to His Essence which is consciousness itself. He knows all because, says the author of *Kaumudī*, He illumines all in relation with Himself. But does this All embrace the past and future? To this it is replied that it does. The past and the future exists in *avidyā* in the forms of bare, immaterial *saṁskāras* and are knowable. This reply of the *kaumudī* would remind one of the theory of *satkārya* of of Sāṁkhya-Yoga school and especially of the *Sūtra* of Patañjali, IV. 12. But in its general setting it seems to be somewhat of a graft upon the system. And one great defect from which this theory suffers is that it interprets omniscience as impersonal (*sarvajñātṛtva* = *sarvajñānātmakatva*) — an interpretation which, however plausible, is not supported by the tradition of Śāṅkara Vedānta. Vācaspati is right, therefore, when he says that omniscience must be personal and explains that even Absolute Consciousness may be personal, when thought of under relation of causality. The theory of Bhāratītīrtha, on the other hand, seeks to explain the omniscience of God on the assumption of His being the witness of the infinite *vāsanās* of *jīvas* as inhering in and modifying the Primitive Nescience (*ajñāna*).

All these views are centred on the fundamental thesis of Śaṅkarācārya, viz, that omniscience, omnipotence, etc. are not *really* predicable of the Supreme Being. It is after and through the operation of Cosmic Nescience that these are attributed to Him. Since His essence is knowledge itself, it is only by a metaphor that He may be called all-knowing. Omniscience and omnipotence are, therefore, pseudo-real concepts and not real. Śaṅkara plainly says: *tad evaṁ avidyātmakopādhiparicchedāpekṣam eve'śvarasye śvaratvaṁ sarvajñatvaṁ sarvaśāktitvaṁ ca, na paramārthato vidyayā'pāstasarvopādhisvarūpa ātmanī śītrīśitavyasarvajñatvādivyavahāraupapadyate.* (under *Ved. Sūtra*, 2.1.14). This is the central teaching of Śaṅkarācārya, viz, the denial of the reality of Śakti (Power) and with it of personality and self-consciousness in the Absolute. The Saguṇa Brahman, of course, is admitted to be personal, and consequently omniscience and omnipotence belong to Him, but then it must be remembered that the Reality, in the highest sense of the word (*pāramārthikatva*), of the *saguṇa* aspect is not conceded. In the system of Śaṅkara, there appears to be an impassable chasm between the two aspects of Brahman. But in regard to the question whether human omniscience, viz, that of the *yogins*, has its origin in the divine omniscience, Śaṅkara emphatically answers in the affirmative (cf. *yatprasādaddhī yogināmapy'atītānāgataviṣayaṁ pratyakṣam icchanti* etc. under *Ved. Sūtra*, 1,1.5).[30]

Śrīkaṇṭha and the subsequent host of commentators on Vedānta have not felt any such difficulty in interpreting the doctrine of divine (and human) omniscience. Their position is more clear on this point. They admit the existence of a *real* Śakti in Brahman and affirm that knowledge is as much the essence (*svarūpa*) of Brahman as its power or predicate (*śaktidharma*). Śrīkaṇṭha observes that the omniscience of Brahman consists in its eternal, immediate and faultless awareness of everything independently of external sense-

[30] This passage shows plainly that according to Śaṅkara the knowledge of God, like that of the *yogin*, is *immediate*, *pratyakṣa*. The theory of *Tattvaśuddhi* therefore is not only erroneous, but positively opposed to the teaching of Śaṅkara.

organs [31] and notes that this is possible by virtue of the supreme Jñāna Śakti (called *Umā* or *Cidambarā*) associated with it. It is to this Jñāna Śakti that the word *manas*, as used in the expression *mana ānandam*, (an epithet of Brahman) is said to refer, so that it means the faculty by which God as well as the liberated souls eternally enjoy the infinite (*niratiśaya*) joy of their beatified nature (*svarūpānandānubhavasādhana*) and which is indeed no other than the Śabda Brahman or *Praṇava*.[32] From this is it obvious that in the opinion of Śrīkaṇṭha the divine omniscience is synonymous with the eternal self-illumination and self-revelation of the Supreme Being, for the All (*sarva*, *nikhilavastu*) which such omniscience is stated to comprehend and illuminate is not external to, but forms and integral aspect of, this Being.

The theory of Rāmānuja and of his immediate predecessors in the field is not substantially very different from the above.[33] He employs the term Puruṣottama as a special name of Brahman, thereby implying personality and will in Him. He describes Brahman as the all-knowing subject whose essence is intelligence and whose eternal power of knowledge (known as Lakṣmī) is intimately related to Him. This power (*śakti*) or attribute (*dharma*) of God is sometimes spoken of as His mind, by which everything is always revealed to Him immediately (*dharmabhūtajñānena sarvaṁ sadā sākṣātkurvata īśvarasya*, etc.),[34] and sometimes as His consort.

[31] *Nityāparokṣāpekṣita vāhyakaraṇaniṣaniṣkalaṅkānubhavanikhilavastutvam idaṁ sarvajñatvam* || (under *Ved. Sūt.*, 1.12)

[32] Śrīkaṇṭha in the plainest language, asserts the identity of Umā or the Supreme Power of Divine Knowledge with the mystic Oṁkāra: *praṇavaparyāyeno 'māśabdena paraprakṛtirūpā parāśaktir ucyate* (*Ved. Sūt.*, 4.22)

[33] *Jñānasya rūpasyai'va tasya jñānāśrayatvaṁ maṇidyumaṇidīpādivad jyktam eva* (p. 53 of *Śrībhāsya*, Srirangam edition).

[34] Varavara's commentary on *Tattvatraya*, p. 44. This is *śuddha*, pure *sattva* and is to be distinguished from the natural *sattva*, which even in its purest condition is bound to have an admixture, however slight, of the two lower qualities. The pure *sattva* constitutes the Divine Mind just as the mixed *sattva* forms the lower mind, with this difference that it is, unlike the latter, eternal and infinite. It is this which under God's will evolves into an infinite variety of forms.

Like Śrīkaṇṭha and Rāmānuja, all the subsequent commentators admit an eternal real Śakti in the Supreme Being and explain the facts of omniscience and omnipotence by means of this Śakti.

-VI-

MĪMĀṀSĀ (PŪRVA)

From the foregoing summary of the orthodox views on intuition and omniscience (human and divine) as well as from the Buddhist and Jaina accounts of the same to which we shall advert in the following pages, it would seem that the doctrine of *Pratibhā*, in some form or the other, has ever been an article of universal acceptance in this country. It is an anomaly, therefore, that we find the Mīmāṁsakas alone maintaining an attitude of bitter opposition to this doctrine. They deny the possibility of omniscience of any kind, either eternal as of God or what is due to contemplation as in the case of the *yogins*.[35] The arguments adduced by them in support of their denial [36] seem to be no more than the stale stock-in-trade arguments with which the common empirical sense of man seeks to overthrow the dictates of the higher mystic consciousness. There must be some deeper reason for the denial. The philosophical

[35] See *Ślokavārttika*, pp. 79-82.

[36] For Jayanta's refutation of some of these arguments, see *Nyāyamañjarī*, pp.103-106. Kumārila is very hard upon those mystics who hold that in the gradual exaltation of consciousness there comes a moment when the restriction of senses to their corresponding objects (*viṣayaniyama*) is no longer applicable. He plainly denies not only the power of sense-organs to apprehend an object which is not relevant to it (*na rūpe śrotravṛttitā*), but even the possibility of there being a central faculty capable of cognising all objects (*ekena tu pramāṇena sarvajñaḥ* etc., *Ślokavārttika*, p. 80). This is nothing but the common-sense view. But it is not tenable for the mystic consciousness, cf. the *Śruti*: *ghrāṇataḥ śabdaṁ śṛṇvanti pṛṣṭhato rūpāṇi paśyanti*. With this Vedic passage may be compared the statement of Saint Martin: "I heard bowers that sounded and saw notes that shone". In regard to Kumārila's objection to the assumption of a central faculty one is reminded of Edward Carpenter's own experience of the mystic consciousness, in which, as he says "All the senses unite into one sense" (see Underhill's *Mysticism*, p. 8).

position of Mīmāṁsā in relation to the other systems must be determined in order to see if we can discover some rationale of this denial. It is evident that the doctrine of omniscience does not somehow fit in with the fundamental assumptions with which the system as a whole starts.

It seems to me that the conception of Śabda or Veda as eternal and impersonal lies at the bottom of the Mīmāṁsaka's whole tenor of thought. From this may be deduced as corollaries many of the views which the system sets forth. The unbroken continuity of world-cycles, the doctrine of self-validity of knowledge, the theory of its causality etc., all these will be found, when closely analysed, to follow from this central conception. The rejection of omniscience may also have something to do with this very fact. According to Mīmāṁsā, it would appear, omniscience is not compatible with personality which is held to be a limitation. The very fact of being a subject involves the inevitable relativity of consciousness, fatal to omniscience; and moreover, when Veda is already assumed to be the eternal source of all knowledge, impersonal and self-revealed, it would be superfluous to posit a Personal All-knowing Being, either human or divine (cf. *āgamasya ca nityatve siddhe tatkalpanā vṛthā*. *Ślokavārttika*, p. 82).

But what are we to understand by the first benedictory verse of *Ślokavārttika*, where Kumārila speaks of the Supreme Being under the name of Mahādeva and describes Him as furnished with the Divine Eye (*divyacakṣus*) in the form of the three Vedas? The meaning of the verse is obvious and even Pārthasārathi who suggested an explanation in consonance with the Mīmāṁsā position could not deny that it really referred to Mahādeva (*viśveśvaraṁ mahādevam*) and therefore to a personal God. The identification of Divyacakṣus with Veda is quite in keeping with the mystical explanation of Veda which is in its essence equivalent to Praṇava and therefore to *Pratibhā* which is the Divine Eye in the highest sense of the word. The *śloka*, therefore, as coming from an orthodox Mīmāṁsaka teacher, remains unintelligible.

-VII-

BUDDHISM

In the Buddhist philosophical literature, so far as I am aware, the term *Pratibhā* is not generally found. But the word *Prajñā* is most frequent, and it occurs there with many of the associations which attach to the word in Patañjali's system.

It is asserted that the ultimate Truth (*paramārthasatya*) the realisation of which is an essential condition for freedom from pain, is not amenable to any of the human sources of knowledge — to the senses or even to reason — but it reveals itself in the light of Supreme Wisdom which arises from contemplation and quietude (*samādhi, śamatha*). Contemplation is declared to be the only means for gaining *Prajñā*, i.e., knowledge of things as they are in themselves as distinguished from what they appear to us.[37] Though the world (*loka*) has little concern with such knowledge, it is considered to be the only way to Deliverance. As in Yoga, so in Buddhism, *Prajñā* is supposed to consist of a series of successive stages, in the last of which it becomes absolutely spotless and calm.

The *Prajñā* is sometimes conceived as an eye (*prajñācakṣ us*), which is said to develop itself when the mind is purified by *samādhi*.[38] In the technical phraseology of the Buddhist literature, the term *prajñācakṣus* does not seem to represent *prajñā* in its entirety but only in one of its aspects, and in this way the different stages of *prajñā* are found represented by corresponding supernatural eyes, viz, (i) *dharmacakṣus*, (ii) *divyacakṣus*, (iii) *prajñācakṣus*, and (iv) *buddhacdakṣus*.[39]

---

[37] *Yathāvasthitapratītyasamutpannavastutattvaparicayalakṣaṇā, prajñā* || *Boddhicaryāvatārapañcikā*, p. 348.

[38] *Śamathapariśodhitacittasantāne prajñāyāḥ prādurbhāvāt supraśodhitakṣetre śasyaniṣpattivat* || *Loc. cit.* Cf. the Yoga view which is similar (*Yoga Sutra*, 1.20).

[39] In the list of the five eyes as given by Childers (S.V. *pañcacakkhu*) we read *samantā cakku* instead of *Dhamma*, but the name *dhammacakkhu* is sometimes retained. It is there described as the power of knowing general things possessed by the Buddha. In the *Nyāyaratnākara* (p. 80), Pārthasārathi Miśra refers to the

In Pāli literature, the word *dhammacakkhu* (spiritual insight), also known as *vipassanā*, is used for the dawning of the spiritual sense in man on conversion. When this is fully developed, the convert is established in the fruit of '*sotāpatti*' and the first stage comes to an end. This eye is characterised as a faculty of true knowledge, undisturbed by *rajas* (*virajām*) and free from obscurity (*vītamalam*). How this faculty is to be distinguished from the so-called divine eye (*divvacakkhu*) does not seem to be quite clear (cf. Rhys Davids, *Dialogues*, p. 95 footnote). That both are supernormal is, of course, plain. But it is sometimes asserted that *divvacakkhu* is able to see visible objects only, though such objects may not be ordinarily within the scope of our faculty of vision (cf. *Kathāvatthu*). In the *Abhidhammāvatāra* also it is said that *divvacakkhu* has *rūpa* for its object [40] as *divvasota* has sound (*śabda*). The fit objects of the celestial sight are held to be of four kinds. viz, things present (*paccuppaṇna*) as well as absent (*paritta*), external and internal (*loc.cit.*, p. 110 verse 1153). This eye is defined as the knowledge (and its faculty) which rises on the *citta* when, in the fourth stage of *jñāna*, it is identified with the object.[41]

Besides these two faculties there is the *paññācakku* (*prajñācakṣus*) which is held in the *Itivuttaka* (p. 52, § 61) to be higher than the *divvacakkhu*.

Buddhadatta, however, divides *cakkus* first into two classes, viz, *māṁsa* (physical) and *paññā* (supernatural), of which the latter is five-fold: (i) *Buddha*, (ii) *Dhamma*, (iii) *Samanta*, (iv) *Nāna*, and (v) *Divva*. From what he says of these powers of supernatural knowlege it seems that it (i) consists on the realisation of *āśayas* and *anuśayas* which are supersensible, (ii) means knowledge of the three-fold path, (iii) stands for omniscience, (iv) indicates the

view according to which *divvacakkhu* is the faculty of Buddha's omniscience: *Buddhapratyakṣaṁ divyacakṣurjanitaṁ sarvaviṣayaṁ bhaviṣyati.*

[40] In this sense it corresponds to the *avadhi-jñāna* and *darśana* of Jaina Philosophy.

[41] *Atthasādhakacittaṁ taṁ catutthajjhānikaṁ matam | taṁ cittasaṁyutaṁ jñānaṁ divyacakkhūti ||* (*Abhidhammāvatāra*, p. 107, verse 1100). For the manner how this eye is developed see ibid., pp. 106-107 and Shwe Zam Aung in his Introductory Essay to the *Compendium of Philosophy*, p. 63.

Eye that is evolved (after conversion), and (v) *divvacakkhu* is synonymous with the Supreme Wisdom or *Prajñā* which arises from *abhijñācitta* (p. 65, chap. X, 635-639).

In the Sanskrit Buddhist literature also, the same five-fold division is to be met with.[42] In the *Mahāvastu* it is pointed out that in vision by the physical eye (*māṁsa*) light is needed; but in the function of the other eyes it is not necessary.[43] *Divyacakṣus* is said to be better than that of the gods etc. *Dharmacakṣus* is characterised by the development of ten psychic powers (including the purity of the *Divyacakṣus*). But all these powers pale before the Buddha Eye which is equivalent to Absolute and Unconditional Omniscience.

There is of course much confusion on the exact significance of the terms in Buddhist literature, for, in course of time and for various reasons, imports have gradually changed. But one thing is certain, viz, that we find everywhere recognised the existence of a higher faculty than the physical sense and that it is resorted to for explaining fact otherwise inexplicable. The physical sense is often erroneous and subject to various limitations; it reports are unreliable. But this higher faculty, call it *prajñācakṣus* or by any other name, is infallible and sees things in their light.

Here a curious parallelism presents itself between the Buddhist philosophy and the Yoga system of Patañjali. Thus it is said that *Prajñā* as a means (*hetubhūta*) viz the realisation of the noble eight-fold path, leads to *Prajñā* which may considered as the End (*phalabhūta*), viz, *Nirvāṇa*. The former is the result of continued practice of the preliminary *Prajñā* consisting in *śruta*, *cintā* and *bhāvanā*.[44] This *śruta*, *cintā* and *bhāvanā* are really nothing but the Buddhist counterparts of *śravaṇa*, *manana* and *nididhyāsana* of the Upaniṣadic literature and of *āgama*, *anumāna* and *dhyanā*-

---

[42] See *Vajrachhedikā*, XVIII; *Dharmasaṁgraha*, LXVII, p. 14, *Lalitavistara*, Mitra's translation, p. 15; *Mahāvastu*, vol. I.

[43] Swami Hariharānanda Āraṇya, in his *Śivadhyāna Brahmacarir Apūrva Bhramaṇa Vṛttānta* (p. 80), points out that there are two ways of having supernatural vision, viz, in the solar or in the lunar light. The former is the light of *suṣumṇā* and the latter the manifestation of sense-power. In the first case also physical light is not needed.

[44] Cf. *Bodhicaryāvatārapañcikā*, pp. 349-350; Takakusu, *Itsing*, p. 163.

bhyāsa of *Yogabhāṣya*,[45] and the *prajñā* or realisation of the path (*mārgajñāna*) of Buddhism corresponds to the realisation (*sākṣātkāra, darśana*) of Vedānta and to the Yoga of the Yoga system.

Now the question is: how is omniscience compatible in Buddhism with its doctrine of flux on the one hand (Realism and Idealism) and of Void on the other (Nihilism)? The Yoga system advocates the *satkāryavāda* and is consequently able to explain the rationale of its intuitive experience on the ground that in its view all the products, however widely separated by time and space, are eternally co-existing in the *Primum Materia* (*mūla prakṛtiḥ*), They are manifested as soon as the barriers, which stand in the way of their manifestation before consciousness, are withdrawn. Patañjalī, in most unequivocal terms, expresses his belief that the past and the future are essentially existent.[46]

That they are not usually *seen* is due to some defect in the seer (viz, *āvaraṇa*) and not to their non-existence. But in the doctrine of Universal Flux, such as that of Buddhism, in which a permanent substrate of change is not admitted, there is logically no room for the past or for the future. And as a matter of fact we find that the advocates of the orthodox Theravāda School actually reject the theories, the seceder (e.g. Sarvāstivādins) holding that the past and the future exist and (cf. Andhakas) that the future may be known.[47]

Still the fact has to be explained that the Buddha, if none else, was believed to be able to make predictions and to know anything however remote in time, if only he willed so.

Thus the *Milinda Pañho* expressly declares in an interesting passage [48] that the Buddha was verily omniscient, in the sense that

---

[45] *Āgamenā'numānena dhyānābhyāsarasena ca |*
tridhā prakalpayan prajñāṁ labhate yogam uttamam ||
under *Yoga Sūtra*, 1.48.

[46] *Atītānāgataṁ svarūpato'sty adhvabhedād dharmāṇām*. Ibid, IV.12.

[47] For the orthodox view, cf. note 4 of the transl. of the *Kathāvatthu* p. 182 (V. 8).

[48] *Āma mahārāja bhagavā sabbaññu na ca bhagavato satataṁ samitaṁ ñāṇadassanaṁ paccupaṭṭhitaṁ, āvajj anaparībaddha bhagavato savvannutañaṇaṁ, āvajjitvā yadicchakam jānātiti* || (Thenckser's Edition of *Milindapañho*, p. 102).

The two kinds of omniscience as implied in this passage correspond exactly to those of the Yukta and Yuñjāna *yogins* as described in the *Bhāṣāpariccheda, Kārikā*, 66.

nothing stood in the way of his knowledge, so that whenever he wanted to know any object he used to reflect upon it (*āvajjitvā*) and at once the object revealed itself to his mind. It is the mysterious power of the Buddha Eye that it can penetrate into any time.[49] Nothing can obscure its vision. In this connection one is also reminded of the interesting description (in Aśvaghoṣa's *Buddhacarita*, chap. XIV) of the Divine Eye (*divyacakṣus*) which the Buddha is said to have gained in course of contemplation during the second watch of the memorable might on his overthrow of Māra. By that wonderful faculty of vision, he saw the entire knowledge world (universe), as if reflected in a clear mirror: *tatas tena sa divyena pariśuddhena cakṣuṣā | dadarsa nikhilaṁ lokam ādarśa'iva nirmale* || (verse 8). Emphasis is here upon the word *nikhilam* which implies freedom from all limitations temporal as well as spatial, and indicates that the vision was simultaneous.

It is really a difficulty which Buddhism (at least its earlier school) does not seem to have successfully solved. All attempted solutions are but make-shifts and show no way out of the contradictions involved.

-VIII-

JAINISM

In the Jaina philosophy, however, no such difficulty arises. Here the fact of omniscience, including the lower faculties of bare clairvoyance, thought-reading etc. claimed for the Lord who possesses it eternally and for the *jīvas* who gain it after a striving, lends itself to any easy explanation. For it is admitted that the *jīva*

[49] Knowledge of the past and future is among the 18 things accruing to a *sādhaka*, according to Mahāvaṁsa, when the Buddha eye is opened for him. Even lower down, *dhammacakkhu* and *divvacakkhu* are capable of such vision into the past or into the future. The fact of Buddha's *jātismaratā* (memory of ante-natal births), so frequently described in the Piṭakas and considered as one of the eight fruits of *dhyāna* or of the power arising from the development of *dhammacakkhu* or as one of the five (or six) *abhijñās*, lends supposition that the veil of Time did not exist of Buddha.

is eternal, that the universe as such is eternal (though subject to change) and that the *jīva*'s knowledge of this universe is also eternal. Even the past and the future object of knowledge are *existent* (*atītānāgatānām arthānāṁ vartamānakālasambandhitayā 'bhave'pi atītānāgatākālasāmbandhitāyā bhāvāt*).[50] Absence of the object from the senses is not a barrier to its being known super-normally; it is the limitation of senses alone that they cannot cognise things not present to them, but in the case of higher perception or intuition, which is not sense-born, the assumption of such limitation is not justified by experience. At any rate, it is admitted that whether present or absent, every object has an existence of its own.

This intuitive experience is said to be two-fold: (i) relative and imperfect (*vikala*), and (ii) absolute and perfect (*sakala*). In the first case the intuition is known as *avadhijñāna* or *avadhidarśana* when its object is a physical substance (*rūpin* or *mūrtadravya*)[51] and as *manaḥparyāya* when it discerns the thoughts of another mind, and in the second case it is exalted into the supreme level and is called *kevalajñāna* or *kevaladarśana* which is a characteristic of the Arhat. Leaving aside the thought-reading for the present, we may observe that both *avadhijñāna* (*ohiñaṇa* in Prākṛta) and *kevalajñāna* are free from the obstructions of time and space, but with this difference that whereas the former is also to cognise only the physical, the latter is directed to both the physical and super-physical (*nikhildravyaparyāyasākṣātkārisvarūpa*) and is simultaneous (*mūrtāmūrtasamastavastugatasattāsāmānya ... sakalapratyakṣarūpeṇai'kasamaye paśyati*).[52] It needs hardly be

[50] Bhatta Anatakīrti, *Laghusarvajñasiddhi*, p. 127.

[51] Devasūrī in *Pramāṇanayatattvālokālaṅkāra*, 2.21, says that *avadhijñāna* is *natural* to gods and hell-beings (*bhavapratyaya*) but may be *acquired* by men and beasts (*guṇapratyaya*).

[52] It may be noted that *avadhijñāna* may sometimes be falsified (*vibhaṅgāvadhi*), and is always relative, but *avadhidarśana*, though equally relative is ever truthful. It is *kevalajñāna* and *kevaladarśana* alone which are in every sense absolute and perfect. The distinction between *jñāna* and *darśana* is emphasised in both the Buddhist and Jaina philosophical literature and it seems that the former corresponds to *savikalpaka* and the latter to the *nirvikalpaka jñāna* of the orthodox systems.

added that this *kevalajñāna* and *darśana* are the synonyms of *Pratibhā*, *Prajñā* etc. of the other systems.

According to Jaina philosophy omniscience or the possession of the faculty of Absolute Knowledge and Supreme Vision is an eternal property (being also the essence) of the soul, which it has apparently lost or allowed to be obscured under the influence of a beginningless series of *karmas*, hence known as a veil of knowledge and vision (*jñānāvaraṇīya* and *darśanāvaraṇīya*).[53] By means of spiritual culture this veil may be withdrawn, and in proportion to its withdrawal the soul will regain its lost knowledge until at last, when all the *karmas* are destroyed, it will become once more omniscient (and omnipotent), being established in its pure and eternal essence.

But what is the nature of this culture which helps in lifting up the veil? To this no definite reply can be given. Different systems, of course, prescribe different methods, but all agree in asserting the paramount importance of Yoga and certain physical austerities. It is said that by these Yogic practices, a tremendous amount of energy, called *tejoleśyāḥ* (akin to electricity and magnetism) is generated in the body.[54] This is of the nature of a fiery force which, when sufficiently purified by continued practice, burns up the cobwebs of the veiling *karmas*. In the *Uvāsagadasāo*, for instance, it is narrated that with the gradual purification and intensification of his personal magnetism by penances the *āvaraṇakarmas* were removed and clairvoyant sight dawned upon *ānanda*.[55] This *āvaraṇakarma* which conceals reality is referred to in the *Yogasūtra* (II, 52) under the name of *prakāśāvaraṇa*, and we can understand that the dawning of the intuitive sense is consequent upon the clearing up of these veiling mists. Carried to its utmost extent, this process of purification naturally ends in the establishment of the power of all-knowledge.

---

53 See Brahmadeva's commentary on *Dravyasaṁgraha*, p. 6.

54 Cf. Hoerule's translation of *Uvāsaga*, p. 50, note 140.

55 *Āṇandassa ... lesāhiṁ visujkramānihiṁ tadāvaraṇijjāṇam karmāṇam svaovasameṇam ohināṇe samuppanne.* Hoerule's edition, p. 33.

-IX-

ITIHĀSA, PURĀṆA AND PROSE LITERATURE

In the *Mahābhārata* the word *Pratibhā* occurs several times, and the context shows that it conveyed the same sense in which we find it used in the Yoga system of Patañjali. Thus in *Śāntiparva* (chap. 316.14) [56] it is contrasted with *apavarga*, thereby implying that it was conceived as an impediment in the way of final release (cf. *Yoga Sūtra*, 3.37). Elsewhere (chap. 239-24) [57] it is expressly enjoined that it is not an acquisition worth coveting, evidently in view of the possible distractions which it may occasion, so that as soon as this power of all-knowing begins to manifest itself it has to be checked. But in some places we seem to hit upon passages which tend to show that a slightly different view of *Pratibhā* was also prevalent. For what can be the true meaning of that remarkable passage which teaches that *Pratibhā* arises only when the *guṇas* have been surpassed? [58]

In the *Śivapurāṇa* [59] the term *Pratibhā* is explained as to be the faultless illumination of things subtle, hidden, remote, past and future. It is said to be one of the supernatural obstacles (*dīvyā upasargāḥ*) in the path of realisation, but though an obstacle, it is nevertheless supposed to be an indication of the proximity of this realisation (*siddhisūcaka*) itself.

In the *Kādambari* [60] we find the world *divyacakṣus*, instead of *Pratibhā*, in use. The sage Jābāli is described there as possessed of

[56] Bangabasi edition (p. 1768). Nīlakaṇṭha's interpretation of the term by *vikṣepa* does not seem to be quite happy.

[57] Ibid, p. 1640. In this passage Nilakaṇṭha explains the word as intuitive knowledge of the contents of all *Śāstras* (*sakala śāstrabhānam*). Hopkins renders it by 'faultness illumination'.

[58] See Hopkins's *The Great Epic of India*, p. 181, *Yoga Technique in the Great Epic* in J.A.O.S., vol. XXII, p. 355.

[59] *Vāyaviya Saṁhitā*, chap. 29.78 (Bangabasi edition, p. 964).

[60] See (a) *Anavaratatapaḥkṣapitamalānāṁ karatalāmalakavad akhilaṁ jagadālokyatāṁ divyena cakṣuṣā bhagavatām* || (Parab's edition, pp. 86-7). (b) *Sa* (i.e. *Jābāli*) *hi bhagavān kālatrayadarśī tapaḥprabhāvād divyena cakṣuṣā* | *Sarvam eva karatalaphalam iva jagad ālokayati, vetti janmāntarany atītāni; kathayaty āgāminam apy artham* ... etc. Ibid., p. 92.

this faculty by which he was able to *see* the entire universe (even the past and the future) as if verily present before his eyes. He acquired the power of omniscience through the gradual removal of impurities from his mind by means of constantly practised penances. The eleventh chapter of the *Gītā* contains the classical example of the working of this faculty. On the eve of that memorable event, the battle of Kurukṣetra, which was to decide the fortunes of India for milleniums to come, Lord Kṛṣṇa graciously awakened this faculty in Arjuna (*divyaṁ dadāmi te cakṣuḥ paśya me yogam aiśvaram*, verse 8) for a short time and thus enabled him to have a glimpse of the supreme vision. Arjuna is said to have seen in Kṛṣṇa's body the whole universe with all its past and future states. It was the vision of many in one (*tatrai'kasthaṁ jagat kṛtṣnaṁ pravibhaktam anekadhā*, verse 13) and in this way resembled a similar vision vouchsafed to the Buddha during the period of his contemplation on the bank of the Nirañjanā — a fact to which we have already referred.

DEVELOPMENT OF PRATIBHĀ: RESUME & RETROSPECT

We have seen in the preceding pages that the development of the faculty of omniscience can not be effected unless the mind is purified and free from the obscuring influence of the disposition clinging to it from time immemorial. What is known as the 'divine eye' is really the mind in its purified condition as the *Chāndogya Upaniṣad* (VIII, 12.5) expressly declares: *mano'asya daivaṁ cakṣuḥ*. And the *Vājasaneya Saṁhitā* of the white Yajus (in the *Śivasaṅkalpa mantra*) also makes a similar statement, referring to the marvellous powers possessed by the purified man. It is apparent, therefore, that every man, in so far as he is gifted with a mind, is also gifted with the possibility of omniscience. As soon as the impurities are removed from it, everything is revealed to it, however distant in time or in space; and even super-sensuous objects are rendered accessible to it. This is the process of Yoga by which *tamas* is eliminated by the active *rajas* from *sattva* (= mind, *citta*) which consequently becomes pure, steady and luminous. This *cittaśuddhi* (or *sattvaśuddhi*) which is invariably followed by the rise of *Prajñā*.

But how are the impurities to be cleared away? The whole question turns upon the practical issues of mystic culture and we can do no more than briefly touch upon the matter in this place. It is intimately connected with what is technically known as the 'rousing of the *kuṇḍalinī* or the Serpentine Power' in man. This power represents the combined *jñāna śakti* and *kriyā śakti* of God and exists in a latent form in every individual man. In the ordinary state it is said to be lying asleep and has its centre, according to the usual opinion, at the base of the spinal column. The awakening of *kuṇḍalinī* is the actualisation of the infinite latent power. It is described as a very arduous process and is supposed to be practically impossible without help from outside. This help comes from the Guru, a spiritually awake person, in the form of an influx of spiritual energy from him. And it is held that this 'infusion of energy', usually called *kṛpā* (grace) or *śaktipāta* in Tantric Literature, acts as a dynamic and releases, more or less quickly (according to the spiritual constitution of the subject), the infinite possibilities of the soul by burning up its veiling *karmas*. This is the process of purification and concentration of mind (*cittaśuddhi*), known as the purging of the soul in mystical literature. As soon as the process comes to an end the Light of *Prajñā* (*prajñājyotiḥ*) or *Pratibhā* begins to shine forth in the manner of a Luminous Eye in the middle of the forehead, just between the two eye-brows, and the man is then said to be converted or regenerated into a god-man. This is the so-called 'Divine Eye' (*divyacakṣuḥ*) or the third eye of Śiva, otherwise known as the Eye of Wisdom (*prajñācakṣuḥ*) or the Eye of *Ṛṣi* (*ārṣa-cakṣuḥ*). Since this eye is opened by the grace of the Guru (*cakṣur unmīlitam yena* in *Gurustava*), the latter is usually called the 'giver of the eye' itself is sometimes spoken of as the Guru.

The centre of this faculty of vision is thus found to be the middle of the two eyebrows, above the root of the nose, where the so-called *ājñācakra* (the sixth member of the six-fold group of psychic centres within the *suṣumṇā*) is located. And this squares with the fact that this is also the seat of the mind.

Concurrently with the opening of this vision, the *yogin* begins to hear the eternal and unbroken sound of *Nāda* (i.e. Oṁkāra), the sweet and all-obliterating Divine Harmony. Like the sweeping current of a rushing flood, this mighty sound carries everything before it and drowns all in its music, until, at last, it ceases itself to be heard and there is the Absolute Silence of *nirvikalpa samādhi.*

When this light and sound are fully realised, but before plunging into the Absolute, the *yogin* is elevated into the highest plane of cosmic life. The *siddhas*, *ṛṣis* and gods are seen and their voices (which are all aspects of *daivī vāk* or *ākāśavānī*) are heard. There exists nothing between him and the rest of the universe. And indeed his whole life is then one continuous Brahmavihāra.

Being himself saved, he now becomes, if he so desires it, the saviour of humanity; and he may also participate in the government of the world or else he may live in eternal and blissful communion with the Lord, forgetful of all besides Him. He may even merge forever (or for a definite time) his self-identity in the Absolute and obtain the peace of *Nirvāṇa*. There are infinite possibilities of the transnatural life, and no two souls need be exactly alike in their destiny, though all may be said to have reached *in one sense* the same Beatific Goal. So long as he is in earthly life either before the falling off of the body or on the voluntary resumption of such life subsequent to his physical death, the virtues of Love and Faith are exemplified in him in their noblest aspects. He is the Ideal of Perfect Humanity which is Divinity itself in a concrete shape and is the source of light and life and joy to the word, deep in darkness and sorrow. It is from him that the 'Scriptures' proceed and the world receives guidance and inspiration.

~2~

ŚĀKTA PHILOSOPHY

-I-

The term 'Śākta philosophy', loosely used in the sense of a school of philosophical doctrines, covers the entire field of Śākta culture in India. Every system of culture has its own line of approach to reality. An enquiry into ancient cultures would show that the cult of Śakti is very old in India as in other parts of the world. And it is quite possible that it existed along with Śaiva and Pāśupata cults in the prehistoric Indus Valley civilization.

In spite of the antiquity of Śākta culture and of its philosophical traditions, no serious attempts seems to have been made in the past to systematize them and give them a definite shape.[1] The result was that though the culture was held in great esteem as embodying the secret wisdom of the elect it did not find its proper place in any of the compendia of Indian Philosophy, including the *Sarvadarśanasaṁgraha* of Madhavācārya.[2]

The reason why no serious attempt was made is said to have been either that it was deemed improper to drag down for rational examination truths inaccessible to the experience of ordinary men, or that no further systematization of the revealed truth than what is contained in the allied works of the Śaiva philosophers was needed for the average reader. This reason is not convincing enough, for if the Upaniṣads could be made the basis of a philosophical system, there is no reason why the Śākta Āgamas could not be similarly

---

[1] Pt. Pañcānān Tarkaratna in his *Śakti-Bhāṣya* on the *Brahma Sūtra* and on the *Iśa-Upaniṣad* (Pub. Banaras, Śaka 1859-61), attempted to bring into prominence what he regarded as the Śākta point of view in the history of Indian philosophy. The attempt is laudable, but it does not truly represent any of the traditional viewpoints of the Śākta schools.

[2] *Sarva-Sidhānta-Saṁgraha* attributed to Śaṅkarācārya, *Ṣaḍdarśanasamuccaya* by Haribhadra and Rājaśekhāra, *Vivekavilāsa* by Jinadatta etc. are similar works, but in none of them the Sākta system is represented, even referred to by name.

utilized. For the function of philosophy is, as Joad rightly remarks, to accepts the data furnished by the specialists who have worked in the field and then to "assess their meaning and significance".

The Āgamas have their own theory as to the manner in which supreme knowledge descends on earth-consciousness. The Scriptures as such are ultimately traceable to this source.[3] The question as to how intuitions of a higher plane of consciousness are translated into thought and language, committed to writing and made communicable to others have been answered by Vyāsa in his commentary on *Yoga-Sūtra* (I.43). He says that the supersensuous perception of *yogins* obtained through *nirvitarka-samādhi* is really an intuition of the unique character (*viśeṣa*) of an object, but being associated with verbal elements it loses its immediacy and is turned into a concept capable of being transmitted to others. This is how, according to him, scriptures originate.[4] The supreme knowledge of *Pratibhā* is integral and cannot be obtained from the words of teachers. It is self-generated and does not depend upon any external factor.[5] The cult of Śakti produced a profound influence on general Indian thought. A topographical survey of India would show that the country is scattered over numerous centres of Śakti-sādhana. It was widespread in the past and has continued unbroken till today.

The history of Śākta-Tāntrika culture may be divided into three periods.

[3] The descent is from *Parā-vāc* through *paśyantī* and *madhyamā* to the *vaikharī* level (see Jayaratha on *Tantrāloka*, I. p. 34 and J.C. Chatterjee: *Kashmir Saivism*, pp. 4-6). As regards the order of descent there are different accounts, though the underlying idea is the same. Cf. *Paraśurāma-Kalpa-Sūtra*, 1. II; *Setu-Bandha* by Bhāskara Rāya, 7.47; *Kāma-Kalā-Vilāsa* with *cidvalli*, 50-3; *Yoginī-Hṛdaya-Dīpikā*, pp. 1-3; *Saubhāgya-Subhagodaya* (quoted in *Dīpikā*, pp. 79-825) etc.

[4] As to how intuitive knowledge is converted into thought, Patañjali holds that it is through association with Śabda. The supersensuous perception of the *yogin* in regard to an object obtained through *nirvitarka-samādhi*, gives rise to an Immediate knowledge of its unique character, but if it is to be communicated to others it has to be interwoven with Śabda and then in that thought form transmitted through language.

[5] See my article : 'The doctrine of Pratibhā in Indian Philosophy' in the *Annals of the Bhandarkar Institute*, 1923-4, Vol VPP. 1-8, 113-32 [Chapter 1 of this book].

(a) Ancient or pre-Buddhistic, going back to prehistoric age.

(b) Mediaeval or post-Buddhistic, rather post-Christian, extending to about A.D. 1200.

(c) Modern, from A.D. 1300 till now.

No works of the ancient age are now forthcoming. The most authoritative treatises available today belong to the mediaeval period, though it is likely that some of these works contain traditions and even actual fragments which may be referred to the earlier period. The mediaeval was the most creative period in the history of the Tāntrika, as, in fact, in that of many other branches of Sanskrit literature. Most of the standard works, including the original Āgamas, the treatises based on them and commentaries on them by subsequent writers, fall in this period. The modern period too has been productive, but with a few brilliant exceptions most of the works produced in this period are of secondary character and include compilations, practical handbooks and minor tracts dealing with miscellaneous subjects.

The Sākta literature is extensive, though most of it is of mixed character. Śiva and Śakti being intimately related, Śaiva and Sākta Tantras have generally a common cultural background, not only in practices but in philosophical conceptions as well. The Āgamas are mostly inclined towards Advaita, but other view-points are not wanting. It is believed that the sixty-four *Bhairava-Āgamas* which were issued from the Yoginī face of Śiva were non-dualistic, the ten *Śaiva-Āgamas* were dualistic and the eighteen *Raudra-Āgamas* were of a mixed character.[6] Besides these, there were numerous other Āgamas, most of which have disappeared, though some have survived in a complete or mutilated form, or are known through references and quotations. Among the works which have a philosophical bearing may be mentioned the names of *Svacchanda*, *Mālinīvijaya*, *Vijñāna-Bhairava*, *Tri-Śiro Bhairava*, *Kula-Gahvara*, *Paramānanda-Tantra*, etc. and also *Āgama-Rahasya*, *Abheda-Kārikā*, *Ājñāvatāra* etc.

---

[6] See Jayaratha on *Tantrāloka*, 1.18. There is reference to sixty-four Tantras in Śaṅkara's *Saundarya-Laharī*, V.37. Lakṣmīdhara's commentary gives a list of the names. Other lists are found in the *Sarvollāsa* and *Vāmakeśvara-Tantras*.

Each Āgama has four *pādas*, of which *jñānapāda* is devoted to a discussion of philosophical problems. It is not to be supposed that the approach to the problems and their solutions in each *Āgama* has always been the same. Very great differences are sometimes noticed, but in a general way it may be said that most of the Āgamas pre-supposed a common cultural heritage. From this point of view, therefore, a real grouping and a classification based upon the specific teaching of each group is possible. At some future date, when a regular history of the development of Śākta thought will come to be written, these differences and specific characters will have to be taken into account.

There are different schools of Śākta culture, among which the line of Śrī-vidyā possesses an extensive literature. The school of Kālī has also its own literature, though not so extensive. The Śrī-kula includes certain *śaktis* and Kālī-kula includes certain others. Both these schools and all the other cults are in a sense inter-related. Agastya, Durvāsas, Dattātreya and others [7] were devoted to Śrī-vidyā and produced a number of interesting works. Agastya is credited with the authorship of a *Śakti-Sūtra* and a *Śakti-Mahimnā-Stotra*.[8] This *Sūtra*, unlike the *Brahma-Śūtra* or *Śiva-Śūtra*, has not much philosophical value. But the *stotra* has its own importance. Durvāsas, who had been ordered by Śrī-kaṇṭha (Śiva) to propagate the Āgamas, is said to have created three *ṛṣis* by the power of his mind and asked them to found an order to preach all shades of philosophical thoughts.[9] Durvāsas himself is known to have been the author of two *stotras* dedicated to Śiva and Śakti, entitled *Parā-Śambhu-Stotra* and *Lalitā-Stotra-Ratna*, which go under his

[7] Nāgānanda is supposed to have been the author of *Śakti-Sūtra*. Another *Śakti-Sūtra* is attributed to Bharadvāja (see *Kalyāna*, ibid., p. 624). The authenticity of these works is not very clear.

[8] A work called *Śrī-Vidyā-Dīpikā* is attributed to Agastya. It contains an interpretation of the *pañcādaśi-mantra* received by him from Hayagrīva.

[9] See J.C. Chatterji's *Kashmir-Saivism*, pp. 23-4; K.C. Pandey, *Abhinavagupta*, p. 72 (cf. also p. 55. Durvāsas is said to have taught the sixty-four monistic Āgamas to Kṛṣṇa).

name.[10] According to tradition Dattātreya was the author of a *saṁhitā* work (called *Datta-Saṁhitā*)[11] in eighteen thousand verses. Paraśurāma is said to have studied this extensive work, and to bring its contents within the easy reach of students summarized it in a body of six thousand *sūtras* distributed into fifty sections. The *saṁhitā* and *sūtras* were both abridged in the form of a dialogue between Dattātreya and Paraśurāma by Sumedhas, a pupil of Paraśurāma. This work may be identified with *Tripura-Rahasya*, in the *māhātmya* section of which the tradition is recorded. The *jñāna khaṇḍa* of this work forms an excellent introduction to Śākta philosophy.[12]

Gauḍapāda, supposed to be identical with the Parama-Guru of Śaṅkarācārya, wrote a *sūtra* work, called *Śrī-Vidyā-Ratna-Sūtra*, on which Śaṅkarācārya commented. It is an important work in the history of Śākta literature but not of much philosophical value.[13] His *Subhagodaya-Stuti* and Śaṅkara's *Saundaryalaharī* deserve a passing mention. Śaṅkara's *Prapañca-Sāra* with Padmapāda's commentary as well as *Prayogakramadīpikā* are standard works.

---

[10] In colophon of the *Lalitā-Stava-Ratna* Durvāsas is called *Sakalāgamācārya Cakravartin*. Nityānanda in his commentary says that Durvāsas, *alias* Krodha-bhaṭṭāraka, is really Śiva himself, the master of the teachers of Āgamas born of the womb of Anurūpā. The *Śakti-Stotra* has been published by N. Sagar in Bombay. The *Para-Śambhu-Stotra*, of which a manuscript was examined by me, is divided into several sections dealing with *kriyā-śakti*, *kuṇḍalinī*, *mātṛkā* etc. Here Paramā-Śiva is described as the world teacher, who reveals *Mahā-mātṛkā* in order to manifest *Brahma-tattva*, which is His own self-revelation, the *Prakāśa* having been hidden so long in His heart. Even in this *stotra* Durvāsas is called Krodha-bhaṭṭāraka. It is said that Somānanda, the great Śaiva teacher of Kāśmīra descended from Durvāsas.

[11] *Datta-Saṁhitā* is referred to in *Saubhāgya-Bhāskara*.

[12] It is evident that the work of Sumedhas (of Hārīta family and known as Hārītāyana) is really to be identified with *Tripura-Rahasya* itself rather than with the *Kalpa-Sūtra* of Paraśurāma as some have done, because the *Kalpa-Sūtra* is not in the shape of a dialogue between Dattātreya and Paraśurāma and is not attributed to Sumedhas, whereas *Tripura-Rahasya* has the form of a similar dialogue and is attributed to Sumedhas Hāritāyana.

[13] See *Śrī-Vidyā-Ratna-Sūtra* with commentary by Śaṅkarācārya (Sarasvati Bhavan Texts, Banaras) edited by M.M. Pt. Narayan Shastri Khiste.

So is Lakṣmaṇa Deśika's *Śaradātilaka* on which Rāghava Bhaṭṭa commented. Somānanda in his *Śivadṛṣṭi* refers to the school of Śāktas as allied to his own school (*Śaiva*) and says that in their opinion Śakti is the only substance, Śiva being but a name reserved for its inactive condition.[14] Though he was a Śaiva in conviction his analysis of *Vāc* is a valuable contribution to Śākta thought. As regards the great Abhinavagupta, he was verily the soul of Śākta culture. He was a pronounced Kaula and his literary activities in the field of *Śaiva-Śākta-Āgama* (as well as in poetics and dramaturgy) gave it a unique philosophical value which has not yet been surpassed by any of his contemporaries or successors. His *Tantrāloka* is an encyclopaedic work on Śaiva-Śākta philosophy based on many earlier works. His *Mālinīvijayavārttika*, *Parā-Trimśikā-Vivaraṇa*, *Pratyabhijñavivṛtī-Vimarśinī* and *Pratyabhijñā-Vimarśinī* are full of extraordinary learning and spiritual wisdom.

After Abhinava, the most important names are those of Gorakṣa, Puṇyānanda, Naṭanānanda, Amṛtānanda, Svatantrānanda and Bhāskara Rāya. Gorakṣa alias Maheśvarānanda was the author of *Mahārtha-Mañjarī*, and also its commentary entitled *Parimala*, *Saṁvid-Ultāsa* etc. He was a close follower of Abhinava. *Pratyabhijñāhṛdaya*, referred to as Śākti-Sūtra by Bhāskara,[15] was commented on by Kṣemarāja, also related to Abhinava. Puṇyānanda's *Kāma-Kalā-Vilāsā* is a standard work on *kāma-kalā* and deals with Śakti in its creative aspect. Naṭanānanda wrote its commentary called *cidvalli*. Amṛtānanda was Puṇyānanda's disciple. His *Yoginīhṛdayadīpikā*, a commentary of the yoginī-hṛdaya section of *Nityāṣ-odaśikārṇava* of the Vāmakeśvara-Tantra represents one of the most valuable works on Tāntrika culture. Other works also, e.g. *Saubhāgyasubhagodaya*, are known to have come from his pen. Svatantrānanda wrote his *Mātṛkā-Cakra-Viveka*, a unique work in five sections devoted to an elaborate exposition of *Rahasya-Āgama* or the secret wisdom of Śākta-Tantras. There is an excellent commentary on his work by one Śivānanda Muni.

---

[14] See *Śiva-Dṛṣti*, p. 94.

[15] See *Saubhāgya-Bhāskara*, pp. 96-97 etc.

Bhāskara Rāya is perhaps the most erudite Śākta scholar in recent times (A.D. 1723-1740) who wrote many valuable works on Śākta Āgama. His best work is probably *Setu-Bandha*, the commentary on *Nityā-Ṣoḍaśikārṇava*. His *Śāmbhavānanda-Kalpa-Latā*, *Varivasyā-Rahasya*, *Varivasyā-Prakāśa*, commentaries on *Kaula*, *Tripura and Bhavanā-Upaniṣads*, on *Lalitā-Sahasranāma* (*Saubhāgya-bhāskara*) and on *Durgā-Sapta-Śatī* (Guptavatī) deservedly famous works and exhibit the author at his best. Pūrṇānanda's *Śrītattvacintāmaṇi* is a good book but contains very little philosophical information.

As regards the Kālī school the following works may be mentioned: *Kāla-Jñāna*, *Kālottara*, *Mahākāla-Saṁhitā*. *Vyomakeśa-Saṁhitā*, *Jayadratha-Yāmala*, *Uttara-Tantra*, *Śakti-Saṁgama-Tantra* (Kālī section), etc.

-II-

The Supreme Reality called *Saṁvit* is of the nature of pure intelligence, which is self-luminous and unaffected by the limitation of time, space and causality. It is infinite light, called *prakāśa*, with an unstinted freedom of action called *vimarśa* or *svātantrya*. This freedom constitutes its power which in fact is identical with its being and remains involved in it as well as expresses itself as its inalienable property. The essence of *Saṁvit* is consciousness free from *vikalpas*, and it is fundamentally distinct from matter. It is one, being integral, continuous, compact and of homogeneous texture and there is no possibility of break in its continuity and admixture of foreign elements in its essence. Being free, it does not depend on anything else for its manifestation and function.

The power may be said to exist in a two-fold condition. Creation, dissolution etc., are in reality consequent on the play of this power. It is always active, its activity being expressed on the one hand as self-limitation (*tirodhāna*) involving the appearance (*sṛṣṭi*) of the universe as such till then absorbed in and identified with the essence of Reality and on the other as self-expression only (*anugraha* = grace) implying the disappearance (*saṁhāra*) of the same and its absorption in the Reality. Maintenance (*sthiti*) of the world represents an intermediate state between *saṁhāra* and *sṛṣṭi.*

Saṁvit is like a clean mirror within which the universe shines as an image reflected in a transparent medium. As the image is not distinct from the mirror, the universe is inseparable from *Saṁvit.* But the analogy between the two needs not be pushed beyond this limit. The mirror reflects an object, but *Saṁvit* in its fullness being creative requires no object outside itself. This freedom or power of actualisation is *svātantrya* or *māyā*. The world thus manifested within the Absolute has infinite-varieties, but the *Saṁvit* remains always the same unbroken unity of existence and consciousness. Reality as universal Being is one, but its specific forms are multiple, just as the mirror is one but the images reflected in it are many. The one becomes many, not under the pressure of any external principle but through its own intrinsic dynamism. Motion seems to be initiated and multiplicity evolved within the primal unity under its influence. For this reason the one always retains its unity and yet creation etc. with its infinite varieties follow. The many is as real as the one, for both are the same.

We are thus confronted with three possible states for consideration:

(a) *Saṁvit* alone, but not the world appearing within it (= *cit*).

(b) *Saṁvit* as well as the world shining within it, without external projection (= *ānanda*).

(c) *Saṁvit*, the world within it and its projection outside (= *icchā*).

In every case *Saṁvit* as such remains one and the same and is not in the least affected. Hence it is called *nirvikalpa*, free from *vikalpas* and modifications. On comparison of the three states it would seem that the first represents a condition in which there is no manifestation within or without. The second is a state of manifestation within, but not without. The third state, being that of *icchā*, means external projection, though in reality *Saṁvit* in itself being full, can have nothing outside it, for even the so-called externality is not really external to it.

That *Saṁvit* is free from *vikalpa* and that creation is *vikalpa* or *kalpanā* is admitted by both Śākta Āgama and the Vedānta. But the question is, how does creation as a *vikalpa* emanate from *Saṁvit*, which is pure and free from *vikalpas*? The Vedānta says, it does not so emanate but is part of a beginningless process (in spite of cyclic beginnings) going on within the domain of matter or *māyā* and superimposed on *Saṁvit* or Brahman which reveals it — a process which is not in any way initiated by it.

But the attitude of Āgama is different. It believes in *svātantrya* or power in the *Saṁvit* to generate movement, though it is only *ābhāsa*, and externality is only apparent. The universe is within this, power is within the Absolute. When power is supposed to be dormant, *vimarśa* is held to be dissolved in *prakāśa* (*antarlīna-vimarśa*): Śakti seems to be sleeping as *kuṇḍalinī* and Śiva is no longer Śiva, but a *śava*, the state being not one of spirit but of lifeless matter. But when power is awake as indeed it always is, the supreme consciousness remains conscious of itself. This self-awareness of the Absolute expresses itsself as 'I' or '*Aham*' which is described as full (*pūrṇa*), since there is nothing outside it to act as a counter-entity in the form of 'this' or '*idam*'. In the technical language of the Āgama, the state of Absolute from this point of view is called *Pūrṇā'haṁtā*. The fullness of *Aham* implies the presence of the entire universe reflected within it as within a mirror. The universe is then one with *Aham*.

Saṁvit is *prakāśa* as well as *vimarśa* — it is beyond the universe (*viśvottīrṇo*) and yet permeates it (*viśvātmaka*). The two aspects constitute one integral whole. This is a-ha-m, the first letter '*a*' standing for *prakāśa*, the last letter '*ha*' representing *vimarśa*; the unity of the two, which would denote the unity of all the letters of the alphabet between '*a*' and '*ha*', is indicated by the *bindu* '*ṁ*'. Thus *aham* is symbolized by *bindu*. The creative act of the Supreme Will breaks as it were this *bindu* and sets in operation the entire cosmic process.

The externalisation referred to above is the manifestation of a non-ego (*an-ahaṁ-bhāva*) within the pure Ego (*śuddha-Ātman*), appearing as external to the limited ego; it is the root Ignorance (*mūlāvidyā*) of the Vedānta. This non-ego is the so-called *a-vyakta* (unmanifest) or *jaḍa-śakti* (matter). The freedom or the spiritual power of *Saṁvit*, known as *Cit Śakti*, is beyond this Ignorance, but to this *power* the Advaita Vedānta, as usually interpreted, seems to be a stranger. As *avidyā* or the material *power* issues out of the spiritual *power*, the ultimate source of all contingent existence, there is no discrepancy in the statement, often found in Śākta works (e.g. *Tripura-Rahasya, jñāna khaṇḍa*) that *power* has three distinct states of its existence:

(a) During the universal dissolution, when the Self is free from all *vikalpas*, Śakti exists as pure *Cit-Śakti*, i.e. *Parā-Prakṛti* (of the *Gītā*). As mirror is the life of the image, it is the life-principle of *jīva* and *jagat* which are sustained by it.

(b) When after *pralaya* the pure state ceases and when although there is no *vikalpa* as such, there is yet a tendency in that direction, the power is called *Māyā-Śakti*.

(c) But when the *vikalpas* are fully developed and materiality becomes dense, Śakti appears as *avidyā* or *jaḍa-śakti* or *prakṛti*. When *māyā* and *avidyā* are subsumed under one name it is called *jaḍa-prakṛti* (i.e. *Aparā-Prakṛti* of the *Gītā*).

It has already been observed that the appearance of the universe in creation (*sṛṣṭi*) follows upon the self-limitation of the divine *power*, and the cosmic end in dissolution (*pralaya*) follows from the self-assertion of the same *power*. After the period of cosmic night is over the supreme will, in co-operation with the mature *adṛṣṭas* of *jīvas*, manifests, only partially as it were, the essence of the Self, whereon the Self is revealed as limited. The appearance of limitation is thus the emergence of not-self, known as *avidyā* or *jaḍaśakti*, called also differently by the names of void (*śūnya*), *prakṛti*, absolute negation, darkness (*tamas*) and *ākāśa*. This is the first stage in the order of creation and represents the first limitation imposed on the Limitless. The erroneous belief, generated through the freedom of the Self, that the Ego is partial (*aikadeśika*) and not full and universal (*pūrṇa*) is responsible for the appearance of this something which, being a portion of the Self, is yet outside of it and free from self-consciousness and is described as not-self or by any other name as shown above.

Thus Supreme Reality splits itself spontaneously, as it were, into two sections — one appearing as the subject and the other as the object. Purṇā'haṁtā which is the essence of Supreme Reality disappears after this cleavage: the portion to which limited egoism attaches being the subject and the other portion free from egoism the object. The object as thus making its appearance is the unmanifest (*a-vyakta*) Nature from which the entire creation emanates and which is perceived by the subject as distinct from itself.

Caitanya is of the nature of self-luminous 'light' (*sphurat*) which shines on itself (*svātman*) and is known as *ahaṁtā* or 'I-ness'. When resting on the non-ego (*anātman*) it expresses itself as *idaṁtā* or 'this-ness'. The essence of *Caitanya* consists in the fact that the light (*prakāśa*) is always revealed to itself. This universal Ego or 'I' stands behind all dualism. The supreme Ego is universal, as there is nothing to limit (*pariccheda*) or to differentiate (*vyāvṛtti*) it, and the entire visible universe exists in identity with it. But this characteristic by its very nature is absent from matter (*jaḍa*), which is not self-manifest. Just as light and heat co-exist in fire, in the same way universal *ahaṁtā* and freedom or *śakti* co-exist in *Caitanya*. This freedom is *māyā* which, though essentially identical with *Caitanya* (*cid-eka-rūpa*), brings out varieties of an infinite kind, but in bringing out this variety it does not in the least swerve from the essence.

The appearance of the universe in pure *Caitanya* has three distinct stages:

1) The first is the germinal state (*bījāvasthā*), when the material power, which is still in its earliest phase of manifestation, is pure. Matter does not assert itself at this stage and consequently there is no differentiation in experience. In other words, it does not yet appear as distinct from *Caitanya*, though potentially it exists. The state is represented by the five pure *tattvas*, viz, Śiva, Śakti, Sadā-Śiva, Śuddha-Vidyā and Īśvara.

(a) The *avidyā*, which has been described above as being *Caitanya* in its limited appearance as an object external to the subject, is called Śiva. In pure *Caitanya*, owing to the play of its own will, an infinite number of limited aspects (*svā'mśaś*) arise.

These are mutually distinct. From this point of view, to every limited aspect of Cit there is a corresponding object external to it, but to the unlimited Cit or Pure Self (*Pūrṇa-Ātman-Para Śiva*) there is no externality. The universal (*sāmānya*) common to all the pure and limited Cit aspect referred to above is called Śiva-*tattva*. The *tattva* is thus a universal holding within it all the individuals (*viśeṣas*), but Para Śiva or Pure Self is transcendent and comprises both the universal and the individuals. Hence Śiva-*tattva* may be more properly described as pure *Caitanya* in its general but conditional form, free from all *vikalpas*, and is to be distinguished from the Absolute proper.

(b) The appearance of Śiva (*parichinna nirvikalpa cit*) as 'I' (*aham*) is called Śakti. Although this self-presentative character (*ahaṁ-bhāsana*) is in the essence of *Cit*, so that there can be in fact no differentiation between Śiva and Śakti as such, the *Cit* is nevertheless known as Śiva in so far as it is free from all differentiating attributes and as Śakti by virtue of its characteristic self-awareness.

(c) When the self-presentation (*ahaṁ-bhāsana*) is no longer confined to the Self but is extended to the not-self or the object (*mahā-śūnya*) external to the self, it is known as Sadāśiva. This state marks the identification of the self with the not-self in the form "I am this" and indicates predominance of spirit over matter.

(d) But when matter prevails and the consciousness assumes the form "This is I", the state is technically called Īśvara.

(e) The term '*Śuddha-vidyā*' is reserved for the state which represents an equality in the presentation of the subjective and objective elements in consciousness.

2) The second stage in the evolution of *avidyā* represents a further development of difference or materiality, when the subtle products of matter and spirit make their appearance. In this mixed condition the mixed (*miśra*) *tattvas*, viz, *māyā*, *kalā*, *vidyā*, *rāga*, *kāla* and *niyati* reveal themselves.

(a) The confirmation of difference due to the free will of the Supreme, which characterizes the second stage, has the effect of reversing the normal relation between spirit and matter. Thus, while in the first stage described above, spirit or *cit-śakti* dominates over matter or *jaḍaśakti* which exists in a rudimentary state, merged in spirit, the second stage shows the preponderance of matter over spirit. Consciousness loses its supremacy and becomes a quality inherent in the material subject. All this is due to the emergence and development of difference in *Caitanya*. This material subject, which is matter prevailing over spirit and related to it as a substance to its quality, is called *māyā*.

(b-f) The five aspects of *māyā* are the five so-called *kañcukas* or wrappings which are the five eternal *śaktis* of Para Śiva in a limited form. The obscuring power of *māyā* acts as a veil as it were upon the omnipotence, omniscience, self-contentment, eternity and the freedom of the supreme Self and thus acting is known as *kalā*, *vidyā*, *rāga*, *kāla* and *niyati* respectively.

(g) The Pure Self as obscured by *māyā* and its five-fold activities appears as *puruṣa* with its limitations of action, knowledge, contentment, eternity, and freedom.

(3) The third or grossest stage in the evolution of *avidyā* is represented by the dense products of the mixed *tattvas*, where matter is overwhelmingly strong. This stands for the group of the twenty-four *tattvas*, from primary *prakṛtī* down to *pṛthivī*, constituting the material order.

Prakṛti, with which the lower creation begins, is indeed the assemblage (*samaṣṭi*) of the disposition and tendencies (*vāsanās*) of all persons with various and beginningless *karmans*: it may be fitly described as the body of the *karma* dispositions of the *jīvas*, considered as inhering in *Cit-Śakti* or Self. This *karma-vāsanā* or *prakṛti* is three-fold according to the experience, which in its mortal outcome is pleasant or painful or of the nature of comatose condition in which neither pleasure nor pain is felt.

The dispositions exist in a two-fold condition, viz, as *avyakta* when they lie unmanifest as in dreamless sleep or as *citta* when they manifest themselves as in dreams and the wakeful state. In the dreamless state there can be no experience of pleasure and pain, because, as the mature *karmans* only can be worked off through experience, the others which are not yet sufficiently ripe are not ready for fructification. It is a fact that *karmans*, when they are matured by time, cause the cognitive power (*jñānaśakti*) of the conscious self to move outwards and have contact with the external world, which is the objective outcome of *prakṛti*. In a state of sleep such movement is naturally absent. But the process of time during which the sleep continues acts on the *karmans* and matures some of them so that the aforesaid power is allowed to come in touch with the outer objects or with their semblances and the sleep is over. The power as thus qualified by the body of *karma* dispositions leading to contact with the objects and consequent experience (*bhoga*) is known as *citta*.

The *citta* differs according to the difference of *puruṣa*, but it is one with the *prakṛti* in dreamless sleep. Thus it may be viewed as *puruṣa* or as *prakṛti* according as the conscious (*cit*) or unconscious (*a-vyakta*) element prevails in it. It is not therefore a distinct category, but falls either under *puruṣa* or under *prakṛti*.[16] The *citta* is in fact the inner organ (*antaḥkaraṇa*) which is known under three names according to the triple character of its function, viz, as *ahaṁkāra* when it feels the ego-sense, as *buddhi* when it comes to a decision and as *manas* when it thinks or cogitates within.

A short note on the Śākta view of *manas* (mind) would not be out of place here. Like the supreme *Saṁvit*, *manas* has two aspects, viz, *prakāśa* and *vimarśa*. *Prakāśa* indicates the resting of the *manas* on, and its contact with other objects; and *vimarśa* consists in mental agitation in regards to that very object caught as a reflection within and expressed in thought as "it is thus", which involves association with past images stored in the mind. What happens may be thus explained: the *manas* becomes first connected with the object through the senses, etc., when the latter manifests itself in an undifferentiated form due to freedom from verbal references (*śabdollekha*). This is *nir-vikalpaka-jñāna* and is always inferable according to those who do not believe in the self-validity of knowledge. According to Śākta Āgama, however, this is mere *prakāśa* (i.e., *darśana*) or bare awareness of the object. At the next moment the external object impinges its form on the *manas* by

[16] See *Tripura-Rahasya*, *jñāna khaṇḍa*, ch. XIV, 33-77).

way of reflection, expressed in the judgement — "It is thus". This is called *vicāra*, a state of consciousness in which a particular object is differentiated from others and is mixed up with conceptual elements. It is *vimarśa* or *sa-vikalpaka-jñāna*. Thus the *manas* has a two-fold state, as mentioned above. The *vimarśa* may be fresh as in case of immediate experience (*anubhava*) or old as in case of memory (*smṛti*) and mental co-ordination (*anusandhāna*). Both the latter states are due to psychic dispositions caused by experience.

The states of consciousness are now easily intelligible. The sleep-state (*suṣupti*), from this point of view, would come under *prakāśa*, viz, *prakāśa* of *nidrā*. It is a form of *nir-vikalpaka-jñāna*. It is durable and not momentary and is regarded as a state of insentiency (*mūḍhadaśā*) due to the absence of *vimarśa*. It is pure *prakāśa*, which is another name for insentiency. The waking state (*jāgrat*), on the other hand, is mostly of the nature of *vimarśa* and is not a state of insentiency. Thus an unbroken series of states of consciousness free from images (*vikalpas*) in dreamless sleep; there arises, during the subsequent state of waking, a series of images.

But what is the nature of *nidrā* which is revealed in sleep? It is replied that it represents the great void to which we have alluded in the earlier pages as identical with the so-called *ākāśa* and which is the earliest externalized manifestation after the divine Ātman caused its first self-limitation. It is formless and unmanifest and is revealed in sleep when nothing else exists. It is the absence of all visible forms conceived as one universal background. This being revealed in sleep, the man on waking feels that he was aware of nothing during this state.

It is a well-known phenomenon noted by Śākta philosophers that even during waking the mind becomes insentient as in sleep at the moment of seeing an object, but this insentiency is not felt as such. The *nir-vikalpaka-jñāna* of the waking hours being momentary the insentiency sinks below (*tirohitavat*) under the pressure of the quick succession of images.

In sleep the *prakāśa* aspect of the *manas* remains, but the *vimarśa* lapses. This is why the *manas* is usually described as being dissolution when an outer object is just seen.

The *citta* is really self as directed towards the knowable object. In sleep the *manas*, being free from images, remains quiet and motionless. Its momentary modifications being absent, it is said to be dissolved. Such a state is therefore discernible in each of the three following conditions, viz:

(1) *Nir-vikalpa-samādhi*, when the pure Self remains established in its self-luminous essence.

(2) Sleep, when the unmanifest or great void is revealed.

(3) Vision of an object, when there is *prakāśa* or revelation of the external object through the usual sense contact.

In all these different states there is an apparent similarity of concentrated *prakāśa* due to non-manifestation of *vimarśa* as "it is thus" (*śabdānubedha*). Thought the same *prakāśa* underlies all the states, the states themselves are not identical, in as much as the subsequent *vimarśa* expressed in the form of mental co-ordination (*anusandhāna*) is different in each case. Thus the *vimarśa* in case of *samādhi* assumes the form "I was silent during this time"; in sleep it is expressed as "I knew nothing during this time"; but in the vision of an external object it takes on the form "It is such an object". This difference in *vimarśa* is not explicable except on the assumption of some sort of difference in the objects concerned. But it does not destroy the unity of the essence, viz, freedom from images of verbal associations on the three states in question. The difference in object is as follows:

The object in *samādhi* is pure self, unmixed with the forms of visible body, etc. The object in sleep is the unmanifest or *avyakta* which is an external formless thing. The object in vision is an external substance with peculiar features and distinguishable from others.

Hence, though the object (*bhāsya*) are different, the bare consciousness (*bhāsa*) or awareness which is common to all is one and the same and is undifferentiated. In other words, though *samādhi*, *nidrā* and the external objects are different from one another, the consciousness in which they are revealed is one. This shows that difference in the object cannot produce any corresponding difference in the consciousness or the essence (*svarūpa*). Difference in essence is possible only through reflection which is absent in all the three cases as they are equally of the nature of pure awareness (*prakāśa*).

Samādhi and sleep being of longer duration are capable of being thought about (*vimarśa*) in subsequent moments, but the case of the vision of an object is different, because it is momentary. In the same manner, momentary *samādhi* or sleep cannot be made an appropriate object of *vimarśa*. Even in waking hours there exists momentary *samādhis* as well as *suṣuptis* which are generally ignored.[17]

-III-

The *Śaradā-Tilaka* (I.7-8), while describing the origin of the manifested world, contains an important passage, which shows the order of manifestation as follows:

(i) Parameśvara, described as '*sakala*' and '*saccidānanda-bibhava*'.
(ii) Śakti
(iii) Nāda (*para*)
(iv) Bindu (*para*)
(v) Bindu Bīja (*apara*)
(vi) Nāda (*apara*)

In the above context the word 'Parameśvara' means evidently the Supreme Divine in which infinite power, Śakti or *Kalā*,[18] lies in eternal union. The divine being is described there as of the nature of an eternal Self-Existence (*sat*), Self-Consciousness (*cit*) and Self-Delight (*ānanda*). During creation what first happens is the manifestation of power (*śakti*) which so long lay hidden in the depths of Being. There is no doubt that this power is characterized by will (*icchā*) which is its first evolute.

[17] See ibid, XVI, 64-94; also chapters XVII-XVIII.

[18] In this context the word '*Kalā*' stands for the supercosmic transcendent power of the Lord and is to be clearly distinguished from the five *kalās* evolved as forces from *bindu* conceived as cosmic matter and force related to the *tattvas* and *bhavanas*.

In the *Śiva-Purāṇa* (*Vāyavīya-Saṁhitā*) it is said that the emergence of Śakti in the beginning of creation is like the appearance of oil out of oil-seeds. It is a spontaneous act, initiated by the divine Will. In other words, it is through the divine Will that the supreme Power which is synonymous with it and remains concealed in the divine Essence reveals itself.[19]

The appearance of Śakti after the great Cosmic Night is like the revival of memory in a re-awakened person after the unconsciousness of sleep. The desire for a vision again of the lost world is associated with a sense of void, which is *māyā*. *Māyā* stands as the beginning of subsequent creation and the divine principle which produces it is its Lord or Controller. The vision of void is accompanied by an indistinct sound called *para-nāda*, which fills the entire space. *Nāda* is of the nature of light. That sound and light co-exist and are related as phases of the same phenomenon is recognized in the Tantras. The first self-expression of the Supreme Will (*icchā*) is the origination of void (*śūnya*) and of the sound and light filling this void. All this comes under the category of Will. The next step is represented by the concentration of this diffused light-sound into a focus (under the secret influence of Will) called *bindu*. It is in this stage that the power of action (*krīyā śakti*) distinctly unfolds itself. The creative principles (*tattva*) are evolved out of this supreme *bindu*. *Bindu* subsequently breaks itself into three; the three parts are known as *bindu*, *bīja* and *nāda*. *Bindu* is the part in which the Śiva-aspect is predominant, while in *bīja* Śakti prevails. In *nāda*, however, the elements of Śiva and Śakti are of equal strength.

What disturbs the equilibrium of the *bindu*? *Śaradā-Tilaka* says nothing in reply to this question. *Prapañcasāra* (I. 42-3) says that it is *kāla* which breaks the equilibrium of *bindu*, and in this view *kāla* is an eternal aspect of the eternal *puruṣa* through which this intimate knowledge of supreme *Prakṛti* is said to be derived. *Prakṛti* knows itself and is self-luminous.[20]

---

[19] *Śivechayā parā śaktiḥ śiva-tattvaikatāṁ gatā |*
tataḥ parisphuraty ādau sarge tailaṁ tilād iva ||

The great *sound* which comes into being when the *bindu* splits itself is known as Śabda-Brahman, as *Śaradā-Tilaka* (I.11-12) and *Prapañca-Sāra* (I.44) observe.

It is well-known that what figures as the pericarp of the thousand-petalled lotus within the crown of the head is the so called *brahma-randhra* which is often referred to as a void. It extends through the *suṣumnā nāḍi* down to the very bottom of the interior of the spinal column. If the mind stays in the void it loses its restless nature and enables one to attain to the realizations of oneself as above the *guṇas*. The Will-power and the supreme *nāda* emerge from this source.[21]

The supreme *nāda* stands for the supercausal or *mahākāraṇa* state of Brahman, which is known as *visarga-maṇḍala*. If the supreme Śakti is called *kula* and the supreme Śiva *a-kula*, the sphere of *visurga* may be described as below them both. But usually it is placed in the upper layer of *brahma-randhra*, below which the regular order are the so-called spheres of the sun, the moon and the great *vāyu* — all within the limits of the thousands-petalled lotus.

The causal state of Brahman is represented by Śabda Brahman or *kula kuṇḍalinī*, figured as a triangle consisting of three principles (*tattva*) viz, *bindu*, *bīja* and *nāda*, issuing from the *para-bindu* under division. The triangular *kuṇḍalinī* would thus appear to be a manifestation of the primary power represented by *para-nāda* and *para-bindu*.

---

[20] *Prapañca-Sāra*, I. 46. The actuating power of *kāla* is suggested elsewhere also by the expression *kālapreritayā*. The *Prayoga-Kramadīpikā* (p. 412) explains the terms thus: *prakṛter eva pralayāvasthāto yat paripakvadāśānāntaraṁ sṛṣṭyunmukhaiḥ karmabhir udbhinnaṁ rūpaṁ yo'sau binduḥ*.

21 The identification of *Mahā-śūnya* with *vyāpini kalā* of *praṇava* is according to the *Svacchanda-Tantra*. But some writers equāte *Mahā-śūnya* with the initial *nāda*. (See Purṇānanda's *Śri-Tattva-Cintāmaṇi*). The terms sixteenth (*ṣoḍaśi*) and seventeenth (*sapta-daśi*) *kalā* of the moon are used differently in different texts. When the supreme *Nāda* is called the sixteenth, or *amā kalā*, the name 'seventeenth *kalā*' is reserved for the supreme power of *Samanā*. But at other times *unmanī* is attributed to the seventeenth *kalā*, when the words *Śakti* and *Śūnya* are used synonymously.

The subtle principles of the cosmic structure issue out of the *kuṇḍalinī* and begin to locate themselves in distinct centres in the forehead and lower down in the sympathetic system. It has already been observed that *bindu* (lower) is Śiva, *bīja* is Śakti and *nāda* (lower) is the product of their union. Bīja or Śakti is virtually the entire alphabet, the letters of which are arranged in a triangular fashion designated in the Tantras as '*a-ka-tha*' triangle — an equilateral triangle the three sides or lines of which are formed by sixteen letters each, beginning with '*a*', '*ka*' and '*tha*' respectively. Thus forty-eight letters constitute the three equal sides of this triangle. This triangle is intimately associated with the principles of *kāma-kalā*. The constituent *bindus* of *kāma-kalā* are thus three — two causal (*kāraṇa*) and one of the nature of effect (*kārya*).

The *nāda* which springs from the interaction of *bindu* (lower) and *bīja* is to be distinguished from Śabda-Brahman which manifested itself during the division of *para-bindu*. The latter may be described as *mahānāda*. The *nāda* contains within itself the indistinct sounds of all the letters of the alphabet, much in the same manner as the sunlight may be said to consist of all the coloured rays known to us. The truth of the matter is that *mahānāda* or Śabda-Brahman, in its manifestation as *kuṇḍalinī*, is located in the body of man and serves as the mechanism for the articulation of sound.

The continued practice of a *mantra* causes it to be sounded in a subtle manner in the *suṣumnā*. The sound expands itself and is blended with the lower *nāda*; it does not and cannot rise up to the *mahānāda* higher up. The focus of *mahānāda* is free from the action of ordinary *vāyu* which cannot rise up to it. It may be of some interest to note that *mahānāda* is associated with *para-nāda* in the *brahma-randhra* above it on the one hand and with the lower *nāda* on the other. The power involved in the lower *nāda* crosses the middle of the two eye-brows (*bhrū-madhya*) and flows down the *suṣumnā* channel. At the lowest point *nāda* is converted into the *kuṇḍalinī*. The forces of the *bīja* as concretized in the latter are all within the lower *nāda*.

The position of *para-bindu* has a special value for contemplation, in as much as it represents the nexus of the divine plane on one hand and cosmic and supercosmic spheres on the other. It is the place where *nāda* extends into *mahānāda* or Śabda-Brahman, beyond which is the divine *nāda* within the Infinite. *Para-nāda* above is supra-mental (*unmanā*) divine consciousness and light, while *mahānāda* below is the source of universal creation. *Para-bindu* stands between the two. It is for this reason considered to be the best centre for contemplation of the Guru.

It may be stated that the *bīja* consists of *varṇas* and that these are driven down to take their respective places in the six centres below, as soon as the downward moving power of *mahānāda* passes through the middle of the two eye-brows and extends into the spinal column. These *varṇas*, the modifications of *mahānāda*, being the blends of *nāda* and *bīja*, are so many actions generated from *para-bindu* which is pre-eminently characterized by activc *power*. *Mahānāda* cannot give rise to the different creative principles unless it passes through the stage of *bindu*.

We need not proceed further to describe the progressive stages of creation. We find in the above analysis, which follows mainly the traditions set up by Lakṣmaṇa Deśika, Śaṅkarācārya and others, the antecendent of *para-bindu*; the *mahānāda* called therein Śabda-Brahman, which follows the disruption of *para-bindu*; and the *nāda* which results from the union of *bindu* and *bīja*. Similarly, there are two *bindus* — *para-bindu* which is produced from the focussing of *para-nāda* and which is the source of Śabda-Brahman, the immediate spring of creative forces: and *apara-bindu* which is the effect of *para-bindu* with the Śiva element prevailing. As regards the *kalā* it would appear that the supreme Śakti which is the eternal asociate of the divine principle and always remains in it, either as completely absorbed in it and incapable of differentiation or as partially emergent, is the highest *kalā*. In a lower sense, however, the name *kalā* is used to signify the *bīja* mentioned above. That is to say, the *varṇas*, symbolized as the letter of the alphabet and conceived as the basic principles of the lower *nāda* or the sound potentials, are *kalās* in this sense. From this point of view the triangle called '*a-ka-tha*', otherwise described as *kuṇḍalinī*, is the *kalā*.

-IV-

The earlier Āgamas also generally support a similar view. The supreme Śakti, the instrument of transcendent Śiva in all His activities (*samanā*) is the totality of all the *tattvas*.[22] It is within that the entire universe lies hidden. From this down to *vyāpinī*, or the great void within the *brahma-randhra*, there is a regular series of *śaktis* representing more and more diminished consciousness and power (e.g. *anāśritā*, *anāthā*, *ananta* and *vyoma rupā*), all being hyper-subtle and described by *yogins* in terms of negation. In fact not a single *śakti* beyond the *brahma-randhra* lends itself to a positive description. The *suṣumnā* canal along which the *nāda* flows up ends in *brahma-randhra*.[23]

The supreme Śakti is sometimes described as *Amā kalā*. It is then intended to convey the idea that it is eternal, ever emergent and of the nature of unalloyed bliss, the other *kalās* which go into the make up of the world being replenished and supplemented by it. When it is free from *visarga* it is not outwardly inclined and rests in itself. In this condition it is called *śakti kuṇḍalinī* or *parā-saṁvit* and is likened to a sleeping serpent resting on itself. But when it is ruffled it becomes *visarga* which is of two kinds, accordingly it represents the precreative flutter called *ānanda* and symbolized as '*a*' and the last creative effort bringing out life or *prāṇa* symbolized as '*h*'. *Prāṇa* or '*h*' is sometimes describes as *haṁsa* or *śūnya*. The two *visargas* are therefore known as higher and lower '*para*' and '*a-para*' graphically represented in nāgarī script as the two points of *visarjanīya* (:). The *Amā-kalā* reveals the two points and flows out in order to manifest forms. Every form in the universe, whether a subject or an object or an instrument of knowledge, is identical with *Amā-kalā*, though it may be made

22 This position, in which *kāla* is called *sāmya*, forms a *kalā* of *samanā* and is eternal (being unaffected by *mahā-pralaya*), is that of the so-called *Para-Brahman*. It is not the state of Śiva. The atoms abide here in *mahā-pralaya*, for they are not yet transformed into the essence of Śiva. The movement of *paśu* as such commences from here. See *Tantrāloka*, VI. 138-167.

23 Cf. *Tantrāloka*, VIII 5.400-5

to appear as different from it. The determinate *prakāśa* in each form implies this difference. Hence *śakti-kuṇḍalinī* expressed in *visarga* is still resting on itself as *Saṁvit* and is free from movement.

Prāṇa-kuṇḍalinī represents the other end where *Saṁvit* has already developed in *prāṇa*. *Saṁvit* is full and self-contained. Its supreme creative act is to be distinguished from the later creative processes, as it means the projection of the Self out of itself into itself. As the source of creation is not anything extraneous to the Self, the latter is the efficient (*nimitta*) as well as the intrinsic cause (*upādāna*) of the effect. Creation takes place within the Self and not within time and space different from it. What is projected or created is also not anything other than the Self. Thus every object in this universe, inner or outer, is a form of the Self. The projection is of the nature of multiple *ābhāsas* manifested as both inner and outer realities. *Saṁvit* thus appears gradually as the different letter-sounds in its process of materialization. These are the multiple forms assumed by *visarga*, the outermost being called '*h*'. The *visarga* which is only '*h*' without manifestation is described in some treatises (e.g. *Kula-Gahvara*) as the principle of *kāma* or unrestricted will. As there is no real difference between the *visarga* and the objective world it is not possible to assume a causal a *vācya* as well as *vācaka*. Infinite manifestation is the essence of *visarga*, though it does not produce any real multiplicity. The supreme Śakti as being responsible for this manifold appearance, viz, delight (*ānanda*), will (*icchā*), knowledge (*jñāna*) and action (*kriyā*) is the hidden spring of *visarga*.[24]

The subtle *visarga* ceaselessly expresses itself, and as *nāda* (or *para-bīja*) existing in every creature it indicates *prāṇa* and its existence is felt within by all, though its special manifestation is confined to specific occasions. *Visarga* is thus the attribute of the Supreme Divine which is eternally free and has the power of the five-fold divine activity, viz, creation, preservation, destruction or withdrawal, grace and alienation.

---

[24] See *Tantrāloka*, III. 136-48.

The Transcendent or *anuttara* ('*a*'), by means of *visarga* (up to '*ḥ*' or *prāṇa*), reveals itself as Śakti ('*ha*') and then returns to itself and abides in the indivisible *prakāśa*, which is its own eternal Self, called Śiva-*bindu* ('*ṁ*') — *a-ha-ṁ*. This is how in the universal consciousness, which is no better than bare awareness, there arises a sense of 'I'. Its relation to the not-self, e.g. body, etc. is an event in time which is psychologically explicable. The Ego-sense in pure consciousness reveals it as one's own Self (*svātman*). The unity of Śiva and Śakti follows logically from the integrality of oneness of this sense which covers both. This is the secret of the fullness of Ego or *Pūrṇāhaṁtā* to which reference has already been made.

The unity of *prakāśa* and *vimarśa* is the *bindu* called *kāma* or Ravi (Sun). The emergence of two *bindus* out of this primordial one is the state of *visarga*. The two *bindus* are Agni (fire) and Soma (moon), conceived as *Cit-kalā*. It is not a state of dualism, but one of union between two inseparable elements of a single whole. The two aspects combined, namely, *bindu* and *visarga* are represented as a significant symbol of divine unity, though it is true that in the ultimate state even these elements lose their own lustre. The interaction of the *bindus* causes nectar or creative fluid to flow out. This is the so-called *hārdha-kalā*, the essence of *ānanda*. The interaction is like the heat of fire acting on butter and causing it to melt and flow. The *one* is *sat*, the *two* is *sat* as aware of Itself, i.e. *cit* (*cit-kalā*) and the *hārdha-kalā* flowing from between the two is the result of self-awareness felt as *ānanda*. The entire science of *kāma-kalā* is thus the science of *saccidānanda* and *Brahma-vidyā* as indicating an eternal creative act. The substance of delight which flows out constitutes the essence of all the creative principles.

Though *prakāśa* and *vimarśa* are identical, it is to be remembered that *prakāśa* is always partless and continuous while *vimarśa* is partless and as well as divisible into parts. Whenever therefore *prakāśa* is referred to as discrete it is to be understood only in a secondary sense. The three *bindus* working together towards a common end form as it were a single triangle.

Prakāśa within *vimarśa* is of the form of a white *bindu*; and *vimarśa* within *prakāśa* is of the form of a red *bindu* called *nāda*. The two *bindus* in union constitute the original *bindu* called *kāma* of which these are *kalās*. The unity of the three is the substance called *kāma-kalā* from which the entire creation consisting of words and the things signified by them originates.

Bhāskara Rāya in his *Varivasyā Rahasya* while speaking of *kāma-kalā* refers to the three *bindus* as well as the *hārdha-kalā*, the nature of which is held to be very secret. The white and red *bindus* represent in his opinion male and female energies.

Amṛtānanda says that *hārdha-kalā* flows from between the two *bindus* and is the wave (*laharī*) of *vimarśa* and *sphuṛattā*. *Prakāśa* is like fire and *vimarśa* is like the butter which melts under it. The flow is the so-called *hārdha-kalā* noted above. The *Baindava-cakra*, made of three *mātṛkās*, is the out-flow of *kāma-kalā* along with *hārdha-kalā*, and it is out of this that the thirty-six creative principles emanate.[25]

-V-

The soul as a spiritual atom thus makes its first appearance when the freedom of divine will is lost behind its own self-created veil through the transition of Śakti from *parā-kuṇḍalinī* to *prāṇa-kuṇḍalinī*. This transition is effected by a graded process in which *śakti-kuṇḍalinī* coils itself more and more tightly through the evolution of *mātṛkās* and *varṇas* and reaches the level of *prāṇa* and *śūnya*. It is a truism that *Saṁvit* is first changed into *prāṇa* before the regular course of subsequent creation represented by the first principles or *tattva* can possibly take place.

The universe of experience consists of a number of *bhuvanas* or planes of life and consciousness made up of *tattvas*. In the Śākta Śaiva Āgamas thirty-six *tattvas* are recognized, out of which twenty-four counted from below are considered as impure, the next

[25] See *Kāma-Kalā-Vilāsa* with Commentary, verses 3-8 pp. 4-9; *Yoginīhṛdaya Dīpikā*, pp. 8-12; *Varivasyā-Rahasya*, pp. 48-60.

seven as mixed and the remaining five as pure. In this scheme *prakṛti* (24) marks the end of impure, *māyā* (31) that of mixed, and Śiva (36) that of pure *tattvas*. Each *tattva* has a series of *bhuvanas* affiliated to it.[26] The *bhuvanas*, in spite of their mutual differences in detail, have the common characteristics of the *tattvas* concerned as predominant, though it is recognized as in the Pātañjala school that everywhere everything is to be found (*sarvaṁ sarvātmakam*).[27] The *bhuvanas* are the abodes of living beings, endowed with bodies and organs made of a substance the materiality of which corresponds to the nature of their *karman* or *jñāna* and the degree of their perfection. The *bhuvanas* of the *pṛthivī-tattva* represent the sphere, known as *brahmāṇḍa*, the *bhuvanas* of the *tattvas* up to *prakṛti* form the *prakṛtyaṇḍa*, those of the *tattvas* up to *māyā* represent the *māyāṇḍa* and the *bhuvanas* of the *tattvas* up to Śakti beyond *māyā* constitutes the *śaktyaṇḍa* which is the widest sphere.[28] Beyond Śakti-*tattva* there is no limitation and consequently no sphere, though *bhuvanas* are said to exist even in Śiva-*tattva* which is identified with *bindu* and *śāntyatīta kalā*.

The *tattvas* are generally supposed to be the ultimate principle, but they are not so, as they are constituted by *kalās* and *śaktis* which represent the multiple units of energy underlying the entire creation, and which considered in their totality represent the ground of self-expression of the transcendent Śiva. Thus the stuff of the universe is Śakti and, in the manner shown in the earlier pages, *prakāśa* with *hārdha-kalā* constitutes the substance out of which the *tattvas* are formed.

---

[26] For the *tattvas* and the *bhuvanas* related to them, see *Mṛgendra-Āgama*, *vidyāpāda*, pp. 344-356, (Ed. Kṛṣṇa Śāstrin and Subrahmānya Śāstrin); *Bhogakārikā* by Sadyojyoti, VV. 109-13; *Ratna-Traya* VV. 89-118. Cf. T.A. Gopinath Rao: *Elements of Hindu Iconography*, II (Pt. 2), pp. 392-7; *Mātṛkā-Cakra-Viveka*, IV, pp. 86-93.

[27] Cf. *Vyāsa-Bhāsya* under *Yoga Sūtra*, III. 14.

[28] For the four *aṇḍas* under *Yoga-Sāra*, pp. 64-5. The different *aṇḍas* are evolved and destroyed by *kālāgni* and created by Brahmā or Śrīkaṇṭha. The *prakṛtyaṇḍa* and *māyaṇḍa* are destroyed and created by Śrīkaṇṭha, Lord of *kāla-tattva*. The highest *aṇḍa* of Śakti is destroyed and created by Aghoreśa. See *Tantrāloka*, VI. 170-182.

The divine attributes of the Self are all diminished, in its atomic condition, when the *cit* appears as *citta*. Of the three well-known impurities or *malas* this is the first, called *āṇava*. It is the state of a *paśu* in which the sense of limitation is first manifested. This limitation makes possible the rise of *vāsanās*, as a result of which the assumption of physical body for a certain length of time becomes necessary to work off these *vāsanās* through experience. These *vāsanās* constitute *kārma-mala*. The *māyīya-mala* is the name given to the source of the triple body, namely, (i) the causal or the *kalā śarīra*, (ii) the subtle or *puryaṣṭaka*, i.e. *tattva-śarīra*, and (iii) the gross elemental or the *bhuvanaja-śarīra*. In fact everything which reveals itself in our experience as knowable and objective comes under *māyīya-mala*. The function of this impurity is to show an object as different from the subject (*sva-rūpa*). All the principles from *kalā* down to *pṛthivī* represent the fetters of *māyā* or *pāśas*. These give shape to body, sense, *bhuvanas*, *bhāvas*, etc. for fulfilling the experience of the soul.[29] Hence what is popularly known as *saṁsāra* extends from *pṛthivī* upto *kalā*, and not beyond the latter. These three impurities persist always in the worldly soul.

This worldly soul is technically known as *sa-kala*, being endowed with body, senses, etc. corresponding to the *tattva* or *bhuvana* to which it belongs. Such souls range from the lowest plane to the plane to the plane of *kalā* and migrate from plane to plane according to their *karmans*. There is another state of the soul in which the *māyīya-mala* as described above is absent, but the other two *malas* continue as before. This is a state of *pralaya* or dissolution in which the soul is free from all the creative principles, is in a disembodied condition and remains absorbed in *māyā*. Such souls are called *pralayākalas* or *pralaya-kevalins*. These are

[29] As regards the three *malas* see *Pratyabhijña-Hṛdaya*, pp. 21-2; *Saubhāgyabhāskara*, p. 95; *Śiva-Sūtra-Vārttika* (1-2-3). The *āṇava* is two-fold according as it refers to the loss of pure *ahaṁtā* in the self and appearance of impure *ahaṁtā* in the not-self. The self loses *svātantrya* and retains *bodha* or it is as *bheda* representing the appearance of multiplicity in unity: it consists of *māyā* and the thirty-one *tattvas* produced from it. *Karma-mala* is *adṛṣṭa* and may be regarded either as merit or demerit (*puṇya-pāpa*). In different texts the meaning of the *malas* is sometimes found to be slightly different.

bodiless and senseless atoms with *karmasaṁskāras* and the root ignorance clinging to them. When, however, the *karmans* are got rid of through discriminative knowledge, renunciation or such other means, the soul is exalted above *māyā* though still retaining its atomic state. It is then above *māyā* no doubt, but remains within the limits of *Mahāmāyā* which it cannot escape unless the supreme grace of the Divine Master acts upon it and removes the basic Ignorance which caused its atomicity and the limitation of its infinite powers. This state of the soul represents the highest condition of the *paśu*, known as *vijñānākalā* or *vijñāna-kevalin*. This is *kaivalya*. Among these souls those which are thoroughly mature in respect of their impurity are competent to receive divine illumination at the beginning of the next creative cycle. The dawn of divine wisdom which is the result of divine grace (*anugraha*) acting upon the soul is the origin of the so-called *śuddha-vidyā*.[30]

The states of the soul which follow are not those of a *paśu* but of Śiva himself, though certain limitations still remain. These limitations are those of *adhikāra*, *bhoga* and *laya* according to the dualists.[31] They are removed in due course of time through

---

[30] The illumination of mature *vijñānakalā* is either intense or mild according as the *kaluṣa* or original taint attached to the soul has run its course completely (*samāpta*) or otherwise; the former types of souls are raised to the status of Vidyeśvaras and latter become *mantras*. The *sakala* and *pralayākala* souls, too, in which the *mala* is mature, are favoured with divine grace and raised to the position of (i) Mantreśvaras, and placed in charge of the different divisions of *brahmāṇḍa* or the planes belonging to *pṛthvī-tattva*, and of (ii) Bhuvaneśvaras or Lokeśvaras, with powers over the planes belonging to the higher *tattvas* beyond *pṛthvī*. The *pralayākalas*, however, where *mala* is immature but *karma* mature, are associated with subtle bodies called *puryaṣṭaka* at the beginning of the next cycle and made to assume physical bodies and migrate from life to life, thus maturing the *mala* through experience. The Śākta or Śaiva belief in three-fold nature of the soul is comparable to the conviction of the Ophites and their predecessors the Orphical in the West — it presupposes a faith that the division corresponds to the degrees of grace and does not imply and essential difference. It is true, however, that according to the dualistic some difference does exist between Śiva and Parama-Śiva. The Valentinian conception of essential distinction in human souls has also its parallel in India as evident from the views of a section of Jaina, Buddhist and Vaiṣṇava writers, but finds no recognition in the Āgamās.

[31] See *Ranta-Traya* by Śrīkaṇṭha, vv. 276-95.

fulfilment of experience, etc., in the *pure order*.[32]

The successive stage of spiritual perfection consequent on the dawn of wisdom are represented by the *tattvas* to which the souls are attached. Thus the lowest stage is that of a Mantra which corresponds to Śuddha-*vidyā*. The higher states are those of Mantreśvaras corresponding to Īśvara-*tattva*, of Mantra-maheśvaras corresponding to Sadā-Śiva, of Śiva corresponding to the *tattva* known under that name. The state of Śiva is really transcendent, being that of pure and absolute consciousness, but the true Absolute is Parama-Śiva, where identity with all the *tattvas* as well as their transcendence are present simultaneously.[33]

Due to the limitation of its powers the Self is bound. The Śāktas hold that there are certain hidden forces latent in *cidākāśa*, known as *mātṛkās* (lit.: mothers of the world), which preside over the *malas* referred to above and over the *kalās* or the letter-sounds of the language. The supreme *mātṛkā*, known as Ambikā, has three aspects, viz Jyeṣṭhā, Raudrī and Vāmā, each of them having a specific function. The *kalās* are the ultimate units of human speech with which thought is inextricably interwoven. The *mātṛkās* beget in each soul in each act of its knowledge, determinate or indeterminate, an inner cognition (*antaḥ-parāmarśa*) and produce a sort of confusion there on account of intermingling with *śabda*. Knowledge in this manner assumes the form of joy, sorrow, desire, aversion, conceit, fear, hope, etc., under the influence of these forces. This is how *bhāvas* originate and govern the unregenerate human soul. *Mātṛkās* are thus the secret bonds which bind down a soul, but when they are truely known and their essence is revealed they help it in attaining *siddhis* or super-normal psychic powers.

These forces function in *cid-ākāśa* so long as the so-called *brahma-granthi* is not rent asunder. This *granthi* is evidently the node of identity between spirit and matter and is the spring of the ego-sense in man. The moral effect of *kuṇḍalinī* is so far clear. It is

[33] See *Pratyabhijñā-Hṛdaya*, p. 8.

[32] The pure order of *śuddha adhvan* represents the higher world of pure matter beyond the influence of *māyā*.

maintained that if the *mātṛkā* is not propitiated and if the node if not removed, it is likely that even after the rise of truth-consciousness the soul may, owing to inadvertence (*pramāda*), be caught up in its snares, get entangled in the meshes of *śabda* and lapse into ignorance or go astray.

The divine Will is one and undivided, but it becomes split up after the origin of the *mātṛkās* which evolve out of the *nāda* co-eternal with this Will. This split in *icchā* or *svātantrya* caused a separation between *jñāna* and *kriyā*, its constitutive aspects. This is practically identical with what is described as a divorce between *svātantrya* and *bodha* or *vimarśa* and *prakāśa*, which takes place on the assumption of atomic condition by the supreme Self. In this condition *jñāna* evolves into three inner and five outer senses, and *kriyā* into the five *prāṇas* and five motor-organs connected respectively with the vital and reflex activities of the organism.

-VI-

The view-point of the dualistic Āgamas may now be summed up. Here the divine Essence or Śiva is conceived as inalienably associated with a Power or Śakti which is purely divine and identical with it. The Essence and Power, both of the nature of *cit* or pure consciousness, constitute the two aspects of one and the same divine principle. Śiva is a transcendent unity. Śakti too is really one, though it appears as *jñāna* or *kriyā* according to the character of the data on which is functions, It is the Will (*icchā*) of Śiva and is essentially one with Him. *Bindu* is the eternal material principle outside Śakti, and the three principles are usually described as the three jewels (*ratna*) of Śaivism and its holy-Trinity. In creation (in pure creation directly and in impure creation indirectly) Śiva's place is that of an agent, Śakti's is that of an instrument and *bindu* serves as the material stuff. Śakti being immaterial never suffers any modification during action, but *bindu* does. The modification of *bindu*, which follows from a disturbance of its equilibrium (*kṣobha*) under the stress of divine Śakti at the end of the cosmic night (*pralaya*) gives rise to five *kalās*, which appear as it were like five concentric circles with greater and greater expansion. These *kalās*, which precede further progressive modifications called *tattvas* and *bhuvanas*, bear the names of *nivṛtti* (outermost), *pratiṣthā*, *vidyā*, *śānti* and *śāntyātīta* (inmost). This represents one line of the evolution of *bindu*, as that of the objective order (*artha*). The other line is represented by the evolution of sound or *śabda*. In this aspect we find *nāda*, *bindu* and *varṇa* as the three-fold expression of *bindu* arranged in an order of increasing externality.

Bindu is synonymous in this system with *Mahāmāyā* and *kuṇḍalinī*. It is pure matter-energy and is to be distinguished from *māyā* and *prakṛti*,[34] which are impure. It is the matrix of pure creation and is the source of two parallel lines of evolution, viz of *śabda* and *artha*, so that it is to be looked upon as a dual nature. The *Pauṣkara-Āgama* says: *Śabda-vastābhayātmā'sau bindur, nā'nyata-rātmakaḥ*.

The order of Śabda creation out of the disturbed *Mahāmāyā* is thus given:

(i) Mahā-māyā	(ii) Nāda
(iii) Bindu	(iv) Sādākhya
(v) Īśa	(vi) Vidyā

In this scheme Mahā-māyā stands for Para *bindu* in its undisturbed condition and *nāda* represents the same *bindu* when the *cit-śakti* has acted upon it. As the action of Śakti upon *bindu* is in a sense constant, it may be assumed that (i) and (ii) are really two aspects (logically successive but in actual fact simultaneous) of the same principle, *nāda* representing the disturbed part of *Mahāmāyā*. If *Mahāmāyā* is *kuṇḍalinī* in its essence, *nāda* is the

[34] In the Śaiva-Āgamas of all the schools which recognize the thirty-six *tattvas*, *māyā* and *prakṛti* are distinguished. They are identified in the *Śvetāśvatara Upaniṣad* (IV. 10): *Māyān tu prakṛtiṁ vidyān māyinaṁ tū maheśvaram*. In the Āgamas generally *māyā* is eternal, but *prakṛti* is not so. For *prakṛti* is evolved from *kalā* which itself is an evolve from *māyā*. But in some places in the Tantras they are differently conceived. *Prakṛti* stands for the material principle in a general way and *māyā* is one of thc *vikalpas* under this category.

same *kuṇḍalinī* in its awakened and active state. *Mahāmāyā* as such has no relation with *puruṣa* or the human soul, but as *nāda* or *kuṇḍalinī* it resides in every *puruṣa*, normal and super-normal.[35]

The truth is that the evolution of *Mahāmāyā* into four-fold *Vāc*, e.g. *parā* or *sūkṣmā*, *paśyantī*, *madhyamā* and *vaikharī* and the obscuration of the inherent divinity (*śivatva*) of every human soul under the veil of *mala* or original impurity working from the beginingless past (*anādi*) are co-eternal phenomena. Transcendence of *Parāvāc* and removal of this veil of obscurity signify therefore a single act, which is only another name of the culmination of the process of divinisation of the human soul interpreted from the dualistic standpoint of the school as the restoration of its lost purity. We are thus in a position to understand why sometimes *Mahāmāyā* and at other times *nāda* is identified with Śiva-*tattva*. (iii) Understood in this light *bindu* would mean *apara* and be a name for Śakti-*tattva*. (iv) the next evolution, *sādākhya*, which is held to comprise Sadā-Śiva-*tattva*, including the human Sadā-Śivas, Aṇu-Sadā-Śivas, five Brahmās, ten *aṇus* (*praṇava* etc.) and six *aṅgas*, stands for a *akṣara-bindu*[36] and denotes *nāda* in its form of gross but undifferentiated sound (*dhvani*). (v) The stage called Īśā represents an intermediate state between the aforesaid *akṣara-bindu* and *vaikharī-vāc* expressed as letters of the alphabet in all their permutations and combinations.[37] The eight *mantreśvaras* and their *śaktis* (eight in number, e.g. *Vāmā* etc.) fall under this class. (vi) The last named *vidyā*, which includes the final stage of sound evolution, embraces all the *mantras* and *vidyās*, all the Āgamas

---

[35] The gloss on the *Sarva-Jnānottara-Tantra* cited by Umāpati in his commentary on a *kārikā* of the *Svatantra-Tantra* (being the 24th *kārikā* of his compendium) says: *Kuṇḍalinī śabda-vācyas tu bhujaṅga-kuṭilākāreṇa nādātmanā svakāryeṇaprati puruṣaṁ avasthitaḥ*. The original couplet runs thus:

Yathā kuṇḍalinī śaktir māyā karmānusāriṇī |
nāda-bindvādikaṁ kāryaṁ tasyā iti jagasthitiḥ ||

[36] Āghora Śivācārya identifies *akṣara-bindu* with *paśyantī vāc* in his commentary called *Ullekhiny* on Śrīkaṇṭha's *Ratna-Traya*, verse 74.

[37] The Īśā stage may be said to correspond to the *madhyamā vāc*, which is characterized by thought (*antaḥ sañjalpa-rūpā*) and possesses an ideal order in its parts.

and the so called *vidyā-rājñīs* (queens of *vidyās*, seven in number), in fact, all audible sensible sounds familiar to us.

It is interesting to observe that *Mahāmāyā* as described above is called Parā-śakti and considered as Ultimate Cause (*Parama-kāraṇa*) of the world. It is also of the nature of *nāda* and is distinguished from the *nāda* lower down as *sūkṣma-nāda*.[38]

The dualists who maintain the doctrine of *nāda* repudiate the theory of *sphoṭa* and other allied theories of verbal knowledge and seek to explain the process of the origin of *śābdabodha* on the basis of this doctrine. Rāmakaṇṭha in his *kārikās* has tried to show that the doctrine of *sphoṭa* is unable to render an adequate account of the meaning of a word. The relation between a word (*śabda*) and its meaning (*artha*) is what is usually known as *vācya-vācaka-bhāva* relation of what denotes or reveals (*vācaka*) with what is denoted or revealed (*vācya*) by it. But wherein lies the denotative character (*vācakatā*) of the word concerned? The object denoted by the word is external, but the word which denotes it is mental (*budhyārūḍha*); the two are distinct and incommensurate. No word is capable of denoting its sense by virtue of its own nature, but its denotative power makes itself felt only when it represents in thought (*parāmarśa*) the object (*vācya*) to be denoted which is external to it. This representation called *parāmarśa-jñāna* is of the nature of what may be called thought-form and reveals the object. Hence some thinkers are inclined to attribute denotative power to this *parāmārśa-jñāna*, in so far as it reveals the object concerned. But the Tāntric philosophers are of opinion that thought *parāmarśa-jñāna* as an intellectual act exists independently of the external object, it is a contigent phenomenon and arises under the action of some causal factors working behind. Such an act does not occur in the case of external objects not previously cognized by the senses.

[38] Sometime the term *sūkṣma-nāda* is applied to *bindu*. The commentary of Bhoja's *Tattva-Prākāśā* holds that *sūkṣma nāda* belongs to Śakti-*tattva*. This view is endorsed by Sarvajña Śambhu in his *Siddhānta-Dīpikā*. Aghora-Śivācārya in his commentary on *Ratna-Traya* identifies *sūkṣma-nāda* with the first manifestation (called simply *nāda*) of *bindu* which is synonymous with *Para-nāda* (see *Ratna-Traya-Kārika*, 22).

Rūpa, *rasa* etc. become objects of mental *parāmarśa* of the speaker. That through which the origin of such *parāmarśa* becomes possible is called *nāda*. *Nāda* giving rise to *parāmarśa-jñāna* (*antaḥ-sañjalpa*) and not physical *śabda* possesses the denotative character (*vācakatā*). The physical *śabda* to which the vocal organ of the speaker gives expression manifests *nāda*. *Nāda* as thus manifested, produces in the hearer the sense of the object meant. *Nāda* reveals all *śabdas* and *arthas*. Hence every act of discursive knowledge is impregnated with *śabda*.

Nāda is multiple, being unique in each individual, and is a product. Every animal soul, (*paśū-ātman*), having a nature of its own, experiences its own *nāda* which arises from *anāhata-bindu*.

-VII-

The Śāktas believe in the importance of self-realization as a means to *mokṣa*. It is said to be of a determinate nature and expresses itself in the form of recognition (*pratyabhijñā*). The sequence of the preliminary state may be described as follows:

(i) Indirect knowledge of the Self through hearing of the teaching of Āgama on the part of a person gifted with all the qualifications necessary for knowledge, e.g. detachment etc.

(ii) Removal of doubts through reasoned thinking.

(iii) Direct knowledge or intuition of the individual self on removal of the false idea which has grown into a firm conviction regarding its identity with the body, etc.

(iv) Lastly, the recognition. It relates to the integral unity between the individual self and the universal one made known through the scriptures. Recognition as thus produced is destructive of the ignorance lying at the root of worldly existence.

The recognition is not erroneous, but is a form of *vikalpa* like other acts of determinate knowledge.

The indeterminate knowledge following from *samādhi* and the aforesaid recognition have the same object. But their difference is due to causal elements. In the case of recognition the instrument in mind turned away from all objects other than the Self and aided by the presence in consciousness of the two objects indicated by the terms 'I' and 'He' in the judgment 'I' and 'He'. In knowledge from *samādhi* no such presence is needed. The recognition "It is the same jar" has for its object an integral substance. Thus the ordinary *vikalpa* having a jar, for instance, as its object and the recognition "It is the same jar" have both the same object, but the result is different on account of difference in causal factors. The indeterminate knowledge is pure, is the support of all *vikalpas* and is in conflict with none, so that it is incapable of destroying a *vikalpa*, like ignorance.

The purity of indeterminate knowledge is due to its freedom from reflection. It is on the background of such pure knowledge that all possible determinations arise owing to appearance of different forms during *saṅkalpa*, just as on a clean mirror reflection emerges due to proximity of the object reflected.

The Śāktas view Ignorance not as absence of knowledge like the Vaiśeṣika nor as inexplicable like the Vedāntin but as a form of *sa-vikalpa-jñāna*. The Āgamas hold that the Supreme Self being of the nature of pure consciousness, what differentiates it from matter is its self-awareness (*sphuradrūpatā*) consisting in freedom (*svātantrya*), through which, as already shown, ignorance (*avidyā*) is manifested and through ignorance, the world.

Ignorance is two-fold, according as it is viewed as a cause or as an effect. As a cause it is non-manifestation of the fullness of one's own self. This fullness is characterized by freedom from the limitations of time, space and form, though it is true that even these elements which are manifested in the light of the Self cannot limit the latter. If the Self which is not limited by time manifests itself as so limited, it is certainly a case of non-manifestation of fullness or *pūrṇatva*. This is the Śākta view of root-Ignorance as already observed. As an effect, ignorance is the manifestation as Self of what is other than the Self, e.g. body, etc. It is only a leaf (*pallava*) in the tree of Ignorance.

Knowledge of the integral Self may be indirect, when it follows from a hearing of its nature from the Āgama taught by the Guru, or direct when it is derived immediately from *samādhi*. Direct knowledge called *vijñāna* can alone destroy the basis of mundane existence. The sense of identity with the body grows into *vāsanā* and become tenacious on account of its long continuance and prevents direct knowledge, even when it flashes for a moment in an impure mind, from producing a firm will (*saṅkalpa*). But when it follows perfection in *samādhi* the requisite firmness is attained and it destroys the above *vāsanā*. There being a strong sense of identity with the body the direct knowledge of pure Self too is unable to overthrow ignorance and to effect *mokṣa* if it is obscured by doubts and errors.

Direct knowledge or *vijñāna* is preceded by indirect knowledge. The place of *samādhi* is between the two. It is maintained that even indirect knowledge has its use, for *samādhi* cannot beget the desired result, i.e. direct knowledge as recognition in the ignorant who have had no direct knowledge. A man, for instance, who has never heard about a gem and known it indirectly through descriptions cannot recognise it as a gem even when he sees it in the jeweller's shop. Only he who has seen it can recognize it, provided that he attends to it. Hence natural *samādhi* cannot produce *brahma-jñāna* in one who has not heard about Brahman.

Advaita-*jñāna* is very rare. It does not and cannot appear until the mind has been purified from the blinding effect of *māyā* through the propitiation of one's own divine Self, by means of meditations or *upāsanā*. The importance of divine grace descending on the soul and purifying it cannot be overestimated.

There is an order of progression in spiritual experience. Svatantranāda in the *Mātṛkā-Cakra-Viveka* points out that on the rise of pure knowledge the knowable become one with the senses, in consequence of which the knowables as such begin to disappear. But as the world still continues, the sense of 'this-ness' as something external to the knower does not altogether vanish. The next position is that of Īśvara when the motor-organs in which the movable objects are similarly absorbed become one with the cosmic body with which the subject as the agent is identified. The *yogin* in this stage is associated not only with an individual body but with the entire universe. In the state of Sadā-Śiva which follows, the senses, in which the knowables have been absorbed, become one with the Self, the true subject. It represents a state of omniscience. In the Śakti stage, the universe, body and the omniscient Self become unified — this is a condition of undisturbed equilibrium between spirit and matter (*cit* and *a-cit*).

~3~

NĀDA, BINDU AND KALĀ

A student of ancient Indian mysticism of the Tantric and Yogic type very often comes across the terms '*Nāda*', 'Bindu' and '*Kalā*'. These are found both in popular works written in the vernacular and in original Sanskrit texts. As the sense of terms is not usually quite clear and free from ambiguity, an attempt is here made to find out the different meanings attached to them in the different schools of thought, in the belief that in the attempt it may be possible to discover a clue to the central idea underlying the expressions.

The *Śāradā-Tilaka*, while describing the origin of the manifested world, contain the following passage:

सच्चिदानन्दविभवात् सकलात् परमेश्वरात् ।
आसीज्छक्तिस्ततो नादो नादाद् बिन्दुसमुद्भवः ॥
परशक्तिमयः साक्षात् त्रिधाऽसौ भिद्यते पुनः ।
बिन्दुर्नादो बीजमिति तस्य भेदाः समीरिताः ॥ [1]

This shows the order of manifestation as follows:

(i) Parameśvara, described as 'Sakala' and 'Saccidānanda Vibhava'.

(ii) Śakti.

(iii) Nāda (Para)

(iv) Bindu (Para)

(v) Bindu (Apara) Bīja

(vi) Nāda (Apara)

In the above passage the word 'Parameśvara' means evidently the Supreme Divine in which infinite Power — Śakti or *Kalā* [2] —

[1] I. 7-8.

[2] In this context the world *Kalā* stands for the supracosmic transcendent power of the Lord and is to be clearly distinguished from the five *kalās*, viz *nivṛtti*, *prātiṣṭhā*, *śānti* and *śāntyatīta*, which are evolved as forces from *bindu* conceived as cosmic matter and force and related to the cosmic *tattvas* and *bhuvanas*.

lies in eternal Union, The Divine Being is described as of the nature of an eternal Self-existence (*sat*), Self-Consciousness and Delight. During creation what first happens is the manifestation of power — Śakti — which so long lay hidden in the depth of Being. There is no doubt that this power is characterised by Will (*icchā*), which is its first evolute.

In the *Śiva Purāṇa*, *Vāyavīya Saṁhitā*, it is said that the emergence of Śakti in the beginning of creation is like the appearance of oil out of oil-seeds. It is a spontaneous act, initiated by the Divine Will. In other words, it is through the Divine Will (*śivecchayā*) that the Supreme Power (*parāśakti*) which is synonymous with it and remains concealed in the Divine Essence (*śivatattvaikatāṁ gatā*) reveals itself (*parisphurati*).[3]

The appearance of Śakti after the great Cosmic Night is like the revival of memory in a reawakened person, after the unconsciousness of sleep. The desire for a vision again of the lost world is associated with a sense of Void, which is *Māyā*. *Māyā* stands at the beginning of the subsequent creation and the Divine principle which produces it is its Lord and Controller. The vision of Void is accompanied by an indistinct sound called *Para-nāda*, which fills the entire space. *Nāda* is of the nature of light. That sound and light co-exist and are related as phases of the same phenomenon is recognised in the Tantras. The first self-expression of the Supreme Will (*icchā*) is the origination of Void (*śūnya*) and of the sound and light filling this Void. All this comes under the category of Will. The next step is represented by the concentration of this diffuse light-sound into a focus (under the secret influence of Will), called *Bindu*. It is in this stage that the Power of Action (*kriyāśakti*) distinctly unfolds itself. The creative principles (*tattva*) are evolved out of this Supreme *Bindu*. The *Bindu* subsequently breaks itself into three, the three parts being known as *bindu*, *bīja* and *nāda*. *Bindu* is the part in which the Śiva aspect is predominant, while in *bīja* Śakti prevails. In *nāda*, however, the elements of Śiva and Śakti are of equal strength.

[3] शिवेज्छया पराशक्तिः शिवतत्त्वैकतां गतां।
ततः परिस्फुरत्यादौ सर्गे तैलं तिलादिव ॥

What disturbs the equilibrium of the Bindu? The *Śāradā-Tilaka* says nothing in reply to this question. The *Prapañcasāra* says:

कालेन भिद्यमानस्तु स बिन्दुर्भवति त्रिधा ।
स्थूलसूक्ष्मपरत्वेन तस्य त्रैविध्यमिष्यते ॥
स बिन्दुनादबीजभेदेन च निगद्यते ॥[4]

From this it is evident that according to Śaṅkarācārya it is *Kāla* which breaks the equilibrium of the *Bindu*. And in this view *Kāla* is an eternal aspect of the Eternal *Puruṣa*, through which His intimate knowledge of the Supreme *Prakṛti* is said to be derived. *Prakṛti* knows Herself and is Self-luminous. The actuating power of *Kāla* is suggested elsewhere also by the expression *kālapreritayā* [5] the *prayoga-kramadīpikā* [6] explains the term thus: *prakṛtereva pralayāvasthāto yat paripakvadaśāntaraṁ sṛṣṭyunmukhaiḥ | karmabhirbhinnaṁ svākāranirūpyaṁ rūpaṁ yo'sau binduḥ ||*

The Great Sound which comes into being when the *Bindu* splits itself is known as *Śabda-Brahman*, as the *Śāradā-Tilaka* and *Prapañcasāra* observe:

भिद्यमानात् पराद् बिन्दोरव्यक्तात्मा रवोऽभवत् ।
शब्दब्रह्मेति तं प्राहुः सर्वागमविशारदाः ॥[7]
बिन्दोस्तस्माद् भिद्यमानाद् रवोऽव्यक्तात्मको भवेत् ।
स रवः श्रुतिसंपन्नैः शब्दब्रह्मेति कथ्यते ॥[8]

It is well known that what is figured as the pericarp of the thousand-petalled lotus within the crown of the head is the so-called *brahma-randhra* which is often referred to as a Void. It extends through the *suṣumnā nāḍī* down to the very bottom of the interior of the spinal column. If the mind rests in the Void it loses its restless nature and becomes a blank — a state usually known as *unmanī* or *nirbīja samādhi*. It is here that one attains to the realization of oneself as Para Śiva above *guṇas*. The Will Power

[4] I. 42-43
[5] *Prapañcasāra*, I. 46
[6] P. 412.
[7] *Śārada-Tilaka*, I. 11-12.
[8] *Prapañcasāra*, I. 44

and Supreme *Nāda* emerge from this source. Evidently, this *mahā-śūnya* is identical with the *vyāpinī*.[9]

The terms sixteenth (*ṣoḍaśī*) and seventeenth (*saptadaśī*) *kalā* of the Moon are used differently in different texts. When the Supreme *Nāda* (iii) is called the sixteenth or *amākalā*, the name 'seventeenth *kalā*' or '*samanā*', is reserved for the Supreme Power (ii). But at other times the term *unmanī* is attributed to the seventeenth *kalā*, when the words Śakti and *śūnya* are used synonymously.

The Supreme *Nāda* stands for the supercausal or *mahā-kāraṇa* state of Brahman, which is known as *visarga maṇḍala*. If the Supreme Śakti is called *kula* and the Supreme Śiva, *akula*, the sphere of *visarga* may be described as below them both. But usually it is placed in the upper layer of the *brahma-randhra* below which in regular order are the spheres of the Sun, the Moon and the great *vāyu* — all within the limits of the thousands-petalled lotus.

The causal state of Brahman is represented by *Śabda-Brahman* or *kula-kuṇḍalinī*, figured as a triangle consisting of three principles (*tattva*) viz, *bindu*, *bīja* and *nāda*, issuing from the *Para-bindu* under division. The triangular *kuṇḍalinī* would thus appear to be a manifestation of the Primary Power represented by *Para-nāda* and *Para-bindu*.

The subtle principles of cosmic structure issue out of the *kuṇḍalinī* and begin to locate themselves in distinct centres in the forehead and lower down in the sympathetic system. It has already been observed that the *bindu* (lower) is Śiva and *bīja* is Śakti, and *nāda* (lower) is the product of their Union. *Bīja* or Śakti is virtually the entire alphabet, the letters of which are arranged in a triangular fashion designated in the Tantras as *a-ka-tha* (अ-क-थ) triangle — an equilateral triangle, the three sides or lines of which are formed of 16 letters each, beginning with *a*, *ka* and *tha* respectively. Thus 48 letters constitute the three equal sides of this triangle which is intimately associated with the principles of *kāma-kalā* — a subject which is outside the scope of the present paper. This constituent

[9] This is acording to the *Svacchanda Tantra*. But some writers equate *Mahāśūnya* with the Initial (*ādhya*). See Pūrṇānanda's *Śri Tattvacintāmaṇi*.

bindus of *kāma-kalā* are thus three — two causal (*kāraṇa*) and one of the nature of effect (*kārya*).

The *nāda* which springs from the inter-action of *bindu* (lower) and *bīja* is to be distinguished from *Śabda-Brahman* which manifested itself during the division of *Para-bindu*. The latter may be described as *Mahānāda*. The *nāda* contains within itself the indistinct sounds of all the letters of the alphabet, much in the same manner as the sunlight may be said to consist of all the coloured rays known to us. The truth of the matter is that *Mahānāda* of *Śabda-Brahman*, in its manifestation as *kuṇḍalinī*, is located in the body of man and serves as the mechanism for the articulation of sounds.

The continued practice of a mantra cause it to be sounded in a subtle manner in the *suṣumnā*. The sound expands itself and is blended with the lower *nāda* — it does nto and cannot rise upto the *Mahānāda* higher up. The locus of *Mahānāda* is free from the action of ordinary *vāyu* which cannot rise up to it. It may be of some interest to note that *Mahānāda* is associated with the *Para-nāda* in the *brahma-randhra* above it on one hand and with the lower *nāda* on the other. The power involved in the lower *nāda* crosses the middle of the two-eye-brows (*bhrumadhya*) and flows down the *suṣumnā* channel. At the lowest point *nāda* is converted into the *kuṇḍalinī*. The forces of the *bīja* as concretised in the latter are all within the lower *nāda*.

The position of *Para-bindu* has a special value for contemplation, in as much as it represents the nexus of the Divine Plane on one hand and the Cosmic and Supracosmic spheres on the other. It is the place where *nāda* extends into *Mahā-nāda* or *Śabda-Brahman*, beyond which is the Divine *Nāda* within the Infinite. *Para-nāda* above is supramental (*unmanī*) Divine Consciousness and Light while *Mahānāda* below is the source of Universal Creation. *Para-bindu* stands between the two. It is for this reason considered to be the best centre for contemplation of Guru.

It may be stated that the *bīja* consists of *varṇas* and that these are driven down to take their respective places in the six centres below, as soon as the downward moving power of *Mahānāda* passes through the middle of the two eye-brows and extends into the spinal column. These *varṇas*, the modifications of *Mahānāda*, being the blends of *nāda* and *bīja*, are so many actions generated from *Para-bindu* which is pre-eminently characterized by active Power. *Mahānāda* cannot give rise to the different creative principles unless it passes through the stage of *Bindu*.

We need not proceed further to describe the progressive stages of creation. From what has been said above, the meanings of the terms *nāda*, *bindu* and *kalā* have been made suficiently clear. We thus find that in the above analysis, which follows mainly the traditions set up by Lakṣmaṇa Deśika and Śaṅkarācārya, there are three *nādas* — *Para-nāda*, the antecedent of *Para-bindu*; the *Mahānāda* called therein *Śabda Brahman*, which follows the disruption of *Para-bindu*; and the *nāda* which results from the union of *bindu* and *bīja*. Similarly, there are two *bindus* — *Para-bindu* which is produced from focusing of *Para-nāda* and which is the source of *Śabda-Brahman*, the immediate spring of creative forces; and *apara-bindu* which is the effect of *Para-bindu* with the Śiva element prevailing. As regards the *kalā*, it would appear that the Supreme Śakti which is the eternal associate of the Divine Principle and remains always in it, either as completely absorbed in it and incapable of differentiation or as partially emergent, is the highest *Kalā*. In a lower sense, however, the name *kalā* is used to signify the *bīja* mentioned above. That is to say, the *varṇas*, symbolized as the letters of the alphabet and conceived as the basic principles of lower *nāda* in the sound potentials, are *kalās* in this sense. From this point of view the triangle called '*a-ka-tha*', otherwise described as *kuṇḍalinī*, is the Kalā.

* * *

The view-point of the Śaiva-Āgama of the dualistic schools may now be taken up for discussion. Here the divine essence of Śiva is conceived as inalienably associated with a Power or Śakti which is purely divine and identical with it. The Essence and Power, both of the nature of *Cit* or Pure Consciousness, constitute the two aspects of one and the same Divine Principle. Śiva is a transcendent unity. Śakti too is really one, though it appears as *jñāna* or *kriyā* according to the character of the data on which it functions. It is the Will (*icchā*) of Śiva and is essentially one with Him. *Bindu* is the eternal material principle outside Śakti, but subject to Its action. It is co-eternal with Śiva and Śakti, and the three principles are usually described as the three jewels (*ratna*) of Śaivism and its holy Trinity. In creation (in pure creation directly and in impure creation indirectly) Śiva's place is that of an agent, Śakti's that of an instrument and *Bindu* serves as the material stuff. Śakti being immaterial never suffers any modification during action, but the *Bindu* does. The modification of the *Bindu* which follows from a disturbance of its equilibrium (*kṣobha*) under the stress of divine Śakti at the end of Cosmic Night (*pralaya*) gives rise to five *kalās* which appear as it were like concentric circles with greater and greater expansion. These *kalās* which precede further progressive modifications called *tattvas* and *bhuvanas* bear the names of *nivṛtti* (outermost), *pratiṣṭhā*, *vidyā*, *śānti* and *śāntyatītta* (inmost). This represents one line of the evolution of *Bindu*, as that of the objective order (*artha*). The other line is represented by the evolution of Sound or *śabda*. In this aspect we find *nāda*, *bindu* and *varṇa* as the three-fold expression of *Bindu*, arranged in an order of increasing externality.

Bindu is synonymous in this system with *Mahāmāyā kuṇḍalinī*. It is pure Matter-Energy and is to be distinguished from *māyā* and *prakṛti*,[10] which are impure. It is the matrix of pure creation and is the source of two parallel lines of evolution, viz, of *śabda* and *artha*, so that it is to be looked upon as of a dual nature. The *Pauṣkara-Āgama* says: *śabdavastūbhayātmāsau bindurnānyatarātmakaḥ* |

The order of *śabda* creation out of the disturbed *Mahāmāyā* is thus given:

---

[10] In the Śaiva-Āgamas of all the schools which recognized the 36 *tattvas*, *māyā* and *prakṛti* are distinguished. They are not identified as in the *Śvetāśvatara Upaniṣad* (IV. 10): मायां तु प्रकृतिं विद्यान्मायिनं तु महेश्वरम् । In the Āgamas generally *māyā* is eternal, but *prakṛti* is not so. For *prakṛti* is evolved from *kalā* which itself is an evolute from *māyā*. But in some place in the Tantras they are differently conceived. *Prakṛti* stands for the material principle in a general way and *māyā* is one of the *vikalpas* under this category. Thus, we read: तच्छक्तितद्गतप्राणिकर्मविषयभेदेनेति ।

(i) Mahāmāyā
|
(ii) Nāda
|
(iii) Bindu
|
(iv) Sādākhya
|
(v) Īśa
|
(vi) Vidyā

In this scheme *Mahāmāyā* stands for *Para-bindu* in its undisturbed condition and *nāda* represents the same *bindu* when the *Cit-śakti* has acted upon it. As the action of Śakti upon *Bindu* is in a sense constant, it may be assumed that (i) and (ii) are really two aspects (logically successive but in actual fact simultaneous) of the same principle, *nāda* representing the disturbed part of *Mahāmāyā*. If *Mahāmāyā* is *kuṇḍalinī* in its essence, *nāda* is the same *kuṇḍalinī* in its awakened and active state. *Mahāmāyā* as such has no relation with *puruṣa* or the human soul, but as *nāda* or *kuṇḍalinī* it resides in every *puruṣa*, normal and supernormal.[11] The truth is that the evolution of *Mahāmāyā* into four-fold *Vāk*, e.g. *parā* or *sūkṣmā*, *paśyantī*, *madhyamā* and *vaikharī* and the obscuration of the inherent

---

प्रकृतितत्त्वस्यैवान्तर्गतो विकल्पोऽयमुक्तः । तत्राचित्शक्तिमात्रं तावत् प्रकृतिः । तस्याः स्वान्तर्गतस्वेशितुकालप्रयोज्यस्वकल्पिततदीयत्रिमूर्तिहिरण्यगर्भाद्यखिलचेतनां सोढुं नानात्वादिप्रत्ययकरमवान्तरशक्तिमात्रं माया ।+++ मायाया अप्यन्तर्गतं तेषां परिज्छिन्नस्वरूप-तादिप्रत्ययकरमविधालक्षणभवान्तरशक्तिमात्रमिह शक्तिः । ++ तस्याः शक्तेरप्यन्तर्गतं यत् तद्गतप्राणिनां प्राक्तननभवोपार्जितं कर्मजातं तदिह कर्म । न च केवलस्य कर्मणोऽवस्थानमिति तत्समवायी सलिलोऽचिदंशोऽभ्युपेयते यत् शैवप्रक्रियायां प्रकृतितत्त्वं व्यपदिश्यते ।

[11] The gloss on the *Sarvajñānottara Tantra* cited by Umāpati in his commentary on a *kārikā* of the *Svatantra Tantra* (being the 24th *kārikā* of his compendium) says:
कुण्डलिनीशब्दवाज्या तु भुजंगकुटिलाकारेण नादात्मना स्वकार्येण प्रतिपुरुषं भेदेनावस्थितो, न तु स्वरूपेण प्रतिपुरुषमवस्थिता ।
The original couplet runs thus:
याऽथ कुण्डलिनी शक्तिर्मायाकर्मानुसारिणी ।
नादबिन्द्वादिकं कार्यं तस्या इति जगत्स्थितिः ।।

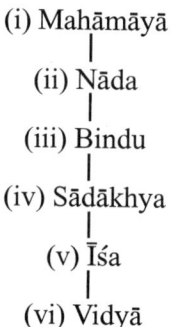

Divinity (*śivatva*) of every human soul under the veil of *mala* or original impurity working from the beginningless past (*anādi*) are co-eternal phenomena. Transcendence of *Parā Vāk* and removal of obscurity signify therefore a single act, which is only another name for the culmination of the process of divinisation of the human soul interpreted from the dualistic standpoint of the school as the restoration of its lost purity. We are thus in a position to understand why sometimes *Mahāmāyā* and at other times *nāda* are identified with Śiva-*tattva*. Understood in this light (iii) *Bindu* would mean *apara-bindu* and be a name for Śakti-*tattva*. The next evolution, (iv) *sādākhya*, which is held to comprise Sadāśiva-*tattva* (including the human Sadāśiva, *aṇu sadāśiva*) five Brahmās, ten *aṇus* (*praṇava*, etc.) and six *aṅgas* stands for *akṣara bindu* [12] and denotes *nāda* in its from of gross but undifferentiated Sound (*dhvani*). (v) The stage called Īśa represents an intermediate state between the aforesaid *akṣara bindu* and *vaikharī vāk* expressed as letters of the alphabet in all their permutations and combinations.[13] The eight Mantreśvaras and their Śaktis (eight in number, e.g., Vāmā, etc.) fall under this class. (vi) The last named *vidyā*, which includes the final stage of sound evolution, embraces all the *mantras* and *vidyās*, all the Āgamas and the so-called *vidyārājñīs* (queens of *vidyās*, seven in number) — in fact, all audible sensible sounds familiar to us.

It is interesting to observe that *Mahāmāyā* as described above is called *Parā Śakti* and considered as the Ultimate Cause (*paramakāraṇa*) of the world. It is also of the nature of *nāda* and is distinguished from the *nāda* lower down (ii) as *sūkṣma nāda*.[14]

---

[12] Aghora Śivācārya identifies *akṣara bindu* with *paśyantī vāk* in his commentary on the *Ratnatraya* (verse 74).

[13] The Īṣā stage may be said to correspond to the *madhyamā vāk*, which is characterised by thought (*antaḥ saṁjalparūpā*) and possesses an ideal order in its parts.

[14] Sometimes the term *sūkṣma-nāda* is applied to *Bindu*, the cause of *akṣara-bindu*. The commentary on Bhoja's *Tattvaprakāśa* holds that *sūkṣma-nāda* belongs to Śakti-*tattva*. This view is endorsed by Sarvajña Śambhu in his *Siddhānta-Dīpikā*. Aghora Śivācārya in his commentary called *Ullekhinī* on Ram Kaṇṭha's *Ratnatraya* identifies *sūkṣma-nāda* with the first manifestation (called simply *nāda*) of *Bindu* which is synonymous with *Para-nāda* (see *Ratnatraya*, *kārikā* 22).

The Siddhāntins who maintains the doctrine of *nāda* repudiate the theory of *sphoṭa* and other allied theories of verbal knowledge and seek to explain the process of the origin of *śabdabodha* on the basis of this doctrine. Rāmakaṇṭha in his *kārikās* has tried to show that the doctrine of *sphoṭa* is unable to render an adequate account of the meaning of a word. The relation between a word (*śabda*) and its meaning (*artha*) is what is usually known as *vācya-vācakabhāva*, a relation of what denotes or reveals (*vācaka*) with what is denoted or revealed (*vācya*) by it. But wherein lies the denotative character (*vācaktā*) of the word concerned? The object denoted by the word is external, but the word which denotes it is mental (*buddhyārūḍha*) the two are distinct and incommensurate. No word is capable of denoting its sense by virtue of its own nature, but its denotative power makes itself felt only when it represents in thought (*parāmarśa*) the object (*vācya*) to be denoted which is external to it. This representation, called *parāmarśa-jñāna*, is of the nature of what may be called thought-form and reveals the object. Hence, some thinkers are inclined to attribute denotative power of this *parāmarśajñāna*, in so far as it reveals the object concerned. But the Tāntric philosophers are of opinion that though *parāmarśajñāna* as an intellectual act exists independently of the external object, it is a contingent phenomenon and arises under the action of some casual factors working behind. Such an act does not occur in the case of external objects not previously cognised by the senses. *Rūpa*, *rasa*, etc. become objects of mental *parāmarśa* of the speaker. That through which the origin of such *parāmarśa* becomes possible is called *nāda*. *Nāda* giving rise to *parāmarśajñāna* (*antaḥ saṁjalpa*) *and not physical śabda*, possesses the denotative character (*vācaktā*). The sense intended to be conveyed is that the *nāda* of the speaker creates in the man hearing a sense of the thing intended to be denoted (*vācyatā*). The physical *śabda* to which the vocal organ of the speaker gives expression manifests *nāda*, which as thus manifested produces in the hearer the sense of the object meant. *Nāda* reveals all *śabdas* and *arthas*. Hence every act of discursive knowledge is impregnated with *śabda*.

Nāda is multiple, being unique in each individual, and is a product. Every animal soul (*paśu ātmā*), having a nature of its own, experiences its own *nāda*, which arises from *Anāhata-bindu*.

~4~

Yoginīhṛdaya and its Commentary Dīpikā

It is well known that the *Yoginīhṛdaya* is the name of the last three chapter (viśrāmas VI-VIII) of the *Nityāṣoḍaśikārṇava*, which forms a part of the Vāmakeśvara Tantra, one of the original Tantras recognised in the Tripurā school of Āgamic Thought. It is regarded as equally authoritative by the Trika philosophers of Kashmir. This is not the place to enter into a discussion as to the exact nature of the relation between the attitude of the Śāktas and that of the Trika Śaivas towards this Āgama, but it is clear that some of the fundamental notions of the two schools regarding *upāsanā*, though closely allied, are different, and this would explain the fact that the same text has been interpreted in a variety of ways.

It will be found for instance on comparison of the *Setubandha* with Amṛtānanda's commentary, that Bhāskara has referred to or quoted from it in several places, and has done so, it seems to us, generally in a spirit of undue disparagement. But in spite of Bhāskara's attacks it will be found that the *Dīpikā* has more correctly represented the traditional view-point and has been as a whole more illuminating.

Puṇyānanda Nātha's *Kāmakalāvilāsa* has already appeared in the Kashmir Sanskrit Series, No. 13. The *Dīpikā*, together with the *Kāmakalāvilāsa*, is calculated to give us an insight into the ideas of the Kashmiri thinkers on the very intricate problems of *upāsanā* connected with the secrets of *kāma-kalā* on one hand and with those of creation and dissolution of the universe on the other.

The *Yoginīhṛdaya*, also known as *Nityāhṛdaya* or *Sundarīhṛdaya*, is supposed to be the best authoritative work on the Divine Mother's inner worship. In the history of relevant Śākta literature we come across the names of twelve well-known traditional lines of devotion connected with this worship, viz those founded by Manu, Candra, Kubera, Lopāmudrā, Manmatha or Kāmadeva, Śiva and Durvāsā.[1] Most of these sects have disappeared in the process of time except the two of Kāmadeva and Lopāmudrā. Of these two the line of Kāmadeva is flourishing.[2]

It is well-known that the *Kāmarāja-vidyā* (of 15 letters) is of two kinds, viz Śākta or Śāmbhava. Of these two the former belongs to the Ūrdhvāmnāya and is free from the defect of impotency through *kīla*, while the latter, which belongs to Purvāmnāya is defective. The *Lopāmudrā-vidyā*, also of 15 letters, is similarly of two kinds (viz Śākta as well as Śāmbhava).

The *Kādi-vidyā*, consisting of 15 letters, is favoured in the *Tantrarāja* and in the *Tripurā Upaniṣad*. The *Hādi-vidyā* too consists of the same number of letters; it is expounded in some Śākta Upaniṣads.[3]

It is said that Durvāsā worshipped the 13-lettered form of the *Hādi-vidyā*. His *Lalitā Stavaratna* has been published. I noticed long ago a manuscript of *Para Śambhu Stotra* attributed to Durvāsā, called therein Krodha Bhaṭṭāraka. Durvāsā also wrote a *Mahimnaḥstotra* in honour of the Goddess Tripurā, on which Nityānanda Nātha, the disciple of Vidyānanda *alias* Śrīnivāsa Bhaṭṭa Gosvāmī, commented.

According to some authorities, *Yoginīhṛdaya* is one of the four principal works of *Kādimata*, the other three being *Tantrarāja*, *Mātṛkārṇava* and *Tripurārṇava*. Subhagānanda Nātha in his commentary *Manoramā* on the *Tantrarāja*, and Bhāskara Rāya in his commentary on the *Bhāvanā Upaniṣad* also admit this. But the latter in his *Varivasyā Rahasya* recognises the *Hādi* interpretation of *Yoginīhṛdaya* as equally authoritative.

---

[1] The *Vidyā* worshipped by Manu consisted of 18 letters and that worshipped by Candra and Kubera was of 22 letters. In some places the names of Nandi and Viṣṇu are found instead of Indra and Agni in the list. Further differences of names and details are also noticed.

[2] It is said in the *Tripura-Rahasya*, *māhātmya khaṇḍa*, that Kāma propitiated the Goddess and added to the glory of the *Vidyā* worshippped by him.

[3] The *Bahvṛcha Upaniṣad* speaks of *Kādi*, *Hādi* and *Sādi Vidyās* in connection with the *Śāmbhavī Vidyā* representing the Supreme Divine Power.

A critical study of the contents of the text conducted along traditional lines as well as on the basis of one's personal yogic experience expressed in terms of the ideological technique accepted in the Schools is the greatest desideratum of the hour, and will, I hope, be forthcoming in the near future. Such a study should include in its scope the mysteries of *cakra*, *mantra* and *pūjā*.

It is well known that the three kinds of worship of the Supreme Goddess, viz the external (*bahiryāga*), *japa*, and the internal (*antaryāga*), are not mutually exclusive, though each represents a special type with its own predominant features. While the *Tripurātāpinī* and other Upaniṣads dwell on the former two, the internal worship consisting in the method of meditation (*bhāvanā*) forms the subject matter of the *Bhāvanā Upaniṣad*. It suggests the manner in which meditation is to be practised on the Śrī Cakra which is located within the *Kāla* Cakra.

These meditations are according to some authorities prescribed in two different ways in the Tantras — the way of the Kādi School and that of the Hādi School. The doctrine of *antaryāga* implies that the *cakras* are to be viewed within the body, though the different ways favour different methods. The *Bhāvanā Upaniṣad* explains the Kādi standpoint. In this connection a reference to the *Nityāhṛdaya* (*Yoginīhṛdaya*), the *Tantrarāja* and the *Bīndu Sūtra* is likely to prove illuminating.

What the *Bhāvanā Upaniṣad* says implies that the human body is to be conceived as the Śrī Cakra, being the expression of one's own self (*svātmā*). This means that while on one hand the body is to be regarded as non-different from the *ātmā*, the entire cosmic system (*bāhyaprapañca*), associated with the body, should also be viewed in the same light. This outer system in its manifestation rests on Time (*kāla*) Space (*deśa*) and a combination of the two. The exponents of the School hold that the well-known fifteen *kalās* of the Moon (viz *darśā*, *dṛṣṭā*, etc.), representing the 15 lunar *tithis* (*pratipad* to *pūrṇimā*) are to be regarded as identical with the fifteen *nityās* (Kāmeśvarī to Citrā). The sixteenth *kalā* called *sādākhyā* should be viewed as one with Lalitā or the Supreme Deity Herself. In other words, one has to feel that what appears in *Kālacakra* is nothing but an expression of what exists eternally as *nityās* in the supreme Śri Cakra itself. The *Tithicakra* or the Wheel of Time is constantly revolving and the Śri Cakra is within it, and not without.

It should also be remembered that from the viewpoint of an esoteric *yogin* the *tithis* are in the last analysis to be identified with the 21600 *śvāsas* supposed to be the average number of breaths per day of a normal human being.

In a similar manner these thinkers deal with Space (*deśa*). According to ancient Paurāṇic cosmology, the entire structure of the world is looked upon as a series of 14 graded division of land and water from Jambūdvīpa on one hand to the Sweet-watered (*Madhuroda*) Ocean on the other, in addition to Meru beyond Jambūdvīpa and Para Vyoma beyond the Sweet Ocean. The *Nityā Maṇḍala* revolves in a way that each *nityā* comes in touch with a particular space division in its annual course, so that, while in the first year the *nityās* start from Meru, in the sixteenth they find themselves starting from the Para Vyoma. This is known as *Deśa-cakra*.

The *Yoginīhṛdaya* has its own method of inner worship, which is not only unique but truly representative of a very old traditional line. The *Cid-Gagan-Candrikā*, *Mahārthamañjarī* and some works of the Krama School of thought possess a valuable literature on this subject, which calls for a close and careful study in this connection.

The *Dīpikā* is the work of Amṛtānanda Nātha, who calls himself the disciple of Puṇyānanda Nātha of Kashmir reputation. Both the preceptor and the disciple are said to have been great *yogins* and were known as *paramahaṁsas*. Puṇyānanda's Kāmakalāvilāsa, to which the author of the *Dīpikā* often refers to, is the work of his Guru.[4]

Besides the *Yoginīhṛdaya-Dīpikā*, Amṛtānanda also wrote *Ṣaṭtriṇśattattvasandoha*[5] and *Saubhāgya Subhagodaya*.[6] In the *Catalogus Catalogorum* (Vol I, p. 29), Aufrecht speaks of two more works as coming from his pen, viz *Ajñānabodhinīṭīkā* and

---

[4] Cf. *Dīpikā*, pp. 11.

[5] Published in the Kashmir Sanskrit Series.

[6] Referred to in the *Dīpikā*, pp. 38, 78, 79 and 135. The work was in the form of Kārikās.

Tattvadīpana (in Vedānta). But it is very doubtful whether the author of these latter Vedānta works was identical with the great Kashmiri teacher of the same name. Weber's assertion (p. 361), referred to by Aufrecht, that Amṛtānanda corrected Kṛṣnānanda's *Tantrasāra*, is equally inapplicable to our author for the simple reason that Kṛṣṇānanda, who was a contemporary of Raghunātha Siromaṇi, Śrī Caitanya Deva and Raghunandana of Nadia (1460-1560 A.D.), was a later than the author of the Dīpikā.

Dīpikā and Setubandha

A reader of the *Setubandha* cannot but be struck with the point of difference between Bhāskara's interpretation and that of Amṛtānanda. Bhāskara refers to the views of the *Dīpikā*, sometimes with approval, but often in a spirit of disparagement. A comparative study of the two commentaries, carried on with a dispassionate mind, is sure to reveal the fact that in spite of Bhāskara's animadversions, Amṛtānanda, as representing the traditional line of explanation, is generally a safer and more reliable guide to the intricacies of this mystic *sādhanā*. Want of space compels me to refrain from dwelling on this point at greater length here and to reserve a systematic study of the question for a separate paper.

Contents of the Yoginīhṛdaya

It is not possible to sum up within the limits of this article the doctrines taught in the work, but considering the importance of the subject, a few words may here be spoken.

The book is divided into three sections, called *paṭalas*, dealing respectively with the threefold *saṅketa* of the Supreme Goddess: (i) *Cakra*, (ii) *Mantra*, and (iii) *Pūjā*.

(i) The *Cakra*, usually known as *Śrī Cakra* or *Tripurā Cakra*, represents the Supreme Divine Power as manifested in the form of Universe, gross, subtle, as well as causal. The *Cakra* consists of nine triangles, five with vertices downwards and four with vertices upwards. The former represents the creative aspect of Power and is called 'Śakti', whereas the latter, called 'Fire', stands for its destructive phase. The origin of the *Cakra* is explained as due to

the Will for self-revelation on the part of the Supreme Power. Śiva and Śakti are known as Fire and Moon, and their equilibrium, where the difference between the two is obliterated, is called Sun, otherwise known as *Kāma* or Supreme *Bindu*. It is said that as in contact with fire *ghee* melts and flows out, similarly the contact of Fire or Śiva (*prakāśa*) cause the Moon or Śakti (*vimarśa*) to melt and flow out. This outflow, from between the two *bindus*, is called *hārdha-kalā*. The *kāma* as associated with the *hārdha-kalā* gives rise to the first *cakra*, called Baindava, which is the source of all kinds of subsequent waves of vibrations, i.e. of all the 36 *tattvas*, in fact of the entire universe. The Baindava Cakra, a triangle in form, comprises the three *mātṛkās*, viz, *paśyantī*, *madhyamā* and *vaikharī*. It is called Baindava in as much as it originates from Bindu — the original or fourth *bindu*, which is in reality nothing but the aggregate of the three *mātṛkās* referred to above and known otherwise as *Sadāśiva* or *Paramātmā*.

The Baindava or inmost *cakra* produces the so-called Navayoni Cakra, consisting of 9 triangles referred to above. The elements of this *cakra* or the nine *yonis* are (i-ii) *Dharma* and *Adharma*, (iii-vi) *Ātmā*, *Antarātmā*, *Paramātmā* and *Jñānātma*, (vii-viii) *Jīva* and object (*grāhya*), and (ix) Right Knowledge (*pramā*). This ninefold *cakra* is, within and without, purely *Cit* (i.e. *caitanyakalā*) and *Ānanda* (i.e. manifestation or rather modification of *pūrṇāhaṁtā*), is free from the limitations of Time, Space and Form. The Baindava Cakra is inner, in relation to which the Nava Yoni Cakra is outer. It should be remembered that the Navayoni is composed of the *vaikharī mātṛkā* only.

The Navayoni Cakra is transformed into the nine *cakras*, viz (i) Tarailokyamohana, (ii) Sarvāśāparipūraka, (iii) Sarvasaṅkṣobhaṇa, (iv) Sarvasaubhāgyadāyaka, (v) Sarvārthasādhaka, (vi)

Sarvarogahara, (vii) Sarvarakṣākara, (viii) Sarvasiddhiprada and (ix) Sarvānandamaya, which correspond respectively to (i) the three-fold Bhūpura, (ii) the 16 petalled lotus, (iii) the 8-petalled lotus, (iv) the 14-angled figure, (v-vi) two 10-angled figures (outer and inner), (vii) the octagon, (viii) the triangle, and (ix) the Supreme Point or *Bindu*.

The Baindava or inmost *cakra* stands for the *Mahābindu* which represents the equilibrium of Śiva and Śakti. This triangle is known as Ambikā and is within the Octagon. Its three sides consist of 15 vowels, viz from *a* (अ) to *aṁ* (अं), and its centre is the letter *aḥ* (अ:). It is presided over by Kāmeśvara and Kāmeśvarī (i.e. *prakāśa* and *vimarśa* or Śiva and Śakti), which are seated as it were on the *āsana* of Sadāśiva or *Mahābindu*.

(ii) The second section dwells upon the *Mantra Saṅketa*. The nine *cakras* spoken of in the first *paṭala* have each a presiding deity, and a *mantra* is really a "ray of *Caitanya*" (*cinmarīci*). It is so called by virtue of its power of delivering (*trāṇa*) a *jīva* on being meditated upon. The nine *vidyās* are named and this is followed by an account of their *nyāsa* in the human body. The *Mantra Saṅketa* is sixfold, i.e. *bhāvārtha*, *sampradāyārtha*, *nigarbhārtha*, *kaulikārtha*, *sarvarahasyārtha* and *mahātattvārtha*. Each of these is described at length.

(iii) The third section treats of the *Pūjā Saṅketa*, as already mentioned. The *pūjā* or worship of the Goddess is declared to be of three kinds, viz (a) *Parā*, (b) *Parāparā* and (c) *Aparā*. The first represents Supreme Knowledge consisting in the realization of the highest unity, i.e. identity with Parama Śiva. The second partakes of a mixed nature, being partly *karma* and partly *jñāna*, and consists in the withdrawal by means of *bhāvanā* of the external *cakras* into the inner undifferenced Light. This is really a gradual elimination of action in the unity of knowledge. The third or lowest form of worship is of the external *cakras*, *āvaraṇa* etc. It starts from the outermost plane or *caturasra* (square) and proceeds by degrees to the central or Baindava Plane; in other words, it is the worship of the whole Śrī Cakra, with all the *sadanas*, *dvāras*, *devas* and others. It is pure action and is confined to the world of difference.

~5~

THE MYSTIC SIGNIFICANCE OF 'EVAṀ'

-I-

Jayaratha, in his commentary on Abhinavagupta's *Tantrāloka* (III. 94-95), quotes the following verse from an unknown source:

एकाराकृति यद् दिव्यं मध्ये षट्कारभूषितम् ।
आलयः सर्वसौख्यानां बोधरत्नकरण्डकम् ॥

What this verse exactly means is not clear from the context of the commentary. Nor does Jayaratha mention the source of his quotation. But a study of the Tantric Buddhist literature, specially of the Vājrayāna and allied schools of the latter age, would make it clear that the couplet is taken from a work of this system and refers to a great mystic symbol current in the same. The commentary of Tilopā quotes this stanza and attributes it to Hevajra. It is evident from a glance at this commentary that Jayaratha's quotation, as it appears in the printed edition, is different and probably also incorrect, so far as the reading '*ṣaṭkāra*' is concerned, the correct reading being 'evaṁkāra'. The reading '*bodharatnakaraṇḍakaṁ*' should also be amended in favour of '*buddharatnakaraṇḍakaṁ*', a reading which is actually found in Hevajra. The meaning of the verse as thus corrected is that what is known as '*buddha-ratnakaraṇḍakaṁ*' or the Essence of Supreme Wisdom — the home of all forms of Joy — is symbolized by a celestial form which looks like *e* (ए) with *va* (व) inserted within it. This symbol; is usually referred to under the name of '*evaṁkāra*' (एवंकार) in Buddhist mystic literature. The Hevajra itself says:

आनन्दास्तत्र जायन्ते क्षणभेदेन भेदिताः ।
क्षणज्ञानात् सुखज्ञानम् 'एवंकार' प्रतिष्ठितम् ॥

which shows that it is within this '*evaṁkāra*' that different Joys, based on different *kṣaṇas*, are believed to take their rise.

The general feature of the symbol is clear enough. The letter '*e*' (ए) is represented as a triangle with its vertex downwards. The letter '*va*' (व) with *bindu* attached, '*vaṁkāra*' (वंकार), is represented as a triangle with its vertex upwards, the *bindu* (point) being in the centre. '*Vaṁkāra*' is described as being within the '*ekāra*' (एकार) — *Bindu* is the common centre of both the triangles and stands for *Yoga* or union of both.

The two triangles, '*e*' and '*va*' are the separate symbols of Śakti and Śiva respectively and are called *Śaktitrikoṇa* and *Śivatrikoṇa* in Hindu Āgamic literature. The usual form of the symbolism is *ṣaṭkoṇa* with *bindu* within. The *Devendra Paripṛcchā-Tantra* quoted in a copy of *Subhāṣita-Saṁgraha*, a manuscript of which was once brought to me for inspection long ago, has two verses relevant to the mystic significance of the great symbol. The verses are:[1]

एकारस्तु भवेन्माता वकारस्तु पिता स्मृतः।
बिन्दुस्तत्र भवेद् योगः स योगः परमाक्षरः ॥
एकारस्तु भवेत् प्रज्ञा वंकारः सुरताधिपः ।
बिन्दुश्चानाहतं ज्ञानं तज्जन्यान्यक्षराणि च ॥

Here we find that '*e*' represents Mother (or *prajñā*, i.e., Śakti), '*va*' Father (or *suratādhipaḥ*, i.e., Śiva) and the *bindu* their union (*yogaḥ*) which is the Supreme *akṣara* (*paramākṣara*), otherwise known as *anāhatajñāna*, the ultimate source of all *akṣaras*.

Kānhapāda, in one of his *Dohās*, says:

---

[1] Also called *dharmakaraṇḍaka*. It is the *mahāmudrā* in which *śūnyatā* and *karuṇā* are unified. It is described as the receptacle (*ādhāra*) of Buddha jewel (*buddharatna*) or the Ultimate Truth (*paramāthasatya*) and as the last ornament (*ābharaṇa*) of a Vajrayānī *yogin*. The *yogin* is said to build up a *karaṇḍaka* in his own body by means of *manas* (mind) and *pavana* (vital principle), when he proceeds, in the language of the *Siddhācāryas*, to marry the *dombī*. In the language of the Siddhānta Śaiva School we may identify this *bindu* with the *akṣara bindu*, otherwise known as *anāhata bindu*, which issues from the Supreme *Bindu* as its second expression, after the manifestation of *nāda*, and which is the immediate antecedent to the physical articulate sound expressed as letter-sounds of the alphabet (*varṇa*, *akṣaramālā*). See Sadyojyoti's Commentary on *Ratnatraya* (verse 22).

एवंकार विढ वाखोढ मोडिउ ।
विविह विआपक बान्धण तोडिउ ॥ [2]
कान्ह विलसअ आसव माता ।
सहज नलिनीवन पइसि निर्विता ॥ [3]

The commentary notes : *ekāraścandrābhāsaḥ, vaṁkāraḥ sūryaḥ, ubhayaṁ divārātrijñānam*; that is, '*e*' (ए) is the Moon or Night and '*vaṁ*' (वं) is the Sun or Day, so that '*evaṁ*' (एवं) stands for Night and Day, or Time (*kāla*). In the yogic language, usually the moon is taken to be the representative of *Prakṛti* and the sun that of *Puruṣa*. This interpretation too would thus corroborate the sense in the above.

It is well-knwon in the Mahāyānic and Vajrayānic Buddhist literature, though it is a mystery the true significance of which can hardly be appreciated outside the esoteric circle, there is a great difference, fundamental in nature, between the two *Nayas* of Mahāyāna, viz, Prajñāpāramitā-Naya and Mantra-Naya. It is said that the truths of the former wisdom were revealed by the Teacher from the heights of Gṛdhrakūṭa mountain, but the secret of Mantric lore were expounded from a distinct place known as Śrī Dhānya. These are really, in my opinion, the names of two *pīṭhas* within the body and should not be confounded with the well-known geographical sites of the same name, with which, for special reasons, they are usually identified.

The *Mūla Tantra*, cited by Naropa in his commentary on *Sekoddeśa*, says:

आकाशे त्वजडे स्वच्छेऽनवकाशप्रकाशिनि ।
विश्वे वज्रालये लयने (?)धर्मधातौ मनोरमे ॥
तन्त्रस्य देशना पूंसां पुण्यज्ञानप्रयोजनम् ।
एकारो गगनालोको धर्मधातुः प्रकीर्तितः ॥
वंकार सुगतव्यूह एकारे सम्यग् विष्टितः ॥

[2] *Caryāpada*, ed. by M.M. Basu, Calcutta University, 1943, p. 32.

[3] Ibid.

This shows that the Symbol '*e*' (ए), within which the figure '*vaṁ*' (वं) is inserted, represents the pure spiritual light of infinite space conceived as *dharmadhātu* (or essence of *dharma*) and that the enclosed figure '*vaṁ*' (वं) stands for the series of the Buddhas who have realized their identity with this *dhātu*.

Elsewhere it is declared that '*e*' (ए) is *bhaga* (*yoni*, triangle of Śakti), Dharmodaya (*Dharmadhātu* revealed), lotus, *siṁhāsana* and *ādhāra* whereas '*va*' (व) is the Ādi Buddha or *Vajra Sattva* seated thereon as its Ādheya:

ए रहस्याख्यधातौ वा भगे धर्मोदयेऽम्बुजे ।
सिंहासने स्थितो वज्री उक्तस्तन्त्रान्तरे मया ॥
वं वज्रो वज्रसत्त्वश्च वज्रभैरव ईश्वरः ।
हेवज्रः कालचक्रश्च आदिबुद्धादिनामकः ॥

-II-

In the Hindu Tantras also the highly mystic character of the symbol is recognised and its interpretation is more or less of a similar nature. As in the Buddhist works, the letter '*e*' (ए) symbolizes, in the form of a triangle (*śṛṅgāṭa*), the Śakti Yantra (*Bhanga*, *Yoni*) conceived as the House of Fire (*vahnigeha*):

त्रिकोणमेकादशमं वह्निगेहं च योनिकम् ।
श्रृङ्गाटं चैव एकारं नामभिः परिकीर्तितम् ॥

It is the secret sphere (*guptamaṇḍalam*) within infinite space (*viyatstha*) and is usually described as the 'mouth of *yoginī*' (*yoginīvaktra*). Its three angles represent the three powers of Will, Knowledge and Action, and within its sacred precincts lies buried, like the *vaṁkāra* in Buddhist literature, the mystery of the so-called *Ciñciṇī-Krama*:

त्रिकोणं भगमित्युक्तं वियत्स्थं गुप्तमण्डलम् ।
इच्छाज्ञानक्रियाकोणं तन्मध्ये चिञ्चिणीक्रमम् ॥

It may be pointed out that the letter '*e*' (ए), even in the early days of its appearance in the Brāhmī script of Aśoka, had the shape of a triangle. From a consideration of phonogenetics it would seem that *e* = *a* (or *ā*) + *i* (ए = अ or आ + इ). The letters '*a*' (अ) and '*ā*' (आ) signify the basic or initial vibration of the Transcendent Consciousness-Power and the bubbling of ineffable Joy respectively, and the letter '*i*' (इ) denotes Will-Power. When these are combined, the result is the manifestation of a triangle:

अनुत्तरानन्दचिती इच्छाशक्तौ नियोजिते ।
त्रिकोणमिति यत् प्राहुर्विसर्गानन्दसुन्दरम् ॥

It is to be remembered, however, that the transcendent (*anuttara* = *a*) consisting of the three *śaktis*, viz *raudrī*, *jyeṣṭhā* and *vāmā*, is of the nature of triangle; so is joy (*ānanda* = *ā*). What is known as the hexagon or the Tantric *ṣatkoṇa* is the result of the union of the aforesaid triangles '*a*' (अ) or '*ā*' (आ) on one hand and '*e*' (ए) on the other. This is symbolized by the letter '*ai*' (ऐ). It is known in the Tantras as the well-known *ṣaḍara*, which is held to be one of the greatest secrets of the Science.

The '*evaṁ*' (एवं) of Buddhist mysticism and the '*ai*' (ऐ) of uTantric mysticism would thus virtually signify the same or a similar symbol and are held to be equally sacred.

~6~

The Problem of Causality — Sāṁkhya-Yoga View

In the history of ancient Indian philosophy the controversy over the doctrine of causality is very old indeed. Although the nature of the controversy has varied from time to time, the fundamental problem has persisted. It is this: What is the relation between the cause and the effect? Does the cause contain the effect in its implicit form or is the effect a new thing altogether? What are the presuppositions of the genetic process? Does it imply simply a gradual unfoldment of what lies within, as eternally existing, or is it a creation *ex nihil*?

We know that various answers can be given to these questions according to the differences of our viewpoint. The Naiyāyika, with his commonsense and realistic assumptions, would naturally be inclined to favour the view which maintains an absolute difference (*atyantabheda*) between the cause (material) and the effect. To him the cause and the effect are two distinct concepts, though bound together by a mysterious tie of relationship; for it cannot be gainsaid, the Naiyāyika would say, that though the effect is distinct from its cause — indeed from everything else in creation — by virtue of its own apparent individuality, it still inheres in it during its existence, and that even when it does not exist, i.e. before its production and after its destruction, its non-existence, technically known as *prāgabhāva* and *dhvaṁsa*, is predicable of its cause alone. As to what constitutes this bond of affinity, nothing is said beyond the fact that it is in the nature of an effect to be thus intimately related to its own material cause. It is an ultimate fact and has to be accepted as such.

This appeal to 'the nature of things' on the part of the Naiyāyika amounts practically to a confession of weakness of his theory. The *yogin*, who is an advocate of *satkāryavāda*, rejects the Naiyāyika hypothesis and affirms that the effect, in so far as its essence is concerned, is identical with the cause from which it comes forth. The so-called production and destruction do not really mean that the product comes into and passes away from existence. Every product being an aspect of the supreme *Prakṛti*, in which it exists somehow involved and identified as an eternal moment, creation out of nothing and annihilation is an absurdity. Production, therefore, is differentiation and dissolution is re-integration. The process of becoming, with which the problem of causality has to deal, does indeed imply a change, but it is a change conceived as the transition of a *dharma* from an unmanifest to a manifest state and from the manifest back into the unmanifest condition. The substrate of change is everywhere and always an existing unit.

The sum and substance of the Satkāryavādin's contention seems to be this. We all must start from the assumption, under the necessity of our thought, that being comes from *being* and *not from not-being*, and that an absolute void giving rise to being is inconceivable. The denial of this principle would land us in contradictions. We conclude, therefore, that the effect is real (*sat*).

In the text-books of the school we find a set of five arguments brought forward to establish the reality (*sattā*) of the effect (even before its origin):

(1) The fact that what is unreal (*asat*) can not be subject to the causal operation (*kārakavyāpāra*).

(2) The fact that an appropriate material (*upādāna*) is resorted to for bringing about a certain effect; in other words, that every material is not by nature capable of producing every effect. This means that the material cause, which is somehow related to the effect in question, brings about that effect. But if the effect were not existing, there would be no relation and consequently no production. An unrelated material is no material at all.

(3) And if the necessity of the relation between the material and the effect be not admitted, it would imply that the fitness of the material is not a condition and that any effect could result from any cause. This would be subversive of all order and so against our experience.

(4) This difficulty cannot be got over by the asumption of *śakti* even, as the Mīmāṁsakas seem to do. They declare that an effect, before its origin, is indeed non-existent (*asat*) and that the cause is therefore indeed unrelated. Still there would be no irregularity, for we admit, they say, that the cause, in so far as it possesses a *śakti* favourable to a certain effect, does produce that effect. As to the question whether the cause possesses a particular *śakti* or not, it can only be answered *a fortiori*, for it is inferred by observation of the effect.

(5) The last argument is that the effect is nothing different from the cause (*kāraṇabhāvāt*). If the cause be existent (*sat*), there is no reason to maintain that the effect, which is only a mode of the cause, should be non-existent (*asat*).

This last argument requires to be expanded. We have already said that according to Sāṁkhya, unlike Nyāya-Vaiśeṣika, the relation between cause and effect is declared to be identity (*abheda*, *tādātmya*) The Naiyāyika, with his pragmatic attitude towards reality, makes utility the criterion of existence (*sattā*) and approaches the problem in a semi-Buddhistic fashion. To him, therefore, the effect, say a jar, is altogether a distinct entity from its cause, clay, for both do not serve the self-same purpose. This is *arthakriyābheda*. Besides this, there are other grounds which, to a realist philosopher, help to differentiate one object from another. These are *buddhi* (=*pratīti*), *vyāpadeśa* and *arthakriyāvyavasthā*. On these grounds, too, the Naiyāyika seeks to establish the difference of the effect from the cause. Thus the notion of jar is distinct from that of clay and, consequently corresponding to this notional or logical difference, the Naiyāyika would say, there must be a real difference in the objective world. In other words, jar and clay, as objective realities, must be mutually different. So, too, differences of names and function point to a difference in reality.

These are some of the stock arguments of the Naiyāyika. But they do not appear to have much weight against the Sāṁkhya-Yoga position. They lose their point as soon as they are aimed at a system in which the so-called Realism finds little support. The *arthakriyābheda* is really no sure test of objective difference, for the same object may have different *arthakriyās*; nor is *arthakriyāvyavasthā* a test, for different collocations of the same cause may serve different purposes. The difference of names, viz clay and jar, is no proof of difference either, for in that case a forest would have to be postulated as different from the individual trees composing it.

The true relation between the cause and the effect, therefore, is that the effect is a *dharma*, an aspect of the cause, and constitutes a mode of it. The primary *Prakṛti* being the equilibrium of the three *guṇas*, the effects or *vikāras* are nothing but various modifications and collocations of it. In essence the cause and the effect are identical for both consist of *guṇas* and it is in difference of collocation (*saṁsthānabheda*) that the difference between the two, as it reveals itself to our consciousness, consists. And this difference in collocation is a peculiar manifestation. That of which it is a manifestation, remains always in the background, unmanifest. In the last resort, the cause, *Prakṛti*, the *Materia Prima*, is the unmanifest, and the effect, the *vikāra*, is the manifested world, always held within the bosom of that unmanifest, universal being.

The doctrine of *satkārya* therefore implies, as we often find in Indian philosophy, that the universe, with an infinite number of cosmic systems belonging to it, is always existing in *Prakṛti* as its aspects. The evolution of a universe out of void has no meaning. The Buddhist, together with the Naiyāyika and Vaiśeṣika, believe that the product has no existence prior to its origination and that it loses its existence as soon as it is destroyed. What this really means and how far it is justified we shall try to explain elsewhere. But we may just observe here that the whole doctrine of *satkārya* is a blow to this position.

To make the Yoga thesis more clear we give here a brief analysis of its concept of substance or *dharmin*. In the technical nomenclature of Indian philosophy, the term *dharmin* bears the sense of "substrate, subject, that in which something is held, that of which something is predicated" and *dharma* means the "aspect of *dharmin*, predicate, content" and so forth. All predication, and therefore all judgment, involves the affirmation (*vidhāna*) or denial (*niṣedha*) of a particular *dharma* with reference to a particular *dharmin*. In fact, every proposition, which is an expression of judgment, bears testimony to the fact of predication. Now, though predication is made–and our entire phenomenal existence is necessarily based upon this — the subject of predication remains always, so far as its naqture and essence are concenred, a point of controversy. When it is said that "the flower is red", the proposition is certainly intelligible to common sense, but on close examination the meaning of the proposition furnishes a topic for discussion. It reveals the same old problem which Nāgasena raised before Menander more than 2000 years ago. What is that to which I am attributing redness? What is meant by flower? Is it a mere bundle (*saṁghāta*, *samudāya*) of sensible qualities or is there a real objective ground, a substrate, to which the qualities are attached by some natural relations? We know that two answers are usually given to this question. The first is that of the Buddhists and in a certain sense of the Vaiyākaraṇas. The second answer comes from Nyāya-Vaiśeṣika. The Vedāntic position on this question is one of compromise between Idealism and Realism, but it tends towards the former. And the Yoga view, too, is more or less idealistic, though with an important qualification.

In other words, the Buddhists deny the existence of a substance away from the qualities and a whole as distinct from the parts. But the Realists, to whom the external world has an objective, extra-mental value, are not satisfied with the view. They posit a real substance in which various qualities inhere and which is not a mere collection of *guṇas* but has an independent existence. So too, with the whole (*avayavī*) which results, as a distinct and independent object, from the combination of parts. In Vedānta, also, the former view is favoured. Śaṅkara, in *Bṛhadāraṇyaka-bhāṣya*, plainly denies substantiality to the atoms and describes them as mere *guṇas*. But the Yoga theory is more clear on the point. It is said indeed that *dharma* is the *guṇa* or a set of *guṇas*, by which the *dharmin* is made known to us and that this *guṇa* may be any of the sensible qualities, viz, colour, sound, etc or any of their combinations. But this ought not to imply that there is any fundamental distinction between *dharma* and *dharmin*. Both of these are at bottom (*paramārthataḥ*) one.[1] They are different only in *vyavahāra*. And since this difference between *dharma* and *dharmin* and between one *dharma* and another is founded on the appearance and disappearnce of the *dharmas* which is due to time-limitation, it is evident that in Eternity, where there is no distinction between past and future, all the *dharmas* are in a sense identical, not only with one another but even with the *dharmin* to which they are referred. This ultimate *dharmin* is the unmanifest *Prakṛti* whose infinite modes (*vikāraḥ*) are the infinite *dharmas*, of which those which are present to our consciousness are called present and the rest are characterised either as past or as future. The *dharmas* are, therefore, only the varying manifestations of the *guṇas*, primary Matter. That is, *Prakṛti* as modified in a particular manner is known as a particular *dharma* or *vikāra*.

* * *

The Yoga philosophy, especially the system propounded by Patañjali and Vyāsa, accepts in the main the views of the rival school of the Sāṁkhyas. The Yoga view of causality is therefore, in all essential features, almost identical with the Sāṁkhya.

From what we have said regarding *satkāryavāda* it must have been made clear that the Yoga (and Sāṁkhya) notion of causality has a distinct character of its own. The word 'cause' means indeed a necessary pre-condition of a subsequent event; this meaning is common to the other system: it also accepts the *anvaya* and *vyātireka* as the guiding principles for the discovery of causality. But the characteristic doctrine remains to be noted.

If we observe the world of change and analyse it carefully, we find that every change involves a double element: (a) a transitional one, and (b) a permanent one. When clay is moulded into the form of a jar, we are accustomed to speak of this moulding as an instance

[1] *Dharmisvarūpamātro hi dharmaḥ dharmivikriyai'vaiṣā dharmadvārā prapañcyata iti, tatra dharmasya dharmini varttamānasyai'va adhvasu atitānāgatavarttamāneṣu bhāvānyathātvaṁ bhavati na dravyānyathātvam* | (*Yoga Bhāṣya*, III. 13).

of change. Evidently here, too, there are two elements present, viz, clay and the forms that apper and disappear in it. The forms are all transitional — they come and go — but the matter, the clay, for instance, is relatively permanent. It is, therefore, said to be the substrate of these changes of forms, through all of which its unity remains unbroken. Before the production of the jar, clay had a definite form, viz, 'lump', which disappeared and made room for the appearance of a new form, viz, 'jar', and the destruction of the jar again is nothing but the disappearance of the 'jar' form and the appearance of a fresh one in its place, and so on till Universal Dissolution, when Matter will absorb within itself all its forms and regain its pristine formless and blank character. But during creation (*sṛṣṭi*) it stands as the background for the play of these countless fleeting forms. From this it will be obvious what the relation between Matter, the *dharmin*, and the form, the *dharma*, is. Every change being a kind of causation, true causal relation must be understood as meaning the relation of the form to the matter, and *not*, as the Buddhists would contend, of one form with another. In the chain of causation, of course, one form may be spoken of as the cause of another,[2] but it is not by virtue of itself but of the matter which is its content. In the technical language of Sāṁkhya-Yoga all causal relation is *Prakṛtivikṛtibhāva*, *prakṛti* being the cause and *vikṛti* the effect.

But the meaning of the term *prakṛti* is very often misunderstood. It is generally supposed to stand for the *samavāyi kāraṇa* of the Vaiśiṣika or for the material cause of the Scholastics. There is no doubt that what is meant by *samavāyi kāraṇa* falls under *prakṛti*, but the latter includes the so-called *nimittas* as well. If we leave aside for the present the question of *asamavāyi kāraṇa*, which is a peculiarity of the Vaiśeṣika alone, we may conveniently divide *prakṛti* into a two-fold aspect, viz: *upādāna* and *nimitta*.

Thus, although *prakṛti* is one, and the question of causal classification is, therefore, out of place in Sāṁkhya, it becomes

[2] In popular parlance, however, one *dharma* may be described as the *dharma* of another.

intelligible why we find mention of a two-fold division of the causal principle. This division is really a concession to the demands of empiric consciousness, and is resorted to just as in Vedānta. truly speaking, Sāṁkhya-Yoga, as much as Vedānta, is an advocate of the identity of *nimitta* and *upādāna*. In other words, the distinction between *nimitta* and *upādāna* is a pseudodistinction, and has no existence on the plane of pure *Prakṛti* which is universal Being and Essence. It is only when *Prakṛti* has evolved herself into the first stadium, into the *Mahat*, that we find this distinction of *nimitta* and *upādāna*, like every other distinction, probably brought out. The functions of the *nimitta*, therefore, is not to serve, as with the Vaiśeṣika, as an external principle of movement, the effectuating factor in the universal Becoming. *Prakṛti* is self-moved (*svataḥparī-nāmīnī*), motion is inherent in it by nature and does not come to it from without. It (as *rajas*) is an aspect of its Being. The efficiency of the *nimitta* consists only in the removal of the *prohibens* in the way of *Prakṛti* (*tamaḥ*, *āvaraṇa*) and in the consequent liberation of the *vikāras*, the form, held so long in confinement within the womb of *Prakṛti*.

For practical purposes, therefore, we may distinguish in our system between two kinds of causes at work, viz, the material and the efficient. What Aristotle designated as formal causes do not seem to posses here a causal character at all. And we shall find that the so-called final causes of Aristotle fall under the category of *nimitta*.

Let us try to understand the position more clearly. We have said that the material cause, the *Prakṛti* qua *upādāna*, possesses an eternal motion inherent in itself and is not an inert substance required to be moved from outside. It possesses *in potentia* infinite forms towards the manifestation of which it has a natural proneness; but this manifestation is held in check by a retarding force, which, as well shall find later on, is identical with the merit or demerit of the *jīva* with whose personal experience the manifestation is directly concerned. As soon as this force is counteracted by an opposite force, e.g., merit by demerit and vice versa, the path of evolution becomes clear and the material transforms itself into the appropriate effect. The block of stone, for instance, contains involved within itself any kind of image, but it is able to manifest a particular image — and this manifestation is called production — only when the particular *āvaraṇa* which stands in the way of its manifestation is removed by the sculptor's chisel. The removal of this *āvaraṇa* constitutes the efficiency of *nimitta*, and is the sum and substance of all causal operation. The *nimittas* do not lend any impulse to the material nor can they bring out what is not implicitly contained in it. The apt illustration in the *Yogabhāṣya* (4.3) of the water in a reservoir on a higher level flowering of itself into the lower fields when a leakage or an outlet is made in the embankment, will clear up our point. Further, since every subsidiary *prakṛti*-finite cause is ultimately permeated by and coincident with pure *Prakṛti*, it naturally follows that every individual thing in nature contains every other thing potentially.[3]

Thus we need not seek for a principle of effectuation in *Prakṛti* outside of its own nature (*svabhāva*). This independence, on the part of *Prakṛti*, of an extrinsic influence is called her *svātantrya* or freedom. Vijñāna Bhikṣu shows (*Yoga Vārttika*, pp. 260-1) that the only possible cause of *pravṛtti* is the nature of the *guṇas*.[4] It is universally admitted that the particles of matter (*aṇu*) are in perpetual motion in space. This motion is the vague vibration characteristic of the atoms and is to be distinguished from the definite motion which brings two atoms together (*dravyārambhaka*) so as to form a substance. This motion does not serve any moral purpose, i.e., does not produce *bhoga*; hence merit and demerit cannot be its cause. Nor is this motion due to a special act of God's will, for it would be assuming too much. It is more reasonable,

---

[3] The arguments in *Sāṁkhyakārikā*, viz *upādānaniyamāt* etc. are in consonance with our ordinary experience which justifies this restriction. An effect, to be brought forth, requires an appropriate material (and appropriate subsidiary causes). This is so, because we are dealing with limited *prakṛti* and with limited human resources. But to the *yogin*, to whom the entire *Prakṛti* is open, it is easy to evolve anything from anything.

[4] Cf. *Yogabhāṣya* under *Sūtra* III. 13:
Guṇasvābhāvyaṁ tu pravṛttikāraṇaṁ uktaṁ guṇānām |

therefore, to think of it as natural. Vijñāna Bhikṣu further points out that the *nimittas* are not found to be necessary and indispensable in the manifestation of an effect, for the *yogin*, by a mere act of his will, can bring forth anything that he pleases and for creation he does not stand in need of any human instruments. Similarly, in the beginning of creation things, e.g. seeds, are produced by God's will merely, without the help of any positive precedent conditions, e.g. similar other seeds. All this goes to corroborate the view that the *nimittas* have not a direct causality in the production of an object. They help, each in its own way, to rouse the evolving power of *prakṛti*, viz, *karma* (merit and demerit) by breaking the *āvaraṇa* which is a *dharma* opposed to itself, God's will by breaking all kinds of *āvaraṇa* beginning with the greatest one, i.e., state of equilibrium, *kāla* by rousing *karmas* etc., and the ordinary instruments, *daṇḍas* etc. by retarding the possibility of manifestation of other effects.

* * *

But what is the aim of all this manifestation? What is its end? An answer to this would furnish us with what Aristotle calls final causes of creation. It is admitted that all movement presupposes an end to be realised; without an end there can be no activity (*prayojanam anuddiśya na mando'pi pravartate*). This end is however variously conceived:

(a) Firstly it is pleasure or pain, which the *jīva* is bound to experience in consequence (i.e. as the fruits, *phala*) of his previous *karma*. In common parlance, this experience is known as *bhoga* and *jīva* as *bhoktā*.

(b) The author of the *Yogabhāṣya* sets forth that this aim is two-fold, pleasure or absence of pain. The former is *bhoga* and the latter is *apavarga*. It is either of these two which is the object of a man's striving (*puruṣārtha*). Pleasure or *bhoga*, when further analysed, would be found to embrace the three varieties of end, viz *dharma*, *artha* and *kāma*. But the supreme end is *apavarga*.

In the *Sāṁkhya Kārikā* (42), it is clearly stated that the *puruṣārtha* actuates the liṅga (*pravartaka*). This *artha* is (a) experience of pleasure and pain on the ascertainment of *viṣayas*, or (b) denial of *viṣayas* on the ascertainment of distinction between *Prakṛti* and *Puruṣa*. In other words, every movement is either towards *viṣayabhoga* or towards *bhogatyāga*, i.e. peace. But as *bhoga* is the necessary precedent of *tyāga*, and must eventually be followed by it, sooner or later, it may be said with reason that the end of all movement is this *tyāga*, which in its highest form is dissociation from *Prakṛti* and self-realisation. It is the "One Event to which the whole creation moves".

The perpetual unrest and agitation which we observe around us will have their close only when this supreme end is attained. The course of evolution, for each individual, will terminate when he realises the essential nature of his own self (*tataḥ pariṇāmakramasamāptir guṇānām*). For apart from the individual for whom it is intended the evolution of Nature has no other meaning. As to the further question whether Nature as a whole will ever cease to evolve we have nothing to say here. This point will be discussed separately in connection with the doctrine of *pralaya*.

Without going into further detail at this point we may note that the conception of causality in Sāṁkhya-Yoga is as much mechanical as it is teleological. Leaving out the other auxiliary factors and confining ourselves to *karman* alone we find that it is both efficient (though negatively so as already pointed out) as well as final. Everything in Nature has its end. It will be found that even the objective inequalities in creation are not explicable except on the hypothesis of the determining principle. A thing is what it is not by chance but, as it were, by necessity. If the external world exists, and has come into being, to serve as the object of experience (pleasure or pain) of a conscious subject and would vanish for him as soon as that purpose is fulfilled, it is easy to follow that its varieties must be occasioned by that principle, moral in its nature, which governs the varieties of such experience; and consequently all instruments and efficient factors must work in subordination to this Supreme Governor. So far, therefore, the whole scheme of Nature appears to be teleological.

But *karman* is not the last word. It is worked off partly in natural course by fruition and is ultimately transcended by the light of Supreme Wisdom which reveals the Self as it is and as distinct from *Prakṛti*. This is the final term of the evolutionary series. From this point of view, too, the scheme of Nature would be found to be pervaded by finality.

This analysis of ours leaves out of account what Aristotle calls 'formal causes'. Though the forms, as conceived in the Sāṁkhya-Yoga and even in the Nyāya-Vaiśeṣika, are not considered to have a causal character strictly, they are not important in the order of creation, so far as the specialities of the individuals are concerned. They will discussed elsewhere.

* * *

It is universally admitted that the world of sensible reality is a world of perpetual change, and it is also practically assumed, as we said, that every change involves a two-fold element, viz, one that is transient and the other that is relatively permanent. The material, which is the subject of change, endures, while the effect comes and goes.

A careful and systematic study of this problem of change led in ancient India to the formulation of three broad theories, viz, *Ārambhavāda*, *Pariṇāmavāda* and *Vivarttavāda*.

The *Ārambhavāda* or the doctrine of origination (genesis) is the view of the Naiyāyika and Vaiśeṣika to whom the effect is entirely a different thing from the productive material. It is immaterial whether the effect produced is a substance or a quality or an action; in all cases it is a new thing altogether and is distinct from the substance from which it arises. This view is a necessary corollary from the *Asatkāryavāda*. That the effect is found to inhere, so long as it continues in existence, in its material cause and is not capable of separation from it, simply proves that there is an intimate relation between the two and not that the two are identical.

A strong argument in favour of *Ārambhavāda* seems to be furnished from the atomic theory. This theory postulates the existence of an infinite number of eternal particles of matter as the ultimate constituents of all substantial products (*kāryadravya*), that is, every product is explained as due to a peculiar combination resulting in contact (*ārambhakasaṁyoga*) of these particles. And since it is impossible to consider the product as a mere grouping of the parts — and the reason why this is impossible consists in the disparity between the two, viz, that the particles are imperceptible and many, while their collection is *perceived* as *one* — it is more compatible with commonsense to suppose that the parts, by reason of combination result in the formation of the *whole* which is a *new* entity, pure and simple.

But what is the bearing of this doctrine on the problem of change? The question is whether change is predicable of the whole (*avayavī*), or of the ultimate particles, or of both.

The Vaiśeṣika says that the particles change and that the resultant whole also consequently changes. This is of the nature of chemical change and is due to the influence of *tejas*. The constant change going on in the world is in the end reducible to this type. In other words, if X represents the whole consisting of parts represented by, say, *a*, *b*, *c*, and *d*, we might say that the change of *a*, *b*, *c*, *d*, into *a*' *b*' *c*' *d*' by the assumption of new qualities would necessarily involve the destruction of X and of the origin of a new whole, called Y.[5] This theory, therefore, assumes a double series of change– one in the parts and one in the whole. But why does not *a* and *c* change into *a*, etc? It is not natural, of course, for this would violate the postulate that no motion is inherent in a thing. To explain this change the Vaiśeṣika assumes the contact of *a* and *c* with the particles of *tejas* which penetrate into the body by means of pores (according to Vaiśeṣika, every substantial product is porous and pervious), break the contact of the atoms and produce in them a change of qualities. The atoms, as thus changed, are united again and form a fresh whole. This *tejas* is not only what we ordinarily call fire. It is ultimately the Solar Energy which, therefore, stands at the root of all physical and chemical changes in the world.

[5] The atoms remain the same, but their qualities change.

But the Naiyāyika does not agree to this. He holds, against the Vaiśeṣika, the solidity of substantial product and its impenetrability by heat-particles which act upon the body as a whole and produce in it change of qualities. Thus, though the substance is constant from its origin till its destruction, it is subject to change so far as its qualities are concerned.

The Vedāntist does not admit with the Vaiśeṣika that difference of size (*parimāṇa*) is the cause of difference of substance; hence the *dharmin*, say, the jar, remaining the same, its former *rūpa* is destroyed and is replaced by a new *rūpa*; similarly the animal organism remaining the same, its leanness (*kārśya*) is due to falling off (*apacaya*) of particles and its fatness (*sthaulya*) may be explained as due to accretion (*upacaya*) of new particles. Thus the body of 'A' when one year old would be identical with his body in his eightieth year, although there may be an entire change of particles and difference of size. In other words, it is the same body in different states (*avasthā*).

The problem of change has received a good deal of attention and careful treatment in the hands of Sāṁkhya and especially of Yoga. *Pariṇāma* means disappearance of one *dharma*, followed by the appearance of another, within the same subject or *dharmin*.[6] The word is used to indicate the process when it refers to the subject, and the result of this process when it refers to the predicate, *dharma*. In popular usages and in later literature this word is found synonymous with *vikāra*.[7]

The *pariṇāma* is three-fold, according as it concerns *dharma*, *lakṣaṇa* and *avasthā*. The definition of *pariṇāma* given above is that of *dharma pariṇāma*. *Lakṣaṇapariṇāma* is the name of the change in regard to *lakṣaṇa* or time-sequence, i.e. past, present and future. The grammatical tenses correspond to this *pariṇāma* in nature. The lakṣana too is not conceived as an ultimate unit and is further analysable into what we may call *avasthā* or states,

[6] *Avasthitasya drayyasya pūrvadharmanivṛttau dharmāntarotpattiḥ pariṇāmaḥ* | *Yoga Bhāsya*, III. 13.

[7] *Upajanāpāyaśālī dharma eva ca vikāra ity uccyate* | *Brahmavidyābharaṇa*, p. 146 (Adv. Mañj. Ed.)

viz new or old. Each such state is supposed to be ultimate and momentary. This kind of *pariṇāma* is not really expressible in language. This being the case, the evolution of Nature may be supposed to consist of a series of such successive moments. In this ceaseless stream of *pariṇāma* everything is being carried away from the future through the present into the past. But the future (*anāgata*) and the past (*atīta*) being nothing but unmanifest *Prakṛti*, every *pariṇāma* is a passage from the unmanifest. This represents a circle, of which one half, viz, passage from unmanifest into manifestation, i.e. from the future into the present, stands for what is known as *visadṛśapariṇāma*, and another half, i.e. return from manifestation into unmanifest, i.e. from the present to the past, for *sadṛśapariṇāma*. This is true of all the three kinds of *pariṇāma*.

Thus the triple *pariṇāma* represents a series of three circles not mutually exclusive but really concentric, *dharmapariṇāma* being the outermost and the *avasthāpariṇāma* the inmost of the group. But *dharma* and *avasthā* are relative concepts merely and are identical. The author of the *Yogabhāṣya* clearly states (III.13) that the change of *dharma* in a *dharmin*, of *lakṣaṇa* in a *dharma* and *avasthā* in a *lakṣaṇa* is the same process, being characterised by modification of the substance and involving a transition of states (*avasthā*).[8]

This change is incessant and uncaused. It pervades the whole realm of Nature. It is said that nothing that is made of *guṇas* is ever, even for a single moment, at rest, and this for the simple reason that *guṇas* are by nature fickle.[9] Even in the state of dissolution when the manifested universe is resolved into *Prakṛti*,

---

[8] *Dharmiṇo'pi dharmāntaram avasthā, dharmasyā'pi lakṣaṇāntaram avasthā ity eka eva dravyapariṇāmabhedeno padarśita iti* | Again : *Paramārthastu eka eva pariṇamāḥ* | Balarāma points out (p. 210, note 2) that the three *pariṇāmas* are really cases of *avasthāpariṇāma* or they are all to be labelled as *dharmapariṇāma*, since all the mutations are in the *dharmin* as their permanent abode.

[9] *Dharmalakṣaṇāvasthāpariṇāmaiḥ śūnyam na kṣaṇam api guṇavṛttam avatiṣṭhate, calaṁ ca guṇavṛttam* | *Yogabhāṣya*, III.13.

this change of mutation still continues — this is *sadṛśapariṇāma*.[10] It is only *Puruṣa* or the Self which is truly immutable, being beyond *Prakṛti*.

Now a *dharma* or state, unless it is present, must be either past or future; but in all these states the *dharmin*, of which these are affirmed, is constant. A *dharma* is a particular *śakti* pertaining to a substance and is inferred to exist in it from its action, viz, from the production of a particular effect. It is subject to mutation, but is never annihilated (cf. conservation of energy). The present (or *udita*, i.e. actual) *dharma* is one which is described as '*svavyāpāram anubhavan*' and '*savyāpāram*'; this is the object of our immediate consciousness, and is differentiated, on the one hand, from the past or *śāntadharma*, which has ceased to be active (*kṛtvā vyāpārān uparataḥ*) and on the other, from the future (possible or *avyapadeśya*) *dharma* which has not yet commenced to operate. Of these *dharmas* the present only is felt as distinct (*viśiṣṭa*) from *Prakṛti* by reason of its manifest character, and one might say that this alone exists. And we know that the Buddhist actually denied the others. The past and the future *dharmas* are not directly known. The truth in the matter seems to be that these *dharmas* rest in *Prakṛti* as in union with it and are not distinguishable, not only from one another but even as *dharmas*. Their essence is the essence of the *dharmin*.

Hence it follows that the *dharmas* are two-fold, according as they are manifest (*abhivyakta*) or unmanifest (*anabhivyakta*) and the *dharmin* is the substance which persists (*anvayī*) in them both and consists of a double nature, viz, it is a *sāmānya* as well as a *viśeṣa* i.e. as a *sāmānya* it persists in and is identical with *śānta* and *avyapadeśya dharma*, and as a *viśeṣa* it persists in and is the same as *uditadharma*. In other words, every effect or manifest product, in so

---

[10] Brahmānanda Bhārati, in his *Saralasāṁkhya*, p. 17, seems to deny that in the state of equilibrium (*sāmyāvasthā*) there could be *pariṇāma*. He says that the admission of *pariṇāma*, even if *sadṛśa*, would militate against the theory of equilibrium of *guṇas* in *pralaya*, for *pariṇāma* (*vaiṣamya*) and *sāmya* are contradictory. Bhārati's objection seems to me unfounded. It rests on a misunderstanding of the meaning of *pariṇāma*.

far as it is a manifestation, is an individual (*viśeṣa*), and considering its past and future unmanifest condition is identical with the universal Being or *Prakṛti* (*sāmānya*). The relation of cause and effect being identity in difference (*tādātmya*), every effect has an individual character (derived from its identity with the cause) by virtue of which it is perceived as one with everything else in nature.

The above will suffice to bring out the meaning of the statement that all things are essentially identical, and consequently all are in all. The root-principle of Yoga philosophy and practice is thus found to be a recognition of the fact that everything is full of infinite possibilities, and personal exertion is meant simply to give them, by removing the obstructions, actuality. As to how this is done we shall discuss elsewhere.

The perpetuity of flux is thus found to be an established fact in Nature. Our mind as well as the outer world are both equally fluent. Let us now try to discover how these momentary changes contribute to various results. The question is: if the *dharmin* is one and suffers changes of state moment by moment it follows that these changes are all uniform, and in that case how are we to account for the varieties of creation? The origin of multiplicity in effects from one or uniform cause is an illegitimate hypothesis. Concerning this it is said that diversity of modification is due to diversity of *krama*. *Krama* is the relative sequence between one *dharma* and another (*dharma* includes *lakṣaṇa* and *avasthā* also) and is ultimately a unit of change. It is the sequence of *kṣaṇas* (*kṣaṇā-nantaryātmā*). One *dharma* may be said to be a *krama* of another provided that it immediately follows it. The *krama* of *dharma* and *lakṣaṇa pariṇāma*s is sensible, but that of *avasthā pariṇāma* is extremely subtle and super-sensuous. None but a *yogin* can perceive the subtle change that a substance is undergoing every moment. But such *kramas*, though ordinarily imperceptible, are not to be ignored. Their cumulative effect, from which they are inferred, is great. It is their permutations and combinations, endless in number, which give rise to this manifold of our sensible experience.

Thus understood, *krama* is a movement of the *guṇas*. Referring to a *dharma*, we may define *krama* as its movement, from moment to moment, from the *anāgata* state towards manifestation (*varttamānatā*) and then towards *atīta*. In the *atīta* or *śānta* stage of the *dharma*, where all movement comes to a stand-still, there is no *krama*,[11] and it is for this reason that it is described as irrevocable. That *krama* belongs to the present *dharma* is universally admitted. But the *yogin* points out that even the *anāgata dharma*, a *dharma* which has not yet come to be manifested and is yet in the womb of *Prakṛti* as an *avyapadeśyadharma*, possesses *krama* and is subject to the law of fluctuation. Had it not been so, an *anāgatadharma* would never have become *varttamāna* at all? An *anāgatadharma* becoming *varttamāna* is tantamount to the evolution of primordial Nature. A detailed study of this point and the secrets of creation will be furnished elsewhere, when it will also be shown that just as lapse into the past is the final term of the life-history of *dharma*, so the *anāgatāvasthā* of the *dharma* is the initial term of its history. And this anāgatāvasthā may be conceived firstly (1) as *Prakṛti*, and then (2) as an ideal *dharma* (*bodha*) i.e. the same *dharma* when it is in the *Mahat* (cf. the original meaning of the term 'conception').

The philosophy of *krama* is very deep. It is said that the *guṇas* being eternal and always in motion by nature, the *krama* of their modification never comes to an end. Their *pariṇāma* is eternal. But their evolutes, viz *buddhi* etc, are not permanent. That is, the *krama* of every substantial product ceases one day when it becomes dissolved. Every product, *buddhi* downwards, is meant to serve as an end or a means to an end of the self (be it *bhoga* or *apavarga*) and is thereby justified in its existence. The realisation of *puruṣārtha* is the *raison d'etre* of the existence and continuance of the manifested world, and as soon as this is accomplished finally by *dhurmamegha* it is resolved into its components, viz, the *guṇa* particles (cf. *Yoga Sūtra*, IV. 32). But this is for one man — for him only who has reached his goal. There are other *jīvas* who may

---

[11] *Yogabhāsya*, III. 14.

The question is : How, then, can the *yogin* call back the past, though he does not usually call back, but revokes only a phantom, an exact duplicate, of the past?

be still in the middle of their journey, some who are still moving outwards in search of *bhoga* or earthly enjoyment and some who, having turned their back upon them, are indeed moving inwards but are yet on the path, struggling in pursuit of the saving knowledge. For such *jīvas* the manifested world (*dṛśya*) will have to continue. And the number of *jīvas* being infinite, there will never come a time when there will be no more a manifest, objective world (*Yoga Sūtra*, II. 22). But this does not violate the possibility of periodic dissolution of the world.

We have seen above that the *krama* of modification of the *dṛśya* ends as soon as the *puruṣārtha* is realised. But as the *krama* has an end, has it also a beginning? The *dṛśya* being only a product or evolute of the relation between *Puruṣa* and *Prakṛti*, the question recurs — What is the origin of this relation and when did it originate? We pointed out that the *anāgatāvasthā* is the beginning of the *krama* of the *dharma*. Does this *avasthā* refer to a definite point of time or is it simply a vague assumption following from the necessity of thought alone? Put more pointedly, the question refers itself to the moral explanation of the bondage and consequent limitations imposed on the self. In reply to this pertinent question, the Sāṁkhya-Yoga, like other kindred systems, asserts that we cannot posit an absolute beginning of this series of *kṣaṇas*, that since every *kṣaṇa* is explicable only on the hypothesis of a preceding *kṣaṇa*, no absolutely first *kṣaṇa* is conceivable. The causal series must be held to be infinite *ab ante*.

Moreover, what is the nature of this relation between *Puruṣa* and *Prakṛti* (i.e. between *Puruṣa* and *Sattva*)? The relation is given in every judgment of ours, which is a function (*vṛtti*) of the *buddhi* and implies a co-ordination of subject and object. Such a co-ordination of two distinct and mutually exclusive principles is not possible except through confusion or non-discrimination (*avidyā*, *viparyaya*). Thus this relation, which is the source of phenomenal consciousness and misery, is due to *mithyā-jñāna*. But the origin of *mithyājñāna* can be explained only as a consequent of another *mithyājñāna* and that of another, and in this way the series would be stretched infinitely backwards and we would not be able to arrive at its first term at all. The *guṇas* being always in relation to the *Puruṣa* (because both are eternal),[12] their effects too must always have been in relation with it. *Dharmiṇām anādisamyogād dharmamātrāṇām apy anādiḥ saṁyogaḥ* | (Pañcaśikhā in *Yogabhāṣya*, II. 22).

But the usual argument set forward in support of the beginningless character of *saṁsāra* consists in the inexplicability of the inequalities of pleasure, pain etc. on the hypothesis of a beginning in time.

The inevitable conclusion which follows from the above is practically a confession of ignorance. However smartly we may tackle the problem, the mystery remains ever the same. Different attempts at solution simply change the form of the difficulty, but the mystery is never fully cleared. Yet from an intellectual and rational point of view, the doctrine of *anāditva* remain the only valid theory on the point.

This doctrine implies that there has never been a first *karman* or a first *mithyājñāna*, in the absolute sense of the term. There has always been a push from behind. The difficulty of admitting a first *karman* would be great. Assuming pluralism and absence of limitations, all *karmans* would be uniform in the beginning and differences would never ensure. According to such a view the selves, before they fell into the meshes of *Prakṛti*, must have been in a free condition, joyous and pure. Why then should they have acted at all? And even if they had acted, why should one have acted differently from another? In such a theory differences have to be assumed in the very beginning, and since these differences are self-explained and do not require an intrinsic ground of

[12] This is the doctrine of *anādisaṁyogaḥ*. Cf. *Dṛgdarśanaśaktyor nityatvād anādiḥ*| (*Yogabhāṣya*, II.22). The Naiyāyikas, as a rule, reject the possibility of contact being without a beginning. According to them *saṁyoga*, which is *aprāptipūrvikā prāptiḥ*, must be due to motion, either of one or of both. But *ajasaṁyoga* also is sometimes admitted. Cf. *Nyāya Vārtikā*, p. 466; for eternity of *saṁsāra* see *Nyāyabhāṣya*, III.1.27; *Nyāya Vartikā*, I.1.2; 1.119, *Nyāya Mañjarī*, p. 499. The relation which is expressed in Yoga as a contact between *Puruṣa* and *Prakṛti* (or rather *Sattva*, i.e. *Citta*) appears in Nyāya as the contact of the Self with the *manas* (*Nyāya Mañjarī*, p. 499) or with the body (*Nyāya Bhāṣya*, 3.127).

justification, why not extend the same lower down in the series? But this would upset the causal principle and end in a chaos of thought. Better, therefore, than introducing differences on the *eternal planes* (*nityadhāman*), it is to explain them in the usual way by referring them to the adequate causal conditions working *in time*. An endless succession is not an illegitimate hypothesis.

Unless the causal series is admitted to be infinite, that is, if the world be supposed to have a beginning in time, we must have to take recourse, as already noted, to the doctrine of accident and chance (*nirṇimittavāda*). In that case, the experience of pleasure and pain on the part of *jīvas* would remain unexplained and there would follow the defect of *akṛtābhyāgama* or fallacy of unmerited reward and punishment. Moreover, the doctrine would involve the possibility of the free souls also returning to bondage. Śaṅkara expresses himself on this point thus: *ādimattve hi saṁsāra-syā'kasmād udbhūtermuktānām api punaḥ saṁsārodbhūti-prasaṅgaḥ, akṛtābhyāgamaprasaṅgaś ca, sukhaduḥkhādivaiṣa-mpyasya nirṇimittatvāt* | (*Brahma Sūtra Bhāṣya*, II. 1. 36). These inequalities are not explicable though Īśvara and through mere *avidyā* (without *karmans* following from the *vāsanās* of the *kleśas*, viz *rāga*, *dveṣa* and *moha*) which is uniform in all (cf. also *Śaṅkara Bhāṣya*, 1.3.30).

This is the burden of infinite *karman* which every *jīva* bears on his back. The escape from this is to obtain permanent peace. How this may be done need not be discussed at this point. The question why one *jīva* differs from another morally, since all are equally burdened with *anādikarman* of an infinite kind, seems to be solved by the consideration of succession (*krama*) in the development or ripening of the *karmans*. The *karmans* being infinite, their permutations and combinations too are infinite. Hence the difference in the different series of lives.

This view is not universally admitted even in India, though undoubtedly this is accepted in all the recognised systems of Indian philosophy. For there are schools which, while conceding that the world as such has neither beginning nor end, deny that a particular *jīva*'s course of existence in it should also be beginningless. They mean to say that as the *jīvahood* has an end at a definite point of time, it begins also in time. It is inconceivable that a line, which is known to end, should have no beginning. If the term '*anādi*' is intended to mean that we do not *know* when the series begins, simply because our own vision does not reach far back, it is all right. It would merely amount to a confession of the fact that our eyes are dimmed with *avidyā* and cannot discover the beginning; but if it means, as it undoubtedly does, that it has no beginning at all, it is nonsense. These thinkers teach that the *jīva* is originally pure and free, and essentially identical with Īśvara, but that through some fault on his part he was thrown into the vortex of *saṁsāra* in which he has been rotating ever since and from which he will be able to escape only when the force (*vega*) with which he fell (which itself was determined by the intensity of the original fault) will have been exhausted. The intensity of his fault determines the length of his stay away in *saṁsāra*. His original fall and his final emancipation are both due to the action of Divine Will, the former known as *nigrahaśakti* and the latter as the *anugrahaśakti* (power of Grace) of the Supreme Lord.

The question, how the *jīvas*, all pure and spotless at first, are at all capable of transgression, and even then, why they transgress in different ways, is answered by saying that they are all 'free' (*svatantra*) at this stage and that their actions are all self-determined. The different series of lives of the *jīvas* may be explained by their original differences on the Eternal Plane. These differences do not require to be explained from without. They follow from the essential difference in the nature of *jīvas*. This is a doctrine characteristic of all the pluralistic systems.

~7~

THE CONCEPT OF TIME

A careful study of the history of philosophical doctrines in the country would reveal the fact that thinkers have had apparently divergent conceptions of *Kāla* from the earliest times. There was a distinct school of thought in ancient India, known as Kālavāda,[1] which held that the ultimate cause of all movements of life and thought is *Kāla*, conceived either as a blind and insentient power, much like the Western conceptions of Fate, Necessity and Destiny, or as the Supreme Conscious Power identical with the Absolute Reality, or even as a subordinate power immediately responsive to the Supreme Will.

The Naiyāyikas, Vaiśeṣikas and Mīmāṁsakas conceived it as a Static Principle, substantial, eternal and ubiquitous in character and held it responsible for our notions of priority and posteriority — temporal sequence of succession — whereas, according to the exponents of Āgama, it is the Supreme Dynamic Principle lying at the root of the cosmic process, both of creation and of destruction. To the *yogin* of Patañjali's school, however, it is only a mental construction based on a sense of succession and has no value in Reality.

---

[1] Dr. Schrader in his famous work on Indian philosophical speculation prior to and during the days of Gautama Buddha and Mahāvira brought together valuable data on the doctrine. Cf. also the present writer's paper on 'Theism in Ancient India' in Volume II of Sarasvati Bhavana Studies. The *Mahābhārata*, in different contexts, gives different versions of this doctrine. In *Śanti Parvan*, ch. 206.11, *Kāla* is placed between *buddhi* (corresponding to Sāṁkhya's '*Mahat*') and Bhagavān Viṣṇu, and is explained by Nilakaṇṭha as '*avyakta*'. Ch. 320. 108 of the same *Parvan*, however, has a different conception and is interpreted by the commentator as '*jīva*':कालोऽविद्याख्य: षोडशगुण उक्त: । तदुपाधिर्जीव: कालसंज्ञ:।। Again, in the same *Parvan*, in ch. 224.46, *Kāla* is defined and described. The commentator understands from this passage that the support of *Kāla* is *tadupādhirjīvaḥ kālasaṁjñaḥ*, and that the *abhimānī* of *kāla* is *sūtrātmā*.

The conceptions of Time (*kāla*) and Motion (*kriyā*) have such an affinity that in several ancient works we actually find them either identified with each other or otherwise intimately connected together.

1. Thus, in the Trika literature, *Kāla*, viewed in the Absolute Parama Śiva, represents His Supreme Freedom (*svātantryaśakti*) looked upon as *Kriyā Śakti* projecting the Universe, till now unified with the Absolute, and making it appear as external to It.[2]

The projection of the universe is, therefore, only the apparent externalisation of the Eternal Consciousness. The so-called creative process (*viśvakalpanā*) is only the outer aspect of the *Kriyā Śakti*, which in spite of its seeming externality retains always its self-contained (*svātmaviśrānta*) nature. The truth is that the Absolute Consciousness first appears as Life or *prāṇa* (i.e. *Kriyā Śakti*), on which as a base is built up the entire fabric of Time and Space. The Space-order is differentiated through forms and the Time order through motions and activities.[3]

2. Sureśvara, in his *Vārttika* (14) on Śaṅkara's *Dakṣiṇāmūrti-Stotra* (II) regards *Kāla* as a form of the *Kriyā Śakti* of the Lord [4] and the root cause of all changes in nature.

3. The ancient Sāṁkhya also held unlike the current authorities who advocate *svabhāvavāda* that the evolution of Nature

---

[2] *Kāla* as thus conceived is to be sharply distinguished from the so called *kālatattva*, which is one of the six *kañcukas* veiling the essential form of the Self as Para Śiva and making Him appear as *Puruṣa*. The same *Kāla* which as a *Śakti* of Para Śiva constitutes His Essential Nature is a principle of limitation from the view-point of *Puruṣa* or *māyāpramātā*.

[3] For a detailed study of *mūrtivaicitrya* and *kriyāvaicitrya* the reader may consult Abhinavagupta's *Tantrāloka (Āhnika* VI), *Tantrasāra* (Āh. VI) and *Īśvara-Pratyabhijñā-Vimarśinī*. The Vaiyākaraṇa too had a parallel view on this two-fold variation (*vaicitrya*). See also *Tripurārahasya*, *Jñānakhaṇḍa*, chapter 14.

[4] The commentator says: कालोऽपि ईश्वरस्यैव शक्त्याकारभेदः ।

Śaṅkara says:

बीजस्यान्तरिवाङ्कुरो जगदिदं प्राङ् निर्विकल्प पुन–
र्मायाकल्पितदेशकालकलनावैचित्र्यचित्रीकृतम् ।
मायावीव विजृम्भयत्यपि महायोगीव यः स्वेच्छया
तस्मै श्रीगुरुमूर्त्तये नम इदं श्रीदक्षिणामूर्त्तये ॥

(*guṇapariṇāma*) is due to the influence of *Kāla* rather than to an inherent tendency within itself. As to whether it is an eternal principle, co-eternal with *Puruṣa* and *Prakṛti*, or a principle of specified origin, there are differences of opinion. Some are of the opinion that what is known as *Kāla* is really *brahmacaitanya* as reflected on *Prakṛti* [5] — *Mahat* and *Puruṣa* both originating from this reflection — but it is *Kāla* which has the power of effectuating the *guṇas* (*guṇakṣobha*). Others think — and this is evidently the more accepted view — that *Kāla* is an eternal principle just like *Puruṣa* and *Prakṛti*. Its character as the source of Nature's dynamism is everywhere recognised.

4. The *Bhāgavata* saying: *kālād guṇavyatikaraḥ* etc. and the *Pāñcarātra Saṁhitā* making a more or less similar pronouncement come under the same category.

5. Rāmānuja, and other Vaiṣaṇava teachers too, entertain almost identical views on the function of *Kāla* in relation to the action of *Prakṛti*.[6]

6. The Śākta teachers also have a practically analogous account of Time, though the presentation is in a different form. It is said in the *Prapañcasāra* (I.24-4, 64) that the Absolute Reality viewed as *Prakṛti* is Pure Consciousness and is the origin of all things. It remains always what it is, and yet when the latent *karmans* of *jīvas* are matured for fructification it becomes, in a part as it were, alienated from itself, externalised and relatively dense. This part is

---

This shows that the universe exists before creation as void of all limitation and as one with the Absolute, and that the Supreme Power, called *Māyā*, gives rise as it were to manifold complications in Time and Space. The universe as thus infinitely diversified is manifested by an act of the Supreme Will as a magic show.

[5] कालः ब्रह्मचैतन्यस्यावस्थाविशेषः प्रकृतिसमावेशकृतः ।

See Rāmatīrtha's reported Sāṁkhya view in his Commentary on the above *Vārttika* (Mysore Edition, p. 53).

[6] The Vaiṣṇava teachers, however, who advocated what is popularly known as the doctrine of *nityalīlā*, assigned a special importance to the transcendent aspect of Time. In the *tripādavibhūti*, the pure spiritual realms, *Kāla* is an eternal being responsive, in the interest of the intensification and variation of the self-delight of the Lord, to His Will.

called *Prakṛti tattva*. When *Kāla* acts on the lower *prakṛti*, the latter is split up into three forms, viz, *bindu*, *nāda* and *bīja*.[7] The cleavage of *Prakṛti* under the influence of Time is the occasion for the origin of what for lack of a more appropriate term is called Sound (*rava*), which is equivalent to what philosophers describe as *Avyakta* or *Śabda Brahman*. It is evident from the above that in this view *Kāla* functions first as the maturer of *karma*-seeds (*karmapācaka*) and then as the energizer of *Prakṛti*.[8]

7. Bhartṛhari's view that the eternal *kalās* of *Śabda Brahman* under the influence of *Kāla Śakti* become the matrices of the diversities in the world-order belongs also to this class.

In the world Time appears as relative. What is known as Eternity is beyond the influence of Time. It is impossible for an ordinary man to arrive at the highest Spiritual Realisation where the time-factor is absent without passing through the graded series of intermediate experiences in time. In the Tāntric literature there is a regular course [9] of spiritual ascension culminating in the Supreme Experience and Power of the Absolute. What is technically

---

[7] For details the reader is referred to Padmapāda's commentary on *Prapañcasāra* (1.21-64), pp. 11-23. See, also *Prayogakrama Dīpikā*, pp. 398-423.

Bhāṣkara Rāya, in his *Saubhāgya Bhāṣkara* (under verse 132, p. 99), observes that the appearance of (*kārya*) *bindu*, *nāda* and *bīja* out of the Causal *Bindu* takes place in succession and that the four stadia of gradual emanations beginning with the Causal *Bindu* as disturbed by *Kāla* are synonymous with the four forms of *Vāk*, viz, *parā*, *paśyantī*, *madhyamā* and *vaikharī*.

[8] Śaṅkarācārya in his *Prapañcasāra* (1.39-40) makes it clear that *Kāla* causes *Prakṛti* to produce *vikāras*. Padmapāda speaks of two forms of *Kāla* — higher and lower (*para* and *apara*). The former is only another name of the Supreme Spirit (*Nārāyaṇa*) and is *jñānātmaka* (Com. on I.28). It is callled *unmanī kalā* and is the very soul of the lower *kāla*. The latter is discrete and consists, in the language of the *Śāstras*, of 15 sections (*parva*) from the minimum *lava* up to the maximum *parārdha*. All empirical time, including what is perceived in the pure regions, comes under the head. The Supreme *Prakṛti* is identified with the lower *kāla* which represents Time in flow. *Prakṛti* knows Herself as She is eternally self-revealed and the *Puruṣa* knows Her as one with Himself. The *Yoga-Vāśiṣtha* (1, ch 25) too, speaks of two aspects of time. Cf. *Mahākāla and Kriyātmaka Kāla* (*kriyā* = *daiva*).

[9] In the school of Bhartṛhari this course is known as *vāgyeṇa* or *śabdayoga*.

described as *dīkṣā* or initiation is only the setting into activity of a great spiritual current which aims on one hand at the elimination of the bonds of difference (popularly called *saṁsāra*) and on the other at communion — or rather unification (*yojana*) — of the self with the Absolute Reality. The latter function, which is positive in character, helps in the manifestation within the Self of the Supreme Experience. The series of vital, psychic and supra-psychic activities involved in the latter process include what is known as *kālatyāga* or transcendence of Time. This is done gradually, and when it is completed Consciousness becomes absolutely pure and gets rid of the elements of succession or even of simultaneity in its contents.[10]

---

[10] It is held that the minimum perceptible time is a *truṭi*, which consists of two *kṣaṇas* or time-atoms and represents one-fourth of the time taken by the eye to blink, and that the maximum is a *Mahākalpa*, which is understood not in the usual sense of life-time of Brahmā, as in the *Purāṇas*, but of the life period of Sadāśiva and is, therefore, named, by way of discriminations, *Parama Mahākalpa*. The *Mahākalpa* is the period during which the Cosmic System (*brahmāṇḍa*) or the impure creation continues in life, whereas the *Parama Mahākalpa* is the more extensive period during which the Pure Order is active. In each case the period of activity is followed by a corresponding period of rest. This is described on the analogy of *ahorātra* or Day and Night. But, beyond Sadāśiva, the Soul as it were of the Pure Order, there is no such division in Time; that is, when the Soul reaches the plane of *Śakti* it is above the dualism of Day and Night. But, even here, the Tantras state, Time exists of some sort — not, of course, discrete Time appearing in creation and dissolution or as Day and Night but Pervasive Time called *sāmya* (cf. *Svacchanda Tantra*, II. 304: *sa kālaḥ sāmyasaṁjño vai*). It is of this *Kāla Sāmya* that the great *Mahākalpa* of Sadāśiva is only a minute part. But even this, exalted as it is, has to be gone beyond in the mystic experience relating to *Samanā* or *Mahāmāyā*, where *Kāla* in its widest emperical though subtle form may be said to exist. The transcendence of *Samanā*, which is the 11th *kalā* of the *Praṇava Mantra*, is another name for transcendence of *Kāla* which function as the source of Mutation. In the experience associated with *Unmanā Śakti* there is no such thing as *krama* or succession, but there is appaarently *yaugapadya*. But beyond it, if we may say so, there being no actual transcendence of *Unmanā*, even this is absent. Only the Absolute remains, shinning upon Itself (though even this description is meaningless in the Ineffable) in its own self-effulgent glory. This is transcendence of *Kāla*.

सर्वकालं तु कालस्य व्यापकः परमोऽव्ययः ।
उन्मन्यन्ते परे योज्यो न कालस्तत्र विद्यते ।।

In fact the contents of consciousness are merged in it just as waves are merged in the ocean. This consummation may be reached by *mantra* as well as by *yoga*. The so-called *kālaviṣuvat* which is the sixth of the seven *viṣuvats* described in the *Nityāṣodaśikārṇava*, is transcendence of time in the spiritual movement from *samanā* upto *unmanā* and is a precursor to the final or Divine Unity realized in *tattvaviṣvat*, which is an extremely delicate affair, involving by means of 10817 subtle vibrations the attainment of Absolute Quiet (*nādalaya*) and perfect Self-Realisation.

There are certain phases of the doctrine, however, which could not be touched except in outline. These include an analysis of *pariṇāma* leading to a systematic treatment of the subject among the Sarvāstivādins, as exemplified in the relevant theories of the great teachers Dharmatrāta, Ghoṣaka, Vasumitra and Buddhadeva, and the view of Sarvāstivādi philosophers as against those of Vibhajyavādins.

~8~

Some Salient Features of Mysticism

Who is a mystic? It is difficult to answer the question. A mystic is not necessarily an occultist, although he may have some occult power (telepathy, etc.) at his command. A mystic need not be an intellectual prodigy, though he may have all the blessings of the Pure Light. That the supra-human Light of Knowledge may be revealed to a mystic is not strange to Western mysticism. St. Ignatius is said to have comprehended marvellously a great number of truths pertaining to the faith or to the human sciences. These truths were so numerous and the light was so bright that he felt as if he had entered into a new and glorious world. The intensity, amplitude, and excellence of this heaven-sent knowledge was so great that all that he had earlier learnt in his life of sixty-two years, whether acquired fortuitously or through diligent study could not be compared to that which he gained at this climacteric moment. Similar is the account of St. Francis Xavier. He also said that he had found himself inundated by the Divine Light, when a veil was as it were lifted up from the eyes of his Spirit and the truth of the human sciences, even those which he had never studied, became manifest to him through a process of intuition. In India too, in the history of mystic illumination, the acquisition of natural knowledge in a super-natural way is not unknown. The great yogin Śivarāmkiṁkara Yogatrayānanda, whom I knew personally and intimately, told me (in 1914) that he had acquired an exact comprehension of the details of the *Mahābhāṣya* of Patañjali in a vision at night lasting for only a very short time. The story is narrated at some length in my book *Sādhudarśana O Satprasaṅga*, Vol. II.

A mystic is not a devotee in the conventional sense, though he may have the most fervent ardour of devotion. He is neither an ascetic, though in the earlier stages he may be found using methods of self-mortification. He may be all these or may be none. A mystic need not always be a visionary, though he may have visions from time to time. In all the well-known instances we come across certain attributes which may be maximally or minimally present in a true mystic or may even be totally absent, simply because these do not constitute his essential nature.

I have found different people with dissimilar temperaments and outlooks inclined to see mysticism in different lights. But all diverse views finally lose their rigidity and agree in implying a sense of vagueness inherent in the concept of mysticism. This indefinable element in mysticism involves a plunge into the profound depths of Being and Consciousness, leading to a clear intuition of Unity and Love, a state which continues even when the mental life and the sense-life are resumed. This is comparable to the *śāmbhavī* pose of the *yogin* in which the senses continue to function, maintaining contact with the so-called external world; but the inner consciousness refuses to take notice of it and persists in the exclusive enjoyment of the bliss of its own light. More or less in the same way, the mystic seems to move in this world of ours and yet he lives in Reality — in a world of his own. Absolute peace and tranquility reign supreme in him. His heart thrills in the delectable experience of self-awareness. It is a state in which the Supreme Union splits itself up into a blessed companionship in which, however, the sense of otherness disappears, but the sense of integrity persists, allowing for the free play of a responsive personality vibrating with every shade of feeling.

True mysticism, as I understand it, implies that the soul is successively awakened (*prabuddha*), and fully awakened (*suprabuddha*), so that the sense of exclusiveness pertaining to each of the normal human states, viz, waking (*jāgrat*), dream (*svapna*) and deep sleep (*suṣupti*), is supplemented by a state of unbroken self-awareness which presupposes the integrations of consciousness (*turīya*). The awakening of the soul involves as its concomitant the disappearance of the sense of alienness of the so-called other world and causes the soul to turn inward, first from the object to the light which shines upon it, then from the light to the subject, the source of illumination, thirdly from the subject to the Transcendental Consciousness and Power, and finally from this, back to the Central Being which stands behind all manifestations. This is the usual process. It is assumed that all powers lead back to the Self-Conscious Will (*icchā-śakti*) which when turned outwards controls immediately the entire machinery of the cosmic movement, viz, the movement of *jñāna* and *kriyā*. This represents for the *yogin* a state of mastery or lordship (*aiśvarya*), a state of perfection implying full control of the outgoing forces. This state represents the majesty of the soul which is now within the Divine Circle, and reigns supreme over the outer creation.[1]

The above state leads on to the higher state of absolute resignation to the Divine Will. In other words, the human will at this point unconditionally surrenders to the Divine Will, or in a sense becomes one with it. In the Tāntrika phraseology, the soul of the *yogin*, now in close embrace with the Divine, enjoys the bliss of union (*ānanda*) and supreme self-realisation (*cit*) — the whole process representing the mystery of Divine Transformation which is beyond time, space and the categories of empirical consciousness. The consciousness of this state involves a blessed union of *para-jñāna* and *parā-bhakti*, or *cit* and *ānanda*, which is universally and eternally the twofold heritage of every true mystic. Neither the senses nor the reason of man can aspire to this ineffable condition which Divine Grace alone can promise and fulfil.

From what has been said about it, it is clear that to an ordinary human being the mystic consciousness cannot mean much beyond what he can comprehend through his intellect. To some, it may vaguely mean nothing more than a state of supra-normal consciousness through which some extraordinary inner powers reveal themselves, ranging from the so-called occult powers to the capacity for having certain exalted vision and similar experiences. The consciousness to which these powers are relevant may undoubtedly be associated with the faith and the quest of a pilgrim, but it is not mystic at all. Mystic consciousness begins with the realisation of the unity behind the diversities of the material world. Higher up, the

[1] We are here speaking of what is known as religious mysticism, both of the 'moderate' and of the 'extreme' type.

diversities begin to melt away and the One Undifferentiated Whole refulgently reveals itself. It is a consciousness in which the physical being reveals. It is a consciousness in which the physical being and all other worldly ties cease to have any validity at all. The glorious, self-luminous Unity reveals within Itself both the seeker and the sought in union, and yet each retains its distinct entity. It is a state in which man and God unite themselves in a close embrace and realise their oneness, showing thus that one is verily inseparable from the other. Beyond this is the Transcendent and the All-embracing One. In Christianity, the Three Persons in the Trinity, separate from each other, represent One single Divine Substance.[2] In the *Bhāgavata* culture of ancient India, the four *vyūhas*, though mutually distinct, represent one single Divine Substance. The relation between Me and Thee is eternally existent in the union, though it is beyond time and above *māyā*. This is a state of true *yoga* in which, as the *Gītā* [3] says, the seeker sees his Beloved in everthing: *yo māṁ paśyati sarvatra*, and at the same time, he sees everything in his Beloved: *sarvaṁ ca mayi paśyati*. It is a state of *parā-bhakti*.[4] Beyond this is

---

[2] We may refer in this context to the belief expressed in Indian sacred literature that at the beginning of creation One Supreme Consciousness reveals itself at once as Master and as Pupil (called by one name now and by another at another time) for the transmission of Supreme Knowledge (*vidyā*). Abhinavagupta in his short commentary on the *Parā Triṁśikā* says:

Prabudhyamānarūpā yadā praśnaṁ nirbhṛtāvabhāsamāna
paramārtha svarūpaṁ karoti tadā prabuddhāvasthā pratipattau
saiva pūrṇarūpā bhairava devatātmikāprativacanadātri sampadyate |

The implication is that the *parā saṁvit* represents both the 'Query' and the Solution' in his 'transcendental Dialogue'. The idea is that 'Query' never arises except in contact with the *parā saṁvit* and so also the 'Solution'.

[3] *Bhagavad Gītā*, VI. 30.

[4] *Bhagavad Gītā* (VII. 16,17) says that of all the categories of *bhakti*, e.g., that of the distressed (*ārta*), the inquisitive (*jijñāsu*), the worldly (*arthārthī*) and the wise (*jñānin*), the last, i.e. of the *jñānī-bhakta* is the best, becdause the *jñānin* is not only eternally united (*nitya-yukta*) but also one-pointed (*ek-bhakta*). Elsewhere it is said (*Gītā*, VI. 47):

yogīnam api sarveṣāṁ madgatenā'ntarātmanā |
śraddhāvān bhajate ye māṁ sa me yuktatamo mataḥ ||

The highest *yogin*, therefore, is one who is not only a *jñānin* but also a *bhakta*. *Yoga* is thus an intimate union of the Lover and the Beloved.

the Supreme Realisation of what in the Āgamas is described as *Pūrṇāhaṁtā* in which the soul of the seeker, now one with the Divine, realises itself in an infinite variety of modes and ways.

There are different ways of approach to this Supreme Experience and there are infinite shades of differences among the various ways. The Supreme Experience is certainly one and the same and yet there is a characteristic quiddity (*viśeṣa*) in each individual, which has an abiding spiritual value. The Divine Presence may be realised as 'that' (*tat*), as a Living Light permeating all and subsisting beyond all. It may be realised as 'Thee' and 'Me', both inseparable from each other, or It may be realised as 'Me' alone.[5] Thus It reveals itself as Third Person as 'That' (*tat*), or as Second Person as 'Thee' (*tvam*), or as First Person as 'I' (*aham*). There is an Impersonal Presence also which is at once elusive and really magnificent. In each case, the soul exists in a state of indifference (*udāsīna*), or as the closest companion, or as one's very self. In the Impersonal, however, there is no trace of I — even the Integral 'I' (*pūrṇa aham*) is absent there. And yet Awareness persists. It is the same as the *bhāṣā* of the *Śākta Āgamas*, beyond the *anākhyā*. Even here there is a 'Beyond' which cannot be called present, yet which *is*, of which we hear so much in Jewish *Kabāla*. As a matter of fact, even the 'Beyond' or 'Beyond-Beyond' is also within the orbit of the absolute (*akhaṇḍa*).

The Tantras recognise three stages in the development of the human soul, corresponding to the three fundamental states (*bhāvas*) of human nature, viz, animal soul (*paśu*), the heroic soul (*vīra*) and the divine soul (*divya*). The human soul in its early stage of development is called *paśu* and is steeped in animal propensities. The mystic might call it the Purgative state. Impurities abound in this state. The mode of life prescribed for the purpose of removing the impurities is technically known as *paśvācāra*, which is strictly dominated by the laws of morality and self-control. In this state, the laws and regulations guiding a strictly moral life become imperative. The second stage, called *vīra*, arrives when the spiritual

[5] Compare: *ekaivāhaṁ jagatyatra dvitiyā kā mamāparā* | (*Durgāsaptaśati*).

energy locked up within the physical frame, is released along with the awakening of *kuṇḍalinī*. In this state there is a wonderful sense of self-awakening, when the *yogin* realises that he has nothing but a spiritual being, bearing no relation as it were to its physical counterpart which he previously used to regard as his own self. In this condition, he becomes aware of a dual form — a non-physical luminous form being the substratum of his *bhāva*, and another equally non-physical luminous form being the object of his *bhāva*. To some mystics, the appearance of these non-physical luminous forms as Lover and Beloved indicates the incipient state of Love, i.e., a state in which Love in its fullest bloom has not yet come into being. Sex-energy is then automatically sublimated and transmuted on account of the fact that the *yogin* rises above the sense of identify with the physical body. In this stage, in some cases, levitation follows. This state is technically known as *ūrdhvaretā*, in which the gravitational pull disappears. This is followed by the third state known as *divya*, which is really a Divine State and is absolutely Unitive.

The persistence of what for want of a better word is called quiddity or individuality (*viśeṣa*) is admitted in each school of Indian thought. It is found in *Nyāya-Vaiśeṣika* as well as in *Sāṁkhya-Yoga*. It is found in the Upaniṣads where it is said that unification (*samāpatti*) is followed by the emergence of one's own form (*svarūpāvirbhāva*). Thus we have in the *Chāndogya Upaniṣad* that the highest light (of the Self) reaches and appears in his own form: *paraṁ jyotir upasampadya svena rūpeṇābhiniṣpadyate.*[6] In the *Brahma-sūtra* we have the same idea.[7]

In the *Siddhānta Śaiva Āgamas* we find that the animal nature (*paśu ātmā*), when purged of the basic impurity (*āṇava-mala*) and even of the impurity incidental to a life of power (*adhikāra-mala*), recovers its pristine purity as Śiva, free from all defilements. All these liberated *śivas* are equally possessed of the five-fold power (*pañca-kṛtya*) of creation etc, like *Parama Śiva* Himself. These

[6] *Chāndogya Upaniṣad*, VIII. 12.3.

[7] *Brahma-Sūtra*, IV. 4.1

śivas are *one* with *Parama Śiva* and yet they are not *Parama Śiva*. It is a wonderful state inexpressible in human language. The orthodox Advaitin in Vedānta, Trika of the Kashmir school or Mahāyāna Buddhism lay emphasis on the One, conceived positively or negatively, as if it were an undifferentiated whole (*akhaṇḍa*). But even in the face of this unity, there appears, according to some schools, an inherent state of what looks like differentiation which is, however, not differentiation (*bheda*) in the true sense of the term but only a logical quiddity or particularity (*viśeṣa*).[8]

The ancient *Āgamas* start from a different point of view and proceed along a different line. The so-called *āṇava-upāya* described in the Āgama literature is a general name for all physical and psychological devices leading to an animation of the soul. These are resorted to so long as the soul's dynamic power slumbering in inaction is not roused into activity and does not begin to function. Different poses, including different *āsanas*, *mudrās*, *bandhas*, *prāṇāyāma*, *japa*, *dhyāna* and so forth go to comprise this group. When this dynamic power, the *kuṇḍalinī*, is awakened and the knot of the lower ego is untied, these methods which are basically crude are no longer necessary. The power now active begins to function in all its dynamism, destroying the cobwebs of vague notions, fancy and imaginations (*vikalpas*), in its ascent through the vital and psychic centres. The upward surge of the power, now free, shoots

---

[8] Even Śaṅkarācārya, the great monist, is said to have maintained this attitude when he said:

Satyapī bhedāpagame nātha tavaivābaṁ na mamā īnastvam |

This implies that even after the establishment of unity (*bhedāpagame*) there may continue a relationship within this unity, according for the experience of 'Thee' and 'Me'.

The *advaita* of Jñāneśvara, as in his *Advaitānubhava*, also mentions this difference. We find the same view is clearly enuciated in *Tripurā-Rahastya* (*Jñāna-khaṇḍa*). There is no doubt that even in the latter there is a 'Beyond', about which nothing can be said or thought. This appears to be the *parama-pada* of the *Gītā* (*viśate tadanantaram*). It may be equated with the *Parama Śiva* or *Parā Saṁvit* of the Śaiva and Śākta Tantras respectively. Yet a great *siddha* like Svatantrānanda and others seems incluned to go beyond this, and place the *Para-vyoman* even beyond *Parama Śiva*. We are reminded, in this context, of the 'Abyss' of Jacob Boehme and of 'Beyond-Beyond' God of Meher Baba's philosophy.

through the vast fields of mundane existence. These fields, under its impact, are progressively more and more purified from the distractions incidental to the lower atmosphere until the gushing surge reaches the illimitable ocean of Universal Consciousness. This is, in brief, the Śākta way. The aspirant under the influence of the divine grace finds his way smooth and does not have to make any special effort to ascend from a lower plane to a higher plane. What he is required to do merely is to stick to his position and keep his inner eye open and fixed as an onlooker at a wonderful show. He should be steady enough, not to be dragged and bogged down into the mire of sloth and unconsciousness. Eternal vigilance, alertness, and self-observation need be his virtues in this upward movement. It may be pointed out that this period of upward movement of *śakti* is marked by a gradual transformation or spiritualisation of the aspirant's body and mind, culminating in the emergence of what is known as the 'Body of Light' (*baindava-śarīra*), corresponding to the 'Spiritual Body' of St. Paul.[9]

---

[9] As an illustration of the process of spiritual transformation, I would like to refer to the case of a living Indian mystic (named 'P'), personally known to me. He has written a detailed memoir of his personal experience from the first awakening of *kuṇḍalinī* to the Supreme Divine Experience possible in the human body. His *guru* was a great saint of Vārāṇasī, celebrated as Siddhi Mātā, who lived a secluded life in the city. 'P' says that in his own case it was found that the awakening of *kuṇḍalinī* was followed by the emergence of a substance which revealed itself most vividly in the *viśuddha-cakra*, after which it began to ascend along the inner path upwards the *ājñā cakra*. Having reached this destination, the spiritual light mentioned above assumed the form of a clear human figure exactly resembling the material body of 'P'. This form was verily the inner self of the *yogin*, waiting at the threshold of the higher awakening ready to be released from the bonds of dense mater. 'P' felt that when the ascent of the Light into the *sahasrāra* and its assumption of a perfect form was complete, the *puruṣa* and the *prakṛti* elements in *sahasrāra* were unified as a result of the ascent of the *kuṇḍalinī*. The above form then merged into the Form of the Spirit, but before the merger was effected, the entire phenomenal world and all its processes dissolved into the world of *puruṣa* and *prakṛti*. This body, in its upward ascent, then, left the physical body and realised, with the third eye now fully opened, that it had entered into pure *cidākāśa*. This opening of the third eye marked the awakening of the spirit of *Brahman*. This body had, thus, three eyes, viz, the two normal eyes of the old unregenerated body, and the third eye which was then opened. The third eye,

It is in the course of the ascent of *Śakti* that one finds, in some exceptional cases, the phenomenon of levitation. The body, being fully merged in the illumined soul, loses its impurities and is no longer subject to the gravitational pull. It then rises up in air and remains poised in space. This is what is called the *sāttvika* body, free, for the time being, from the effects of *tamas*. The characteristics of *sattva* are said to be levity or lightness (*lāghava*) and illumination (*prakāśa*), both of which are manifested in this state. There are two aspects of levitation which may be noted here. In some cases the physical body, under the influence of the Inner Light, is actually raised up as referred to above; but in other cases the physical body remains unconscious on the ground: but a luminous duplicate issuing from it rises up, keeping itself in touch with the original body by a silver cord. In the latter case, the physical body remains unconscious and all consciousness concentrates on the duplicate floating body of light, strong or mild. But cases of levitation are

---

when it was opened once, never closed again. In the earlier stage, this third eye had looked like a long vertical stroke of a spiritual light above the middle of the two eyebrows. The manifestation of this form was a clear evidence of spirit apart from matter. The supernal views in the *cīdākāśa* floated before the spiritual body. But they were visible to it only when its eyes were all opened and when the vision of the Self (*ātmadarśana*) took place, beyond the stage of *sahasrāra*. In that state waves after waves of joyous experience came as a part of *nītyalīlā*. This was a state of *Brahman* in which the spirit enjoyed the delights of *vaikuṇṭha-līlā* in the *cidākāśa*. The next step beyond this was one of absolute calm and serenity when the Spirit was ensconced in a peace that passeth comprehension. It was a higher state in Brahman, beyond which was the next higher state of Infinite Void (*mahāśūnya*) in which the spiritual body became fully subject to an irresistible upward pull. In this state, the past *kārmic* forces of innumerable lives revealed themselves. The *mahāśūnya* state was followed by an entry into *para-vyoman* through its passage into what is known to the *yogins* as *bhramara-guhā*. The spiritual form became completely purged and purified in the *bhramara-guhā* before its entered into *para-vyoman*. Even in *para-vyoman* where the vision of the Absolute is perfect, there are numerous stages through which the spiritual body has to pass. Ultimately the *hlādini-śakti* of the Supreme Lord asserted itself and the Spirit began to enjoy the Divine Union in a state of Eternal Blissfulness. In this Union he observed that the Spirit and the Divine appear alternately as what we may call Active and Passive Partners in the Supreme Union. This was followed by an admission into the supreme stage of Perfection in which One alone shines and enjoys Itself through Itself.

known to occur also under the impact of an Outer Light, which is the fountainhead of Power, entering the physical body from above. In this case the body is lifted up and kept poised in space for some time, either in a static position or moving it through long distances. The question of ravishment, considered as an aspect of ecstatic union, deserves to be carefully studied in the light of the varied experiences of the *yogin*. The experiences of a *vīra sādhaka* of the *kaula-mārga*, in union with *Śakti*, come under this category. The onset is usually sudden and the entire physical body remains either totally immobile or may seem to have disappeared altogether. The path of esoteric mystic culture based on this suddenness of illumination is known as *sāhasa-mārga*.

The *Śāmbhavī* way refers to the highest *upāya* by which even this upward movement of *Śakti*, leading the seeker on from sphere to sphere, without any effort on his part, comes to an end. The seeker, in fact, is now in a state of perfection — the river itself has merged in the Ocean and is no longer subject to the movements of its earlier stages. The soul in this stage is one with the Universal Consciousness and is possessed of the *śākta-deha*, enjoying now the fullness of Supreme Light and Power. The soul by itself is not aware of this fact. It is the *Śāmbhava* way which aims at the manifestation of this awareness. This stage marks the union of Śiva and Śakti in which the Supreme 'I' reveals Itself to Itself (*pūrṇāhaṁtā*).

The *Śāmbhavī-vidyā*, as known to the ancient *rāja-yoga* school, represents the supreme hidden lore which has been continuously guarded through the ages as a secret treasure in all esoteric schools of Vaidika and Tāntrika Yoga.

The so-called *dhārā-yantra* [10] referred to in *Amanaśka* is really an advanced form of the above *Śāmbhavī-vidyā*. Watchfullness (*anusandhāna*) is described in the above work as the key-note of this mystic process.

It should be remembered that in plenary mystic experience, the mind reaches complete stillness. It is a state of God-realisation;

[10] *Ūrdhramuṣṭiradhodṛṣṭirūrdhva pādopyadhaḥ śiraḥ* |
dhārāyantra vidhānena jīvanmukto bhaviṣyati ||

but it is not a perfect realisation. It is only an ecstatic state which ends as soon as the mind wakes up from its stillness. It is followed by a state when God-realisation is not affected in the least, even after the revival of the mind. The next higher state is when the *Parā-Saṁvit* emerges in its fullest glory. This state is reached only by very fortunate souls. In this glorious state, perfect freedom is attained so that the re-emergence of the mind and the world or of other things associated with them makes no difference at all. It is well known that the Persian mystics used to draw a distinction between the *Majzub* and the *Qutb*, standing for the mystic absorbed in God and the pole or centre respectively. In the state of perfect freedom no such distinction has any validity.

Those who are familiar with the *Virūpākṣapañcaśikā* are well aware of the successive stages through which the awakened soul has to pass in order to reach the highest state of God-realisation in which the soul attains the apex of Divine Majesty and Glory. The seven stages of spiritual progression of a Bodhisattva signify the successive stage through which the mind sanctifies and elevates itself and reaches the highest peak of Boddisattvahood. The seven stages recognized by *Yoga-Vāśiṣṭha* and described in other works like *Bodhaśāra* mean a similarly graded progression towards Perfection.

It should always be kept in mind that every aspirant going ahead along the spiritual path follows his own spiritual pattern, and it is not necessary that all the patterns should be uniformly alike and similar.

~9~

Philosophy of the Nāthas

The supreme ideal of Yoga *sādhanā* as conceived in the Nātha School seems to differ from the conceptions of Patañjali, of the earlier and some later Buddhistic systems and even to a great extent of Śaṅkara's Vedānta. Nevertheless we must observe that the Nātha ideal is analogous to what we find in the Āgamic system of non-dualistic thought in ancient and medieval India.

This ideal is described in one word as *sāmarasya*, which implies obliteration of traces of all kinds of existing differences, not by a process of transcendence as in Sāṁkhya, or of sublation as in Vedantic Māyāvāda, but by a positive process of what may be described as mutual interpenetration. This ideal underlies the principle of unification between Puruṣa and Prakṛti, or between Śiva and Śakti. The attainment of this deal is the Supreme Unity of Parama Śiva, where Śiva and Śakti are one undivided and indivisible whole. It is called Mahāśakti in the language of the Śāktas and represents the Absolute of the Śākta Āgamas. It stands for the *samatā* of the Avadhūta *yogins*, which is really a unification from the logical point of view of *tattva* and *tattvātīta*, i.e. the one and the Beyond.

A cursory glance at the ancient spiritual literature of India would reveal the fact that in almost all the systems associated with Āgamic culture we find a strong insistence on the ideal of *sāmarasya* in some form or other. By way of illustration I may refer to the Tantric Buddhism of the Kālacakra school, in which the union of *pajñā* and *upāya*, technically known as *vajrayoga*, is strongly emphasised. Thus the *Hevajra Tantra* says:

samaṁ tulyam ityuktaṁ syāt tasya cakre rasaḥ smṛtaḥ |
samarasaṁ tvekabhāvam eternātmani bhanyate ||

The *vajrayoga*, which is the ideal of Kālacakra Buddhism, represents in fact the state of Supreme Oneness.

The Vīra Śaivas of the Jaṅgam School also recognise this ideal in their own way. A brilliant exposition in the form of *sāmarasya bhakti* representing the self-luminous unity of Delight realised after a course of continued *sādhanā* is to be found in Mayīdeva's *Anubhava Sūtra* and in Prabhudeva's works.

The *Svacchanda-Tantra* which is one of the earliest Āgamas available to us furnishes a detailed account of the several stages in the process of the unification which ends in Supreme *Sāmarasya*. In this process seven grades are mentioned and described.

Svatantrānandanātha, the author of *Mātṛkā Cakraviveka*, was a brilliant exponent of the Siddha school. He explains this doctrine in his own inimitable manner. He says:

māyāvalāt prathamabhāsi jadasvabhāvam
vidyodayāt vikasvara cinmayatvam |
suptyāhvayaṁ kimapi viśramanaṁ vibhāti
citrakramaṁ cidacideka rasasvabhāvam ||

Here in this context the *sāmarasya* referred to is between *cit* and *àcit*, i.e. between Consciousness and Unconsciousness, which neutralise each other and appear as one. He illustrates this with an interesting example of a pictorial representation, which in reality is one, but which appears to one onlooker as representing an elephant and to another as representing a bull according to the view-point taken.

In the yogic *sādhanā* of certain Tantric schools, especially those affiliated to the Ardhakālī line, we are told that the twelve-syllabled *mantras* constituting the complete *pādukā-mantra* of Sri Gurudeva represent respectively the *unmanī* and *samanī* aspects of the Absolute. The former suggests the upward motion in the direction of the Supreme *Puruṣa* (*ha*) with the Supreme *Prakṛti* (*sa*). The latter suggests that the Supreme *Prakṛti* (*sa*) which descends from the glance (*īkṣaṇa*) of *Para-Brahman* or *Unmanī* Śiva floods with Delight the Supreme *Puruṣa* (*ha*) in the course of its descent. These symbolize in the undivided Absolute Consciousness (*cit*) both the upward and downward movements of the Divine. Behind *Unmanā* and *Samanā* there is only one single

Essence, for *Puruṣa* and *Prakṛti* are ultimately one and the same Brahman, one symbolised by the triangle with its vertex upwards and the other by the triangle with its vertex downwards. The familiar diagram of *ṣaṭkoṇa* as an interlaced figure signifies this union which is represented (they say) by the twelve-petalled lotus above the pericarp of the *sahasradala* lotus. In fact, the conception of *Guru Pādukā* in its highest expression is the conception of *sāmarasya* par excellence.

It is said:

> *svaprakāśa śivamūrti rekikā*
> *tad vimarśa-tanu-rekikā, tayoḥ* |
> *sāmarasya vapuriṣyate parā*
> *pādukā paraśivātmano guroḥ* ||

This indicates that the Divine Guru or Para Śiva has three *pādukās*, two being lower and one higher. The two lower *pādukās* symbolize the self-luminous Śiva on one hand and his self-reflecting Śakti on the other. The higher *pādukās* is the integration in the form of *sāmarasya* of the two in the Supreme Unity.

It may be noted in passing that even the realisation of the Christian Trinity is only a partial manifestation of the truth of *sāmarasya*. The great Spanish saint Teresa of Avila once realised this through Divine Grace and tried to express it in her own language, in course of which she said that at first an illumination shining like a dazzling cloud of Light appeared before her followed by the emergence of the three persons of the Trinity. She felt that the three Persons were all of one Substance, Power and Knowledge and were one God. The vision was not the result of the function of the bodily eye nor even of the eye of the soul. It was an intellectual vision of an intimate kind. Henry Suso, the disciple of the great German mystic Meister Eckhart, referred to the union of the soul and God. He spoke of God as saying: "I will kiss them (the suffering saints) affectionately and embrace them so lovingly that I shall be they and they shall be I and the two shall be united in one for ever." Elsewhere it is said: "The essence of the soul if united with the essence of the Nothing and the powers of the One with the activities of the Nothing" (*The Little Book of the Truth*, edited by J.M. Clark, page 196). This is exactly like the union (*saṁyoga*) of *Liṅga* or *Paramātmā* with *Ātmā* of the Vīra Śaiva School.

From what has been said above it is abundantly clear that, in some form or the other, *sāmarasya* is the ideal, not only of the Āgamic culture, but also of many other spiritual *sādhanās*.

It now remains to be seen how the Nātha *yogins* received this highest consummation of Oneness. It is said that the true process of *sāmarasya* begins only when the Sadguru's grace has succeeded in effecting Mental Quiet (*citta-viśrānti*). The real *sādhanā* cannot commence until the mind is rendered quiet and free from disturbances incident on a sense of identity with the body. The mind being at rest, the Divine Bliss and an experience of Pure Infinite Glory dawn on the soul which is awakened from its agelong slumber. The sense of duality disappears in the serene light of undifferentiated Unity. This light, unbounded and one, brings out the powers of consciousness. The Universal Consciousness, being once awakened, produces in the *yogin* a perfect knowledge of his own Body, which results in the illumination and stabilization of the Body concerned (*dehasiddhi*).

In other words this Body becomes immortal and immune from the ravaging effects of Time. The yogi is now an adept (*siddha*). This luminous Form which is the essence of *caitanya* has to be made, as a further step, one with the Universal Uncreated Light of *paramapada* already revealed. This is done through a continuous process of investigation into the real nature of *Ātmā*. It is to be remembered that *sāmarasya* should not be a momentary attainment, but a permanent possession, in the sense that no reversal (*vyutthāna*) may ever occur. Before this state (*nirutthāna*) is made permanent after *sāmarasya* is once attained, some successive moments in the supreme experience are noted:

(i) The Transcendental Reality is revealed as the universe. In other words, the difference between what is Formless and what has Form disappears for ever and it is co-eternal with the vision of the universe in *Ātmā*.

(ii) In the transitional stage there is a tendency in the Powers to move out. This has to be restrained and the Powers kept as contained within the *Ātmā*.

(iii) The *Ātmā* is realised as a continuum of unbroken *prakāśa* with the Supreme Dynamism.

(iv) As a result of all this there is a unique vision of Being which is unborn. This is the Supreme Integral vision which marks the stage of *nirutthāna*. It is a vision of Eternity when infinite varieties are seen as an expression of the One and when the One reveals Itself in every point of the Infinite.

It seems true that the Nātha *yogin*'s view of *piṇḍa siddhi* and Patañjali's idea of *kāyasaṁpat* are not exactly the same, though it is true that in each the control of the elements is the result. The ideal of *vajradehā* was behind both and dominated the Tantric Buddhist also. In 'Nāthism', the fact that *piṇḍa siddhi* results from a vision of *Paramapada* and is an antecedent of the two indicates that, though Patañjali's *kāyasaṁpat* aims at physical purification to its utmost extent, it can never be equated to the natural purity of *Puruṣa* and continues to remain an inalienable property of *Prakṛti*.

In this light it may be presumed that the criticism of Gorakṣa Nātha's ideal of *piṇḍa siddhi* by Prabhudeva, as found in legends current in South Indian Śaiva schools, has to be explained as the outcome of sheer sectarianism.

The Nātha ideal is first to realise *jīvanmukti* through *piṇḍa siddhi*, which secures an Immaculate Body of Light free from the influence of Time, i.e. a deathless undecaying spiritual Body of Light, and then to realise *Parāmukti* or the highest perfection through the process of mutual integration, *samarasīkaraṇa*. The Bengali Nātha work entitled *Haḍamālā*, a comparatively late work of the Nātha school of Bengal and published by Prafulla Chandra Chakravarty in his book on '*Nātha dharma O Sāhitya*', also points out that the complete course of Nātha spiritual culture did not end with the attainment of *siddha deha* through drinking of nectar after the completion of the process technically known as transcendence of the Moon; it was a state of *jīvanmukti* as free from death. It is only a prelude to the realisation of the highest ideal of perfection through the culture of *Oṁkara*.

~10~

Faith in God

-I-

Why should we have faith in God?

Before answering this question I should like to point out how we come to have faith in all those objects the existence and functioning of which we are compelled to recognise from the worldly point of view for sundry reasons. As regards the exact meaning of the word 'faith', the questioner only knows in what sense he has used it. This much is, however, certain that what is usually called faith has two stages, an analysis of which would greatly help to elucidate my view in regard to its cause. When we hear something from one who is worthy of our credence, but have not the capacity to examine what he says or to take any practical step in regard to it, we are naturally inclined to take his words as true. In my childhood, when I heard many a miraculous tale from my old grandparents, when I was simple-hearted and my mind was more or less a blank tablet so far as the impressions of the world are concerned, all the scenes described in those stories were depicted before my mental vision as real ones, owing to the vividnesss of my imagination. My knowledge of the world as well as my reasoning faculty having not yet sufficiently developed, I was unable to judge what was possible and what was not. The result was that nothing appeared impossible to my mind. If my grandmother told me, for instance, that a certain tree was haunted, my limbs would actually tremble with fear as I passed by that tree in the evening or at the dead of night. The mere mention of a ghost was really sufficient to produce in my mind a belief in its existence. No argument was needed for the purpose, nor had I any inclination to verify the statement. What I mean to say, however, is that both the above illustrations point to a certain stage in the life of a human being when the mere mention of a word, while conveying to one's mind the meaning thereof, produces a firm belief in regard to the object denoted by it. A particular individual may possess such a guileless and clean heart that the mere utterance of a word will at once produce in his mind a living picture of the object denoted thereby. This explains the process according to which a certain scene or object is revealed before the eyes of an innocent child at one's own will by fixing its eyes on its nail (*nakha darpaṇa*) and uttering the name of that object. A critical study of the works on Vedānta woud reveal to us how direct knowledge results from the mere utterance of a sentence or word. The matter has been variously discussed in different places. We need not discuss here how the utterance of a word presents the object denoted thereby before the mental eye of the listener. Occidental scholars have sufficiently thrashed this point. The Indian scriptures, too, have disclosed many secrets about this phenomenon. Many of us may be knowing how in hypnotism the person hypnotised witnesses marvellous scenes under the suggestive influence of the words of the hypnotist.

This should suffice to make it clear that a docile and comparatively receptive mind is a congenial soil for sowing the seed of faith. That is why little children and ladies are more credulous than men who are expert in reasoning. Although this faith may be characterized as 'blind', its existence cannot be denied. The seed of such a faith in God can be sown in a docile mind in childhood, either at home or in society, through example and precept and through discussion and intercourse with good people. In India faith in God used ordinarily to get rooted in one's mind from early infancy. The mind of young children would be influenced to a considerable extent by the ideas of their parents and other elders.

Therefore, if anyone should ask of me what the root of faith is, my reply to him is that it is the effect of a word uttered by a person worthy of our credence on the childlike simplicity and receptivity of one's mind. This is faith not illumined by the bright lustre of knowledge. Nay, this sort of faith flourishes only in the faint light of ignorance. On the full dawn of knowledge it totally disappears, as it is not based on real truth. In other words, blind faith or faith without any real basis, in fact, is thus scared away by the frightening look of reasoning and argument and, being dimmed by worldly strife and stress, is lost for ever and merged in the womb of nature. Even though born in the early stages of evolution of life, it cannot continue to a later stage. Here, however, a note of warning has to be sounded. A faith may be called blind when it is not illumined by the light of one's own knowledge. Nevertheless, if the seed of faith is sown in the heart of an infant by the words of some high soul who has attained enlightenment, it may develop gradually into consummate knowledge. In other words, this type of faith, though not immediately illumined by the child's own knowledge, is not, as a matter of fact, based on ignorance.

Thus, extent and intensity of childilike faith are commensurate with the authenticity of the words of the person who has been recognised as worthy of credence. If at any moment it is discovered that the man supposed to be worthy of credence is not so and that his words are not authentic — if such a knowledge is brought about with the aid of perception or inference — the previous faith is shaken. What is true of a child is also true of the primitive stage of human evolution or society.

Blind faith, with its basis in truth, has many virtues. It easily prompts one to action without the help of argument or reasoning. Later on, when the due performance of an action brings forth the desired fruit, it becomes stronger and unshakeable. In other words, simple faith leading on to definite knowledge soon becomes free. Fallacious reasoning or the intricate net-work of arguments of non-believers are then no longer able to undermine it. It is this type of faith on which the real advancement of humanity or the evolution of human life depends. If, however, there is a tinge of falsehood at the bottom of this faith, it cannot bring forth the real fruit, nor does it lead to right action. It vanishes in the bright light of reasoning, reflection and true perception just like summer clouds which melt away under the sun's rays. It cannot retain its hold on the human mind for any considerable period of a man's life.

Then the question arises, "Why should one have faith in God?"

In answering this question we have to note that faith in God has two asepcts — one which may be called its rudimentary form, and the other, which represents the highest (i.e. most highly developed) form, resulting from direct knowledge through a prolonged course of spiritual activity and having its root in the deepest recesses of the heart of man.

In connection with the first or the rudimentary stage of faith it is necessary to take note of the fact that the elder as well as personages who have got experience in spiritual matters have all acknowledge the existence of God. They have also preached it time and again for the good of the world at large. So long as their theories are not refuted by the convincing arguments to the contrary, it is but natural for many of us to believe in them in obedience to the particular tendencies of our mind. But once a seeker after truth has made real progress in spiritual discipline he gets at every step proofs to show that the simple faith which he has once hugged as real is undoubtedly so. As one advances on the path of inner life, one comes across such unusual occurances and repeatedly and unmistakably witnesses such miracles in his life which compel a thoughtful person to acknowledge some highly powerful Intelligence as the controller of the whole visible universe as also of the supersensual world. The life of an ordinary person generally follows a course in which there is hardly any remarkable incident or miracle. But on his coming into contact with a person of extraordinary powers such wonderful incidents begins to occur in his life as are altogether beyond the knowledge and experience of an ordinary person. These incidents are of different kinds. Some of them are nothing more than a mere play of sentiment. But there may be other incidents which, though not wholly divorced from sentiment, have nevertheless a basis in the facts of the outer world. I shall try to elucidate my point by means of an illustration.

Suppose a man travels for a long time though a distant and uninhabited tract of foreign land or woodland region at the dead of night. He walks on till he gets tired and dejected and, knowing not what to do, even despairs of his life. There is none to watch or help this forlorn traveller, none to support him; and, what is worse, he has no provision with which he may sustain himself during the journey. The tract is unknown to him, the road also is unfamiliar; the destination is too far off, and, looking around as far as his eye can see, he is unable to find any trace of a dwelling or of a human being which may inspire him with hope and courage. He is fatigued with wandering all day long and has no energy left to carry him further. The darkness of the night has enveloped all surrounding space. The attack of wild beasts is also apprehended. Above all, the pangs of hunger are taking the life out of him. So far I have depicted the condition of the traveller only from the point of view of his physical body and the physical world. Besides this, he might also be suffering from mental and other kinds of worries. In such a teribile plight, when he perceives the dark shadow of death approaching, he, in the twinkling of an eye, beholds a glorious divine form, wearing a countenance full of affection, mercy and tranquillity, makes its appearance before him in the solitary place and, taking away all his fear, addresses the following soothing words to him, "Why are you afraid, dear? Look at the light glimmering over there. Go there and all your wants will be supplied. I shall be with you. There is no room for fear." On hearing these reassuring words, the man looks in front of him to find a lamp burning in a cottage thatched with leaves and a man sitting inside, as if waiting for him. He gets shelter there, is provided with food to satisfy his hunger, receives protection against danger, is put on the right track leading to his destination, and gets besides a companion for the journey. We can easily imagine the feelings that will surge in his heart when he gets all this help. However staunch an atheist he may be, and whatever doubts he may have in his mind as to the existence of God, he will have to acknowlege with a grateful heart that there is surely a Higher Power beyond the scope of human thought, which is illimitable and auspicious, which is always watching over a man's life, and which manifests itself in sore need and protects him like a loving friend. It is immaterial whether this Power is termed God or anything else. But there is no doubt that it is supernatural, all-intelligence, all-love, and extraordinary in all respects. Many such events may sometimes occur in the life of a man as cannot be explained by the ordinary relation of cause and effect. The sole object of these, however, is to do good to the person in question.

I need not dwell here on the career of spiritual discipline in the life of a seeker for truth. For a true seeker on entering the realm of self-disciple begins to tread the spirituals path, and is bound, as he proceeds, to perceive the divine existence and power times without number. Even though he proceeds with simple faith, he gradually acquires such knowledge and powers as no longer keep his faith confined within the limits of the rudimentary form, but, on the contrary, help to make it all the more firmly established.

Thus, as a result of efforts made during the present life or as the fruit of his past actions, man is enabled actually to perceive many of His glories and mercy and thereby to entertain an unshakeable faith in His benevolent existence. The question as to what the origin of the rudiments of faith is, as also why and how right faith is produced, have already been answered. Simplicity of heart is at the bottom of the former, while the varied experiences of life and a variety of visions connected with the divine reality are the causes of the latter.

It cannot, however, be expected that all the people in this world will believe in God. A view of the world, as it is, will tend to show that, even though subsisting in the form of a seed in every human being, faith does not manifest itself in an equal measure everywhere. There is a time for its manifestation. I have already pointed out that education, culture, example and precept, scriptures, and the teachings of high souls produce faith in a pure heart. But the element of time also has to be taken into consideration. So long as a man feels quite satisfied with the acquisition of material and transitory objects, or, in the event of his failing to acquire them, wistfully looks to the physical world for help, his attention cannot be arrested by the existence of a power which is beyond the ken of our senses. If all our ambitions could be achieved by our exploiting the visible world, why should we look to an invisible power for their satisfaction? On the one hand, a human being, revolving with the wheel of birth and death, enjoying the fruits of his various actions, acquiring varied experiences and having his plans thwarted, in spite of strenuous efforts of various kinds on his part by incessant obstruction and adverse circumstances, gradually realises the limitation of his power. On the other hand, he also continually perceives the ineffectualness of the power of the world. As his aspirations develop, he arrives at a certain stage of soul life when he begins to realise that nothing that the world could afford would satisfy him. It goes without saying that such a stage cannot arrive without the aspirant having undergone a prolonged course of inner growth. When, however, such a stage does actually arrive, he experiences a sense of utter helplessness. The emergence of this feeling of utter helplessness in a man's life constitutes the most auspicious moment in his upward career. From this very moment his eyes are turned away from the world and he begins to look up to some unknown and inscrutable Power presiding over the universe. In other words, his eyes get naturally diverted from the orbit of the objective world and become directed towards the centre of an infinite power with an intensity proportionate to the intensity of his aspirations. Of course, all this is not done in the regular way or even consciously. For the fact is that so long as the importance of man's ego is constantly being enforced in so many diverse ways, it is hardly possible for him to consider himself as being in a state of perpetual subjection to, or dependence on, a Higher Power, and to regard himself as backed by that Power. When, however, the force of this egoism gets gradually weakened by the forces of action and reaction of the world, and the hollowness of mundane power is realised, the existence and function of the Divine Energy as working within and without the universe becomes manifest in the natural course or things. That is why a man cannot relly believe in the existence of God so long as the time is not ripe for the same, that is to say, so long as the tendency to enjoy worldly pleasures does not become extinguished.

The *Srimad Bhagavadgītā* says that four types of beings betake themselves to the Lord, that is, those who are in affliction (*ārta*), those who seek for knowledge (*jijñāsu*), those who seek to attain some worldly objects (*arthārthī*) and those who are wise (*jñānī*), i.e. who have attained spiritual knowledge. But this statement by itself does not convey the whole truth, for we come across persons in this world who do not turn their eyes towards God even when they are in sore distress. Letting these alone, the history of the world does not absolutely point to the fact that all those who seek for knowledge are always God's devotees. Similarly, those who hanker after some worldly gain would rather seek the help of those who are wealthy from the point of view of the world. They would hardly think of looking to the Lord of the universe for help in attaining the object of their desire. And lastly, even those who are possessed of mere wisdom untouched by devotion are not able to dedicate themselves to the feet of the Lord, who is the fountain-head of all wisdom. It is a far cry to expect that a man who has not to his credit exceptionally meritorious acts brought over from a previous existence, or who is not blessed with the special grace of the Lord, should ever feel his mind naturally drawn towards Him. Therefore the Lord, by the use of the word *sukṛtinaḥ* in the above context, has made it clear that the mind of a person cannot be drawn towards the Lord even though he may be in affliction, or a seeker for knowledge, or taken up with a desire to attain some worldly object, or possessed of wisdom, unless he has to his credit some exceptional deeds of spiritual merit achieved by him in the past life or lives.

Hence it must be understood that time is not ripe yet for those who cannot bring themselves round to believe in God, while, in the case of those in whose minds faith in God has taken root, this has been accomplished through the instrumentality of the teachings or *āptas* or spiritual adepts, by education and also association (with those who believe in God). This faith will go on from strength to strength as they advance on the path of spiritual activities and are able to arrive at the realization of truth.

-II-

What is the harm in not believing in God?

My view of the matter may be shortly stated as follows:

If faith in God has any spiritual value whatsoever, then

assuredly it stands to reason to say that disbelief in Him must lead to harm. But, having stated this, we must take it also that just as faith cannot be brought into being by a mere fiat of the will, so also disbelief cannot be eradicated through mere ratiocination or a process of argument. As I have already pointed out, it is only when a man discovers a limit beyond which he cannot go, and when the realises that his efforts coming into conflict with some inscrutable Power are liable to frustration at every step, and when further it dawns upon him that the power and resources of what we are accustomed to call the outer world are not unlimited but finite, then naturally his mind finds itself helplessly drawn toward some transcendent Power beyond the realms of the finite. But, so long as this state does not manifest itself by a process of natural development, it is clear that any attempt to cultivate faith in God by a sort of force is futility itself. However much it may be true that if one is able to put faith in God he at once steps into the path of Eternal Life and is thus enabled by easy stages of advance to proceed towards the Goal of the supreme good, still, so long as this faith does not grow up in the heart by a process of natural development, one must in all humility yield to the forces of disbelief, notwithstanding that such disbelief is harmful.

Suppose one believes in God, and another does not. Both the cases, if we but care to look into them with an eye of penetrating judgment, will be found to come under the all-embracing dispensation of the Lord who is All-good. In order words, even disbelief in Him does not stand outside His laws. Let us take the case of a person who today by a stress of good fortune has been able to put his feet on the ladder of Faith in God. Now, if we are able to probe into the history of his long, long past, as recorded in previous lives, we shall find him living the life of a non-believer at some time or another. It cannot be argued that since creation all human beings started on their earthly career as believers in God. The stages that have to be passed are these: first, indifference to all faith; then it gets transformed into active disbelief; and last of all, the same disbelief becomes transformed into Radiant Faith.

There are personages who are endowed with an inner sight — the vision and the faculty divine — who do not judge of the degree of purity of a man's heart by his visible conduct and outward behaviour. It is they who certify that one who is a downright non-believer today may and does tomorrow rise to the heights of a transcendent devotee, if and when his present stock of *karmic* enjoyment and sufferings gets exhausted and he is able to revert to his past habits of renunciation. A study of the history of the ancient Christian church will reveal that Paul, who was once regarded as a formidable opponent of the Christ, was later recognised as one of the most trusted followers of Jesus. We come across numerous such instances in the history of every religion.

What has been stated above should not be taken to mean that I am supporting disbelief. What I mean is that disbelief also constitutes a necessary stage in the life of a human being. Even disbelief ultimately gets transformed into faith, and therefore in truth it is not an evil thing. Those, however, who cannot see far into the future look upon the present as the only stage that counts. They therefore are led to think that disbelief in God is likely to prove harmful. Thus it appears that looked at from the point of view of the wise, endowed with an all-comprehensive divine vision, even disbelief has a value which cannot be discarded. Of course, judged from the point of view of those who cannot see beyond the present and whose vision is therefore limited, disbelief is harmful, and therefore always depreciated. Therefore, in reply to the question, "What harm is there in not believing in God?", it may be stated that even though disbelief is harmful from the spiritual point of view, nevertheless, seeing that it is necessary for man's progressive uplift, it cannot, as a matter of fact, be regarded as a positive evil. In other words, if disbelief in God is only a preliminary stage leading on to faith, then the harm accruing from it is only temporary, and must be accepted as such in view of the ultimate good. Nevertheless, judged from the lower point of view, disbelief in God is at the root of the worst evils.

Jesus says:

"He that believeth and is baptised shall be saved, but he

that believeth not shall be condemned." (Aristion's Appendix — Mark, 16-16)

The *Bhagavadgītā* also says:

...saṁśayātmā vinaśyati

That is to say, the sceptics are doomed. Thus it appears that in the scriptures of every religion faith in God has been eulogised and disbelief condemned. Those who have an insight into the profound truths of the supersensual world know how the mind gets transformed and moulded according as it comes under the influence of particular dispositions or beliefs in relation to particular subjects. For the disposition or belief of the mind determines the character of the achievement. Whatever the subject of one's belief, the mind automatically fixes itself on it and soon becomes one with it. If it is accepted that God is the truth, and if the mind can believe in it and so become wrapped with it, then, no matter whether this faith is not grounded in knowledge, by reason of the power of this faith itself, a definite relationship is established between the human mind and God.

As a direct result of this the divine energy begins to act upon it in a thousand unperceived ways. This faith which is founded on reality becomes instrumental in leading a man onward by slow gradual stages to a realisation of the Truth Absolute. Thus, if there is faith in God, the believing soul is able to come within the orbit of Divine Attraction and so gets drawn to Him every moment. It is under this influence that he leaves behind him the attractions of the world. By virtue of this faith, rooted in Truth, the believing soul is able to shed its faults — whatever their number — almost effortlessly. From this we can understand the extent of harm flowing from disbelief. Therefore, so long as the human soul does not come to repose faith in the everlasting Ineffable Essence, it is idle to hope to attain to the blessedness of immortal life.

The connection with the Eternal Substance not having been established, the *jīva* has to undergo a course of endless journeys from birth to birth. If this is so, what greater misfortune could happen to him? The fruit of faith is life everlasting of Light and Bliss. The fruit of want of faith is subjection to the Power of Death and Darkness — because of its remoteness from the Light — and its many-sided corruptions.

It should nevertheless be borne in mind that this solution is from the point of view of those who look at things from the objective side. To one who is endowed with transcendental vision no trace of evil is visible, for Death in his eyes is but a reflection of immortality.

-III-

What arguments are there in proof of the existence of God?

Before attempting to answer this question it appears necessary to premise that whatever arguments may be advanced from the point of view of the world's judgment, either to prove or to disprove the existence of God, not one of them is likely to be accepted universally as absolutely true. Thus, for instance, we find that Udayanācārya in his *Kusumañjalī* has refuted the arguments disproving the existence of God and marshalled arguments in favour of His existence, as judged by the standard of the adherents of the Nyāya School of philosophy. Following in his wake in succeeding times many others have discussed the same topic. Utpalācārya in his work entitled *Siddhitraya*, in one of its sections under the caption *Īśvara-siddhi*, and Abhinavaguptācārya in his treatise entitled *Īśvara-Pratyabhijñā-Vimarśinī* have both, as protagonists of Śaiva scriptures of the Kashmir School, given an elaborate exposition of the philosophy of Godhead. Further, Yāmunācārya in his treatise entitled *Siddhitraya*, Lokacārya in his work known by the name of *Tattvatraya*, as also Vedantadeśikācārya, Śrīnivāsācārya and a number of others in many different places have all from the point of view of the Śrī Vaiṣṇava philosophy explained the Doctrine of Godhead.

Thus, the protagonists of every sect have composed works in which in discussing the Divine Principle they have thrashed out the arguments for and against the existence of God conformably to their sectarian views.

Coming down to present days we find that savants who believe in the existence of God with all their knowledge of modern science have composed works in support of their belief.

There is no doubt that a diligent study of these many-sided discussions will have the effect of sharpening the intellect; but the point is whether they have the least effect in helping one to grow even by an inch towards a living faith in God. What I have stated in reply to the first and second questions should enable us to understand that it is not possible to establish a real faith in God merely on the strength of arguments. It may, of course, be admitted that on the basis of well-founded reasoning an inferential knowledge of the essence of the Divine Being may be gained. But it is difficult for reasoning to establish itself so as to be able to appeal with absolute effect to the varied types of reasoning mind. The reasoning employed by the Naiyāyikas to prove the existence of Godhead is according to the Mīmāṁsakas not true reasoning, but only a semblance of it. To infer an intelligent agent from a given effect is not according to the Mīmāṁsakas a non-controversial matter. And so is the case everywhere.

The truth is that, just as a weapon is effectual only when it is wielded by a powerful man who is proficient in its use, so also arguments put forth by exalted souls who have attained self-realisation have a special efficacy. An argument put forward by one who has acquired direct knowledge of a subject and who has the ability to demonstrate a doubtful point under special circumstances, if necessary, is most powerful for convincing others, even though it is only an argument. Had it not been so, the mystery of God or any other supersensual object would have been unravelled by reasoning long ago. Hence the arguments which are advanced in favour of the existence of God must be regarded as relative only. For they cannot be employed under extraordinary circumstances and, even if applied, they will lose all their force.

By the term 'God' is meant the Supreme Being, the creator, the preserver and the destroyer of the universe, the bestower of reward and punishment, the embodiment of Truth, Knowledge and Bliss, and possessed of infinite powers. A state of equilibrium of the energies subsisting in that Being is what is known as the *Brahman* aspect of God. When this equilibrium is disturbed, one or other of these energies comes into prominence, overpowering the rest, and is seen functioning. In this way endless energies are working in the universe. When creation comes to an end, these energies lose their manifest character and shine forth as one with their source. Whatever has existence in the World has its origin, subsistence and end in God, so that, so long as the world subsists, the divine existence, which is the support of the world, much in the same manner as a lake is the support of the waves, will have to be sought and discovered. Nay, it will also have to be discovered that the universe is at bottom non-different from the Divine Essence. The existence of God as the preserver, controller, witness, and even as the enjoyer of the universe at the time of its subsistence is worth investigating. Besides this we shall have to realise that the ultimate source from which the energies emanate in the form of art and science is also God. In this way we shall have to arrive at an idea of the existence of God as the director of all energies.

A critical examination of the visible universe would reveal that a powerful supersensual energy subsists within the phenomenal, physical and visible world. No activity is possible without energy. If we manage to stem the energy current by some method, the activity which is a result of that energy will also disappear. The human body is a perpetual scene of activities such as perceiving, hearing, grasping, moving about, giving and so on: there is no doubt that these are inspired by energy. The physical world is also a scene of diverse activities such as the blowing of winds, the thundering of clouds, lightning flashes and so forth. As activity presupposes the existence of energy, the diversity of activities would force us to accept a variety of energies. It may however be observed that homogeneous energy generates heterogeneous energies. It is not that the various energies are only interrelated: the same basic Energy and no other is seen working behind each. One and the same Primary Energy is manifested in various forms, and functions differently through various vehicles.

Nityaiva sā jaganmurtīstayā sarvamidaṁ tatam |

The truth of the above dictum from *Durgā-Saptaśatī* has had to be acknowledged with reverence even by the scientists of the present century.

But the question is: What is the real character of this Energy? It need not be said that science has not so far been able to give a satisfactory answer to this question. The day when the secret of the oneness or wholeness of this energy will be known is yet too far off. The finite aspect, however, has been amply investigated in the scientific world. The final conclusion arrived at is that it is Energy which, losing its subtle aspect, gets manifested as dense matter. And then it comes to have properties impossible to trace in its original form of pure or undifferentiated Energy. In truth, physical matter is but a form of energy made, so to say, captive and made to submit to fixed laws. For as long as energy is not captured by means of some contrivance, physical form cannot be evolved out of it. On its being released from this captivity, that is to say, on the grossness being taken away from the physical matter, its existence reverts to the original form of pure energy. Hence energy and matter or material existence, though representing different phases, have at botom a unitary life energy which in its differentiated state is noticed everywhere in the universe and at every moment. Ordinarily no one can perceive energy in its pure aspect with one's unaided faculties; but, should some superior personage give us a vision of it, the fettered human being would not be able to bear its transcendent splendour. Ordinary people can only infer the existence of Energy from its material manifestation, transformation, ripening and similar other functions. Freedom to proceed further is not vouchsafed to ordinary individuals, nay, not even to scientists swearing by physical science. Those philosophically disposed and resolute spirits, that do not drift along with the current of time but are ever striving by means of discrimination to probe into the finer essence of visible existence, have ultimately to admit that behind the veil set up by this world of material appearances there is a vast world of invisible appearances. But the real question that confronts us is, what is the nature of this Supreme Energy? Is it pure, undifferentiated consciousness, or is it devoid of consciousness?

Before proceeding any further we have to decide, in the first instance, whether this Energy has any relationship with the Energy represented by human will, that is the power of volition. For knowledge, on one hand, and activity, on the other, cannot be brought into mutual relation except through Will. Activity which follows from Will implies the existence of energy. What connection has this Will-power got with the Great Energy, a small fraction of which is behind the endless activities of the vast universe, deserves our foremost consideration.

From the ordinary point of view, the worldly activities can be classified under two heads, viz (1) voluntary and (2) non-voluntary. Action which is preceded by volition is voluntary, and any other action is non-voluntary or spontaneous. The automatic functions of the human body are mostly of this latter type. Many of us, however, know that all these involuntary actions, too, can be brought under the control of our will by special effort and long practice. Hence even such of our bodily actions as are not voluntary can be made such in course of time.

It can be easily understood that if the will-power of man is regulated and purified it can be made to regulate all the functions of the body. If it is possible to initiate, retard or change the course of any bodily action by force of will, the conclusion becomes irresistible that will is at the root of all such actions. If, however, it were possible even for actions outside the body to be regulated similarly by the will-power of a given individual, then no doubt could possibly be entertained as to the power of will being at the root of all outside activities. Of course, the degree of will-power that has to be exercised is not uniform in all cases, as the activities that follow from its operation are not the same everywhere. Thus the energy which is responsible for all activities in the world outside as well as in the life of the inner world is essentially of the nature of will. This is the sum and substance of the conclusion I seek to establish. The different forms of physical energy with which we come in contact are all, as a matter of fact, but different phases of will-power. Were this not so, our will-power could not work against them. The force of gravitation, the electric power, the power which mutually attracts and draws away atoms, in fact, all powers can be brought under the control of a pure and regulated will. It need hardly be explained that wherever any of these powers is less intense in degree than the human will brought to bear upon it, the will-power is able to overpower it. But if, on the other hand, it is stronger than the will, the will is unable to assert itself. What was conscious will in the past manifests itself in the present as unconscious Energy: there is no difference between the one and the other. It is intelligible, therefore, that if the will is sufficiently trained into strength, it can easily counteract the so-called physical and other energies which are, at bottom, only acts of will crystallised into unconsciousness. The laws of Nature are only the generalised expression of this energy functioning in the world. The antinomies involved in *adṛṣṭa* and *puruṣakāra* or Necessity and Free Will represent only the contrast, as shown above, between Law and Will. Will manifests itself in the realm of consciousness, and Law in that of unconscious Nature. The two are fundamentally identical.

When the light of our ordinary knowledge becomes gradually purified into pure or transcendent lustre, it is found that even below the deepest depths of unconsciousness there is an element of consciousness lurking. In other words, the zone of consciousness becomes infinitely expanded and everything is illumined. It then appears that all forms of energy are at bottom the expression of an all-embracing Universal Will. This Supreme Will is Divine Power, which has been spoken of in the scriptures as Jagadambā or the Universal Matrix (*Magna Mater*). The author of the *Śiva-Sūtras* says: *Icchāśaktirumā kumārī.*

The light of truth as to the ultimate origin of the universe has not yet been discovered by science. Had it not been so, this root-cause would have been recognised by it as identical with Will; it could have discovered the intimate relationship subsisting between the individual human will and the Divine Will and so paved the way towards reaching the realm of pure consciousness or intelligence. It is because it has had no conception of this Supreme Energy as Will that it has not been able to discover the principle of pure intelligence at the root of all manifest existence. The only way to ascertain whether this Divine Energy is but a name of the Divine Will is to determine whether by purifying and controlling the individual human will it is possible to exert a controlling influence on material energy.

If it could be demonstrated that the energy involved in matter could be acted upon by the human will, it would show that energy and will are essentially non-different. That the power of human will is able at least partially to act with effect upon forms of external energy is not unknown to modern scientists. A perfected *yogin* — even one who not being such is nevertheless advanced far into the realm of yogic discipline — can control material energy in any way he likes. Instances of this kind are not altogether wanting even at the present day.

The fact is that out of the bosom of the Supreme Being and Pure Intelligence arises, as by an inherent urge of its nature, the Divine Will (like waves rising from the storm-tossed ocean breast) from which again, according to a fixed course of development, issue forth manifestations of Divine activity constituting the world of life and matter. It is this Supreme Intelligence or Pure Undivided Self-luminous Consciousness (with its Will-Power operating in the manner described above) that goes by the name of God.

The will pertains to God sometimes as a latent capacity (i.e. without manifesting itself in forms of activity); but when it becomes dynamic, it gives birth to the world of phenomenal existence with its endless panorama of forms. If we are to ascend by philosophical reasoning from the world of matter to the heights of Supreme Intelligence and Consciousness, such as constitutes the Godhead, we must try to establish a nexus or connecting link between the two; and this nexus is the intermediate principle of Will.

A close examination of the chain of cause and effect in the universe will show that no effect can appear without a cause; nay, cause and effect must need be in the same proportion. It is essential to keep this in view while trying to determine the nature of an effect. Indian philosophers have based their theory of *Karma* (action) on this principle. Broadly speaking, the idea underlying the theory of *Karma* is that a particular *karma* bears fruit according to its nature and extent, so that a *karmic* cause can be inferred from the fruit quite as much as a fruit from a *karma*. When we see the wonderful play of joy and sorrow in the world of life and look for their cause, we become constrained to recognise this special *karmic* factor. The extraordinary factor which morally accounts for joy and sorrow is called *karma* or *saṁskāras* (impressions) generated from present actions or brought over from the past. No other factors in the external world can give rise to joy or sorrow. The fact of the matter is that every effect is attributable to a plurality of causes, most of which are ordinary, while a portion thereof is uncommon or extraordinary. The assemblage of ordinary factors may be there and yet it may not be able to produce a given effect because of the absence of the extraordinary factor which is thus the primary cause. There may be numerous causes responsible for joy and sorrow; but they cannot in themselves produce them except through an extraordinary factor which is technically known as *karma*. *Karma* as producing joy or misery in a particular individual must be related to him only; else the cause and effect would become unrelated. It is not possible in a material world governed by the law of cause and effect that *A* should commit an act and *B* enjoy the fruit thereof. None else than the man who thrusts his hand into the fire burns it.

Similarly, he alone who performs good or evil actions as an active doer reaps the fruits thereof in the form of happiness or misery in the capacity of an enjoyer. Thus we find the objects of enjoyment may be present in abundance and yet it may happen that there may be many who have not the good fortune to obtain them for purposes of enjoyment, the reason being that the particular or extraordinary *karmic* factor or factors that would have led to such acquisition was in the case absent. On the other hand, we sometimes find that many secure unexpected and abundant worldly enjoyments without any effort or exertion, nay, sometimes even without the necessary desire and knowledge. Just as a plant cannot grow unless we sow the seed thereof, so also the fruit, viz happiness and misery, cannot manifest itself unless there is working an unseen *karmic* factor brought over from the past. A tremendous active force is present in an endless variety of forms behind the countless millions of solar systems which are drifting with the current of time, bearing numberless varieties of living beings on their bosom and providing them with their respective happiness and misery.

It is true, *karma* brings its own fruits; but it is no more than a blind physical energy, unable to function without the guiding presence of an intelligent principle. Even in the world of our experience energy is nowhere found to work independently. It is no better than a blind instrument required to be moved into action by the motive power of the self-conscious agent behind. We may cite the illustration of fire which possesses the power to burn. It is true that it burns combustible objects only by virtue of that power, but an intelligent being is required to utilise the fire in order to make it burn a particular object. Fire of itself cannot burn it. The force of action is a blind force which under its own law gives rise to pleasure and pain; but it requires to be actuated by a intelligent agent. There is no doubt that the subject which feels pleasure or pain is identical with the one which is responsible for the previous action leading to this experience.

Although an effect results from a cause in more or less a mechanical fashion, it cannot assume the form of an object of enjoyment in respect of a particular individual except under the controlling influence of a higher presence endowed with a will-power. That is to say, though the individual soul experiences pleasure and pain in accordance with its previous actions, it does so under the supervision of the Cosmic Self without whose will nothing can happen in Nature. This Universal Self is the silent witness of actions as well as their fruits and it is under His Will that a particular action develops into joy or sorrow for the experience of the individual soul concerned with that action.

It is thus clear that neither the actions of an individual nor the experience to which those actions lead are explicable except on the assumption of an intelligent principle, pure and universal, working from behind. How this principle inspires or guides things may be elucidated by means of an illustration. For instance, a man who is endowed with the power of vision perceives colours of various kinds in broad day-light. Behind each individual act of vision there is variety in the visible object on one hand, and the power of vision of the seer on the other. But the actual vision cannot be adequately explained by the working of this two-fold causal factor: the illuminating power of the bright light must also be taken into account. In the same way, the fruit of actions performed by a particular individual is no doubt reaped by the same individual; but both action and the enjoyment of its fruit would have been impossible, had they not rested on the intelligent Divine Principle. It is extremely difficult for those who do not believe in God but who regard *karma* only as responsible for its fruits, to account for the diversities of experience.

The controlling Power which regulates the inviolable causal relation is identical with the Supreme Principle referred to above. A close analysis clearly reveals the fact that there are laws working in each of its spheres — laws which are extremely complex and unintelligible. Nevertheless, the laws of one sphere are found to be so closely related to those of another that the conclusion becomes irresistible that there is only one law in the heart of Nature, manifesting itself in diverse forms in diverse spheres. The discovery of the uniformity of laws throughout the universe as well as in the realm of knowledge constitutes the highest achievement of science. From the existence and operation of one and the same fundamental law in spheres of knowledge distinguished from each other, every thoughtful person is led to infer the existence of a Unique Being behind the endless varieties of the universe. This Being, which is the source of all laws, can hardly be anything but intelligent; and there is no denying the fact that It is the ultimate controller of the universe. Hence even those who are advocates of Laws of Nature are constrained to admit, though in an indirect manner, the existence of a Supreme Intelligent Principle. Of course, for the sake of argument, it may be urged that a law does not necessarily imply a regulator. For if the law is believed to be eternal *ab ante* and if it is proved to be really inviolable, the assumption of a maker or promulgator is hardly necessary. The above contention is not altogether groundless. The truth is that the law is neither eternal nor immutable, as it is believed to be. A person of ordinary knowledge may not be able to observe either the beginning or any aberration of the law in question; but as the knowledge gets more and more refined, it is gradually realised that the law has a beginning and that it is also liable to change. It need not be said that under such circumstances the inflexible character of law is thrown to the ground. Those who can understand this can also realise that what is law for a non-liberated soul is only the play of free-will on the part of a higher being, gifted with hither power and knowledge. The Mighty Being, whose will manifests itself in the world in the form of laws, is the Lord of the world. Physical science can only discover the existence of a law; it can have no knowledge of the Being whose Will expresses itself as law. The main reason for not accepting the law as eternal is that both its beginning and its end are, on occasions, observed to owe themselves to an act of will. Will power or any other force cannot act upon an eternal and immutable principle. Of course, from the worldly point of view the law can be recognised both as eternal and inviolable.

Those who study the history of the world with a view to adding to their knowledge know that from the worldly point of view neither knowledge nor activity is observed to have a limit of its evolution. Energy, though unmanifest by a nature, is manifested through a particular channel or medium and performs functions in the way relevant to its nature. The medium of expression not being uniform, the manifestation of energy is manifested more or less according as the medium is more or less pure and receptive. The same law is working in the realm of knowledge as well as in the sphere of activity, the only difference being that the medium of one is different from that of the other. Like unmanifested knowledge, unmanifested activity is also infinite. That which is not manifest or patent does not suffer from any obstruction, nor does it perform any function. Hence the extent to which manifest knowledge or activity is capable of functioning is determined by the nature of the medium through which it is expressed. If the medium is impure or covered with extraneous matter it will not allow the energy to manifest itself fully. As soon as the coating of extraneous matter is removed therefrom, the impediments in the way of manifestation of the energy are also removed. Hence the manifestation of knowledge and activity in a pure stuff which is free from obscurity and contact with extraneous matter is infinite, unimpeded and endless. This, in reality, is another name of God. Both knowledge and activity are manifested to a certain extent in every living being. Were it not so, a sentient being could not be differentiated from insentient matter. This knowledge and activity gradually develops and is fully manifested in a supreme medium. The perfect knowledge and activity or intelligence as revealed in an absolutely pure medium is described as God in the sacred literature.

Those who seek to arrive at the truth on the basis of a close analysis of uncommon, though perfectly natural, phenomena are well aware of the fact that on certain occasions to certain persons the future reveals itself with as much vividness as the past or remote events are sometimes found to do. It is needless to cite specific instances in this context.

Such occurrences are not rare; but that such things actually happen has been corroborated in several ways. One gets non-plussed while trying to unravel this mystery. Should such scenes as have not been enacted in the drama of creation and such incidents as have not occurred anywhere on the face of this earth and are to take place long afterwards in the eyes of the world, be clearly perceived just now, no thoughtful person would be able to explain or rationalise this phenomenon without being confused. It is extremely difficult to comprehend how a thing which has no real existence in the present moment, not only empirically but even phenomenally, can at all be present in consciousness. It is not difficult, however, for a past event to appear in the present experience of a particular individual. For, if we admit that an impression is left on the mind by a piece of knowledge gained and action performed, and if we acknowledge that the same can be revived under an exciting cause, the perception of past events may, to a certain extent, become intelligible. Of course, a universal knowledge of the past would not be possible unless a universal substance in which all impressions are imprinted is assumed. This compels us to recognise the existence of a comprehensive and relatively eternal basis. This would be identical with the universal soul as set forth by the advocates of the unity of the individual soul. The multiple souls of different times and places will only be so many phases of this single universal soul. Hence the utmost that a knowledge can testify to is to establish the existence, not of God, but of the collective universal soul. A vision of the future, however, cannot be rationalised without the existence of an eternal Divine Principle. For the perception of an object or a series of objects which has not yet manifested itself in the stream of time cannot be accounted for, as in the case of visualisation of the past, through a revival of impressions left on the mental stuff. These impressions inhere in the Subtle Body and develop as memory or even as actual vision under the reviving influence of exciting causes. There is no doubt that the degree of clarification of this impression determines the degree of perspicuity in the knowledge derived, so much so that what appears as a memorial and representative image may attain to the lucidity of direct perception. But in the intuition of the future the Mind or the Subtle Body has no part to play.

The truth is: currents flow down, though in a partial manner, from the eternal causal plane, and express themselves as events in time. This flow of causal energy from the future to the present is in reality a tendency of the causal factor towards its self-manifestation as an effect. An entity or an action, when not yet manifest, is comprised under the causal aggregate. Hence it is not possible to find out a trace or even a semblance of the existence on a causal plane in the Mind or the Subtle Body. As this existence has not yet flown, as it were, in the stream of time and come to be realised in the present consciousness, there is no impression left on the Mind corresponding to this. And it is for this reason that it leaves no reflection on mental substance. It is clear, therefore, that a vision of the future depends neither on the Mind nor on the impressions pertaining to it.

Now the question that presents itself to the mind is, how then, can such a vision be possible? The great sage Patañjali says in reply to this question that the future is not in reality something different from the present. What is future for us cannot be so for one whose knowledge is more comprehensive: it is but present for him. By following this line of argument we can understand that no object or occurrence can be called future with reference to that knowledge which is most comprehensive, that is to say, which has no limit. Truly speaking, what is future to us is present to the Eternal Consciousness, which transcends all time limitations; so is the case with the past. The plane of consciousness on which the so-called past and future are eternally present represent the supreme state of Conscious Existence, above all distinctions involved in time, circumstances, ideas and actions. This is the causal plane of the mystic literature, and the principle that controls this plane from its centre is known as God. It is for this reason that a perception of the so-called future by an individual soul need not be wondered at if, in an inconceivable manner, the soul concerned is identified, though even for a moment, with God. For what is future to the individual soul is revealed as present to it on the Divine Plane. This proves the fact that knowledge has such a pure state that what appears as future to a limited consciousness is manifest therein as eternally present. Had an eternity such as this not been in existence, it would never have been possible for an individual soul to have a perception of the future. Hence a well-authenticated instance of pre-vision as described above would be enough to convince one of the existence of an Eternal Principle.

Two main causes are seen operating in the production of an effect. In analysing the universe, too, two causes have likewise to be recognized. The stuff of which the universe is made, known under the different names of *paramānas*, the *guṇas*, *māyā* or *kāla* are recognised as insentient, but a material cause which is insentient cannot transform itself into an effect without the relation of an intelligent or sentient being. This intelligent agency is the efficient cause of the universe, under the influence of which the Primordial Stuff gets agitated and transformed into a variety of forms. Those who believe that Matter for its evolution does not require the efficiency of an Intelligent Principle are naturalists; for to fall back on Nature without adequate investigation into the cause of a phenomenon is not in keeping with the canons of Logic. The existence of God as the efficient cause of creation is thus clearly proved. From a higher point of view, however, it will appear that ultimately there is no real difference between the efficient and the material causes, for one Intelligent Principle assumes different forms of its own free will and is manifested as the multiplex universe.

It is universally acknowledged that a tremendous revolution is going on everywhere and at every moment in the world around us. But change can be understood only in reference to an unchangeable or constant spectator. There must therefore be an eternal witness of this perpetual and universal flux. The pure and universal consciousness which is unconcernedly aware of all the plays of Nature is the all-intelligent God.

What has been said above regarding the existence of God is only in the nature of arguments. Many such arguments have been presented in the scriptures and have also been advanced by Western scholars who are of a theistic trend of mind, and several others of a similar nature may be brought forward, if necessary. But there is very little hope of anyone being persuaded by these arguments into a true belief in God. Reasoning is intended to strengthen the indistinct faith which springs up in the pure and receptive heart of a person as a result of listening to scriptural texts or the words of a great soul who has got direct knowledge of matters concerning the existence of God. No arguments, however strong, will suffice to generate faith in a person who has none, and who does not therefore recognise Authority as a valid source of knowledge. Reasoning is primarily concerned with the production of a sense of rationality or reasonableness in regard to a particular point discussed in the sacred books or by adepts possessed of immediate knowledge. In other words, reasoning will have done its duty when it has shown that the matter about which the heart naturally entertains a faith in response to the words of a reliable person is perfectly amenable to reason and within the region of possibility. Having accomplished so much, the seeker after truth is required to have, through a regular course of self-discipline, a direct realisation of the truth taught by great souls, which had so far been an object of unwavering faith to him and rationalised by arguments. Yoga play the most important part in this discipline, of which Action (*karma*), Knowledge (*jñāna*), Devotion (*bhakti*), etc. are so many different phases. When the attainable object is perceived in its entirety with the help of *Yoga* (concentration), all doubts and misconceptions vanish of themselves. As soon as a vision of the soul, the illusory (*māyika*) difference between the subject and the object being eliminated, the pure Light of the Self begins to shine on itself and gets established as an indivisible and self-luminous Existence. To those who are traversing the path of spiritual discipline the existence of God is not revealed by dry reasoning. Until we transcend the plane of our present knowledge, the world or our own self or anything beyond them will continue to appear to our consciousness exactly as at present. If, however, it so happens that through an inscrutable working of Divine Dispensation the power of Grace is transferred to our mind and brings about a sudden change in the level of consciousness, we shall find that our existence and knowledge will immediately assume new and unforeseen forms. However materialistic and agnostic a man may be, the operation of the transcendent power of Grace can instantly convert him into a new man altogether. It is in this manner that true God-vision or true knowledge has taken its rise in the world; it has never been accomplished by means of reasoning and logic or by hair-splitting discussion.

As a matter of fact, there are many such profound experiences in the life of a man which take no time in changing his angle of vision.

- IV -

In the fourth question it is asked what incidents have occurred in my personal life whereby belief in the existence or mercy of God may have been strengthened. With apologies I must state that I am unable to give publicity to my personal experiences. Of course, this much I can say that I do get response from above — and that unfailingly — on applying myself in the proper way. I have been saved in extraordinary ways from such troubles as could not be averted by ordinary means. Whenever I recall these, and they are numerous, to my mind, my heart is overwhelmed with a consciousness of the Divine Mercy and Love. I cannot possibly recount the ways in which I feel His blessed existence and power every moment in the realm of Knowledge, Action and Emotion.

These matters are so sacred and secret that I do not feel inclined to discuss them in public. My personal nature is as credulous, on one hand, as it is sceptical on the other. But whatever I have experienced in life or am experiencing, has never been, and is not accepted as true, until I have subjected it to severe tests. I hold that if what I believe to be true is eternally true, its lustre would be all the brighter by test and would not suffer in any way. Without passing through the illusory and the empirical existence with knowledge, one cannot make headway towards that which is eternally true. Through His mercy and through the worthy Master's Grace the road leading from the illusory to the empirical and from the empirical to the eternal existence has been revealed to this humble soul and opened to a certain extent. But when under personal effort His eternal nature will be awakened within, I shall perceive Him in every phase of Nature. And by the perfection of eternal Yoga in the form of Action, Knowledge, Devotion and Love I hope to attain by stages His indivisible Existence, Knowledge and Bliss, and to be able in the long run, while winding up this earthly existence, to abide in His supreme Essence which embraces all forms and is still beyond them. It is all due to the Master's Grace.

गुरोः कृपैव केवलम्

guroḥ kṛpaiva kevalam

~11~

Mother

This article is about the great Bengali saint Śrī Ānandamayī Mā (1896-1982), of whom the author was a staunch devotee. M.M. Gopinath Kaviraj spent the last years of his life in Ānandamayī Āśram, Varanasi.

- I -

What is the mystery of Mother's Being and Personality?

But, it hardly becomes us, children as we are, to analyze and dissect our Mother, nor is it possible for us, crying ourselves for light in the darkness of night, to shed any light on Her.

I sympathise with those to whom Mother is verily a riddle. She is so very unlike ordinary or even extraordinary persons known to us that it is extremely hard to make any positive statement about Her with any degree of confidence of accuracy. We know that similar difficulties leading to misunderstanding were experienced in the case of some of the supremely great persons of the past, and that as a result many of these persons actually felt that they were not truly appreciated and were even misunderstood by those among whom they lived and for whom they worked. Śrī Kṛṣṇa, for instance, complained that most people — some of the gods as well — not knowing his true nature, looked down upon him as an ordinary mortal. Gautama, the Buddha, too, in a subsequent age spoke in the same strain, saying that very few people understood him properly.

That Mother's life, even Her earliest life, should abound in extraordinary incidents is not suprising — we are accustomed to such incidents in the lives of genuine saints, mystics and *yogins*. They exist and have their place of honour in those lives. But all these pale into insignificance before the wonderful poise and bliss of Her sweet but magnificent personality — a personality which, strong as it is, blends into the Impersonal, nay, is utterly un-differentiated from it.

It is well-known that the illumination and liberation of saints and mystics presuppose an earlier stage of ignorance and bondage, followed usually by a period of aspiration, personal exertion and austerities. This stage is usually found in the present life itself, or, in exceptional cases, in a pre-natal state of existence. But in the case of Mother, we are told that such a prior state of ignorance never existed at all. The possibility of an ante-natal embodied existence is ruled out on Mother's definite assurance that Her life is not subject to the laws of natural causation and that She has no prior life to account for Her present existence. And even what looked like a path of discipleship in Her pre-marital life was not, as we shall see presently, more than a playful representation of self-imposed discipline in which She condescended to take part merely as a matter of sport. It had no meaning for Her subsequent life in any way.

Among the well-known mystics of the world we seldom find any in whom we do not observe a period of gloom and subjective torture antecedent to the descent of Light. Mother had no experience of darkness in Her Life, either of the soul or of the spirit, nor had She any experience of the descent of Light except as a matter of play. It is said that from Her very birth She was aware of what she had ever been and what she would always continue to be, and that there was no possibility of a deviation from Her self-conscious stature for a single moment.

Her self-knowledge, we are assured, did not arise under the impact of an extrinsic element outside of Her self — it was always with Her, being a state of Her Nature. It was there already in its fulness, requiring no effort on Her part, nor any grace from above, to bring it into greater perfection.

-II-

Ordinarily three sources of illumination are recognized, viz (a) *Daiva*, (b) *Ārṣa*, and (c) *Pauruṣa*.

In the first case knowledge dawns on the soul absorbed in contemplation of some heavenly form, as illustrated by the knowledge of Arjuna coming from Śrī Kṛṣṇa. This contemplation may or may not be accompanied by the descent of self-conscious grace from the form of the deity concerned; and in the case of descent of grace it may be gross, subtle, more subtle, or even the subtlest, depending on whether it is effected through touch, speech, vision or mere thought. Apart from the difference in degree of grace there may be difference in the quality of the grace infused, according as it result in the unification or otherwise of the soul with the source of its knowledge. There are cases known to history where such knowledge is not found accompanied by conscious grace at all, e.g. the knowledge of the analysis of the five-fold sheath of the soul which was received by Bhṛgu from Varuṇa, or the particular *Vidyā* which Yama imparted to Naciketā.

The *Ārṣa* variety is called *pratibhā*. It is not derived from anybody's verbal instruction, but is produced from within spontaneously. Its classical example is Triśaṅku, who was engaged in continued *upāsanā*, identifying himself in thought with the Supreme Brahman. This gave rise in due time to the actual intuition of *Brahman*.

The third of *Pauruṣa* type is the normal variety in which a human Guru communicates his wisdom to a human disciple, as Śuka Deva did to Parīkṣit. This type of *Brahma-jñāna* arises in one devoted to one's teacher on account of the virtuous acts of one's previous lives having come to maturity. In this case too the possibility or otherwise of conscious *śaktipāta* from the human teacher as an accompaniment is to be considered. Whether there is *śaktipāta* or not, the alternative of *upāsanā* or its absence is also there. The quantitative classification as in the other types is possible even here.

We can easily dismiss the first and the third, as both of them imply the origin of knowledge from a separate source, divine or human, and as they refer respectively to one who meditates on God or who is devoted to Guru. The second variety is also discarded as it refers here to cases of persons who, having attained to some degree of perfection, have subsequently experienced a fall from the height. It is not true *jñāna* at all. As regards genuine *pratibhā*, we shall revert to it later.

-III-

Now what is the nature of the self-knowledge which was innate with Mother?

It is clear from what has been said above that though self-knowledge, on the analogy of lower knowledge, has its roots within, its exciting cause is usually outside, as it is initiated by forces working without us. But it may also be, as already pointed out, due to initiation from within, in which case the external agencies would be no more than merely propagating forces. History records instances of illumination of both these types. The Divine Grace is the most important factor, not only in the awakening of religious consciousncss in man but also in its subsequent development in him till the union with the Divine is accomplished. Granting this as a necessary pre-condition of active spiritual life, what is needed in ordinary cases is the operation of a mediating factor through which such grace may become accessible to man. For the bodily and the mental mechanism of an average individual is not capable of bearing the strain involved in the direct transmission of Divine Grace. As a rule God's Grace is said to act on a receptive vehicle free from contact with matter, i.e. on an unembodied soul in a pre-creational state. But if the soul in the process of creative evolution happens to take on a body of impure matter it can no longer receive grace directly from the Divine source, but receives it only though a medium. The medium would be an embodied being whose body may be of exclusively pure matter or of pure matter mixed with impure. Baring the immaculate bodies of the heavenly brotherhood entrusted with the guardianship of the world and with the task of imparting knowledge in the beginning of creation, we have to consider in this context the hierarchy of Teachers consisting of three well-known groups (*ogha*), viz *Divya*, *Siddha* and *Mānava*. The *Divya* or celestial and *Mānava* or human correspond loosely to the *Daiva* and *Pauruṣa* mentioned above. Between these two the Āgamas place the *Siddha* or superhuman group. This medium serves the purpose of an *Ācārya* or Guru to the uninitiated seekers after Knowledge.

Thus, Grace acts freely and immediately in the case of souls which are not clogged with material vestments. This is possible where Grace does not require any external support for its manifestation (*nirādhikaraṇa anugraha*), and it acts indirectly through pure bodies on recipient souls endowed with bodies of *māyā*. This is an instance of Grace acting through a support as its medium (*sādhikaraṇa anugraha*). By the term 'Grace' we should understand here the special Grace of the Lord and not the general grace which confers benefits other than Supreme Realization.

There are thus two ways of approach to Grace in Indian cultural tradition, and the two ways generally meet and seem to be really two aspect of one and the same way. Both are concerned with one's outlook on Guru as the Principle of Divine Grace, functioning in one view by itself, and in the other through its concrete expression in a manifested form available for the purpose. In fact there appears to be no substantial difference between the two trends of thought. In actual practice the object of veneration is held from both these standpoints to be above the entire creation. But one should remember an important point in this connection which is likely to be lost sight of. During Manifestation each of the different aspects of Pure Order beyond Time, where the sequence is only logical, involves complexities in its features, but in the simple Unity of the Eternal Self-luminous all complications are conspicuous by their absence, for the Transcendent is above all categories. For instnace, Guru as an abstract principle is one of the eternal varieties. The Universal Being pervades All and is one with All; by virtue of its presence it occupies every position simultaneously and is identified with each, and yet it retains its transcendent character and uniqueness. An individual human being, on the other hand, by virtue of spiritual elevation, may very well occupy the position of a Guru for the time being and perform the function connected with this position. This, however, is tentative and endures so long as the merit of the incumbent is not exhausted, whereupon he retires giving place to another individual of the same kind who continues the function and keeps the chain unbroken. This shows that Guru is both human and divine, human in view of the transitional character of the medium adopted by the Divine Power for its own purpose, and divine in consideration of the Supreme Principle of Compassion which is eternal and inspires the medium concerned. The Power of God functions through a man or any other embodied being. For this reason it is enjoined that even a secondary Guru, human, super-human and even celestial, should be looked upon by the disciple as divine. Strictly speaking, the Divine Being is free from all attributes incidental to contingent existence and does not deserve to be called by any of the names associated with human activities.

Those in whom the supreme intuition does not arise from within have naturally to depend for its origin either on illuminated persons or on Revelation. But to one in whom it flashes up spontaneously, revealing Truth fully and immediately, external aids are held to be unnecessary. Such a man is believed to be a master of every phase of spiritual life and possesses the ability to impart it successfully to the needy. It is said that the process of his so-called self-initiation is in reality a process of introversion of senses and their subsequent unification with the true Self which awakens the latent divine consciousness. This is the secret of his self-acquired authority. He never feels any urge for resorting to external teachers for interpreting the sacred word, for his inner sense reveals it to him. This is an illustration of how Pure Light, free from intellectual and conceptual elements, comes into manifestation. In the matter of communicating his wisdom to others, he is guided solely by the consideration of the receptive capacity and other qualities of the seekers. Thus, if the minds of the recipients are absolutely pure, the beneficent Will of the Master is by itself sufficient to kindle their spiritual sense. But if they are not so pure, external accessories of a formal character consistent with their inner demands may have to be conceded to suit their requirements. Such a unique person is a Guru unto himself and is known as *Akalpita Guru*, possessed of Full Knowledge and Power manifested from within.

But when this self-derived knowledge and power is imperfect, he has to remove it and bring the knowledge into perfection by some means or other, e.g. though a mental act, viz *bhāvanā* or contemplation or *japa* or yoga. Thus by constantly turning in his mind the thought that he is verily one with Brahman or by repetition of a potent *mantra* or by some such means he has to supplement the knowledge he has acquired from within. Such a person is called *Akalpita Kalpaka*. The difference between the two is that while in the former or superior type of self-illumination the co-operation of the mind, *prāṇa*, senses or body is not essential, in the latter it is indispensable.

A superficial observer might find in Mother's self-knowledge some resemblance to the illumination of one of the two types mentioned above. If Her subsequent course of life be interpreted as a real process of *sādhanā* intended to bring into perfection what She has derived from Her inner Self, it would come, they say, under the second category. But, if it means simply an outer expression of what She found within and does not convey the usual significance attached to *sādhanā*, it would fall under the first category.

A little reflection would, however, show that Mother's case is exceptional and does not come under any of these two categories. The mere fact that Her knowledge did not originate from a Guru does not take us very far into its mystery. In Vedic tradition we hear of one Triśaṅku as being blessed with such spontaneous illumination due to his deep contemplation on his self as identical with the Supreme Brahman. Recently we know of Jacob Boehme (1575-1624 A.D.) of Germany, the 'God-taught philosopher', as blessed with some sort of intuitive *jñāna* directly from within or from above.

In the history of mysticism we come across cases of a sudden as well as of a gradual process of the on-coming of Light without the intervention of any mediating agency. The illumination differs, of course, in kind, quality and degree in each case. The self-evolved gnosis of the *Akalpita Yogī* stands also on a similar footing. But we must bear in mind that all this is a result of an intensive action of grace. For from a careful study of work on mystic theology, especially of the *Tantras*, it appears that there are three degree of grace in respect of its intensity, viz high, medium and low, each of these being sub-divided into three similar classes. Thus in a general way we may speak of nine degrees in all, the first being the most intense and the ninth the mildest. The second degree of grace under this classification would by its descent enable the recipient soul to have self-knowledge without the aid of an external Guru. It purges and transforms the soul instantaneously. What is technically known as *anupāya* or *śāmbhava upāya* belong to this class. Here the *upāya* or means is no other than the Supreme Power itself or its first manifestation as the cosmic will. It is certainly higher than *jñāna* as well as *kriyā*. But it is nonetheless a means to an end and not an end in itself, and is intended to convert an animal soul or *paśu* into the divine Self or Śiva. Its sole objective is to divinise the soul or rather to reclaim it into its divine status which lay always inherent within itself.

Mother's self-knowledge, as already pointed out, is not easily explicable on the analogy of the case referred to above. It canot be interpreted in terms of the experiences of saint and sages. Hence the difficulty of estimating Mother's personality. We cannot ignore the fact that She was never subject to ignorance and the question of having grace even in its highest degree can never arise in Her case. She played the role of a *sādhikā* in Her earlier years, no doubt, and during this period She seemed to have passed through all the stages of a real *sādhikā*. In this play She started with ignorance and proceeded through various austerities, observing silence, regulating diet, practising *japa* and yogic exercices and performing *pūjā* and other similar rites. Dawn of knowledge formed also a part of this play. A sense of agony and dryness of the soul followed by the bliss of union had their own places in this self-enacted drama. The whole affair was an imitation of *sādhanā*, and it was so arranged that it had all the air of naturalness in it. Her self-knowledge, fortified in its unshakable purity, stood behind this play of self-assumed ignorance and the dramatic impersonation of an ordinary *sādhikā* in quest of supreme Realisation. One should not take it as an illustration of divided self and of its activities — it is rather the outcome of an eternally vigilant and self-conscious will playing the double part of impersonation of a *sādhikā* passing through the shadows and light of a disciplined life, and of the still Witness behind observing and directing its own play on the stage.

Some people are inclined to regard Mother as an *Avatāra* or incarnation of a god or goddess. This view, whatever its merits may be, is supposed to be free from the difficulties noted in the earlier view. But what is an *Avatāra*? It is the descent of Energy to the earth level from the pure causal plane with the object of bringing order into a troubled world, establishing righteousness and restoring moral balance to humanity. The Energy which comes down to an *Avatāra* is distinguished from what descends to a man on the ground in that its connection with the source remains unbroken, whereas in the case of a man it is discontinued. Notwithstanding this, its relation with the source is like that of a part with the whole, and even when the descending Energy is continuous with the source, it is only a projection and nothing more. The original source lies outside the field of the descendent energy. The very expression *Avatāra* means descent and presupposes a higher source from which the descent is made. All the *Avatāras* as such have their respective centres, their proto-types so to say, in the *Para Vyoman* (Highest Heaven) or *Mahā Vaikuṇtha*, and these are different modes of the Central Energy of the World Administrator.

We are not concerned here with the particular god or goddess of which she is claimed to be an *Avatāra*. The difficulty is everywhere the same. Even if the god or goddess be taken to be divine in essence the difficulty remains. Knowing Mother through personal contact in the light of what She says about Herself indirectly from time to time, I cannot bring myself to believe that this view would solve the difficulty. If *Avatāra* is understood in the sense in which a Buddhist would consider a *nirmāṇa kāya* in relation to *dharmakāya* it would be a different matter. But even then some difficulty would persist.

If the *nirmāṇa kāya* is considered to be a projection of *dharmakāya*, the difficulty of *avatārahood* would remain as before. If the absolute unity of all the *kāyas* of the Buddha is recognized as a fact, the difficulty may perhaps be removed to some extent. We should then be left with the supposition of the *Ādi Buddha* as it were and not with any of the historical Buddhas appearing in time. In the case of a historical Buddha, we have a long history of strenuous *sādhanā* extending over a series of successive lives with a view to eradicate the fundamental obscurations and cultivate the basic virtues and seeds of knowledge. As a result of this, the historical Buddha was endowed with four-fold knowledge, viz *ādarśa jñāna*, *samantā jñāna*, *prātyavekṣā jñāna*, and *kṛtyanuṣṭhāna jñāna*. In Mother all these types of *jñāna* are believed to exist from the very beginning. Of these the first kind means a general vision of all things of all times without any let or hindrance. It is like a mirror reflecting on its bosom the entire creation. The second kind refers to realization of the essential equality or sameness in all beings. The third variety of *jñāna* enables one to have a sense of absolute certainty in regard to everything in existence. The fourth *jñāna* has a bearing on the world and its good, and is devoted to the service of humanity. It is a knowledge of manifesting an infinite number of *nirmāṇa kāyas* in response to the different needs of different persons.

Some people are disposed to look upon Mother as a *Vilāsa*, a self-project in time and space of the Timeless Divine. I do not know how far this view is tenable. If the conception Nārāyaṇa (of Vaikuṇṭha) as a *Vilāsa* of Śrī Kṛṣṇa (of Goloka) be the true conception of *Vilāsa*, which involves loss of power and knowledge in relation to the original, we shall find it difficult to explain her own statements regarding Herself like the following:

"Yet here the aforesaid holds good, for this body responds strictly to the line of thought and to the spirit in which a question is asked. Consequently, what is the opinion of this body and what is not? If there is a line of approach there must be a goal to which it leads and beyond that is the unattainable. But where the distinction between the attainable and the unattainable does not arise is THAT Itself. What you hear depends on how you play the instrument. For this body the problem of difference of opinion in no wise exists." [1]

This statement cannot apply to a *Vilāsa* for obvious reasons.

Is She then the Divine in its *svayaṁ rūpa*, in its plenary and perfect Form? Is She then a visible expression of the Absolute Itself? Is She the outer manifestation, within a self-imposed veil, of the Inner *Ātmā* of the world, of all of us, revealed to us clothed in a human form simply to draw us towards Herself away from the turmoils and tumults of fettered existence? Who can say?

It is believed by some that Mother has come down on a definite mission, viz to awaken divine consciousness in man and bring love and peace into the present world. But some deny this on the ground that Her actions are purposeless in the sense that they are actuated by Divine Will directly and not by a personal will of Her own as an ordinary individual. In any case it seems clear that a descent or manifestation so remarkably great as this cannot fail to have a great consummation in its own course. She never claims to be a Teacher, though she sometimes seems to function as such indirectly, for the Teacher is one who has the limitation of teachership attached to him on account of his pure *vāsanā*. But the Mother is free from every kind of *vāsanā* as such from the very beginning. She claims to be Herself alone — nothing more and nothing less. In a sense She is perhaps the very Truth which the Teacher promulgates.

We are often told that Mother has no mind and no body. The meaning of the statement does not seem to be clear, at least to some of us. To me it means that the statement is intended to convey the sense that as an ordinary body or physical organism, together with its term of existence as a vehicle of worldly experience, is due to one's prior *karmas* maturing for fruition and having their

---

[1] *Words of Sri Anandamayi Ma*, p. 119.

roots in ignorance, Mother, on account of Her immunity from these causal factors, cannot be said to bear the burden of such a body and of such a mind. It means that even a pure body and a pure mind cannot be really attributed to a person who is eternally free from ignorance and *karma*.[2]

In all cognate schools of Indian thought we are familiar with a similar conception of the relation between *karma* and body. In Jainism, for instance, we are told that *jīvanmukti* follows on the wake of the cessation of what is called *ghātī* or obscuring *karma*, viz, *karma* which deludes, obstructs and obscures knowledge and intuition. But the *aghātī karma*, which gives rise to experience of pleasure and pain, determines one's term of life and status and builds one's body, continues.[3] Even a *Tīrthaṅkara* is not immune from this. When even these are destroyed there is an absolute cessation of *karmas* and the body ceases to exist. It is a bodiless state of *Ātmā*. *Kevala jñāna* emerges at the end of *ghātī karma* which implies the end of impure mind (and of impure body), while Perfection arises at the end of *aghāti karma* which means the cessation of pure body and pure mind as well.

Similarly in Buddhism we find that an *Arhat* or *Jīvanmukta* is liberated from *kleśas* and is consequently free from a defiled mind. But this is not an essential character of the *Arhat*, for even a person in *nirodha samādhi* as one in the meditation on nothing-

---

[2] It is evidently for this reason that the human body of Sākyamuni was pronounced illusory in the ancient Buddhist work *Sadharma Puṇḍarika.* The view of this work on the life and achievement of Gautama Buddha has been ably summed up by Poussin and is reproduced below: "Although completely divine, Sākyamuni is not God, he is Buddha from the beginning, he is the father of the worlds, the father of the future Buddhas and Saints, the universal Providence in order to save human beings and to lead them to *Nirvāṇa*. He appears in a human form which is illusory; he is born, teaches and enters *Nirvāṇa* — as least as far as ordinary men can see; but in reality, while illusory Sākyamunis are appearing in this world, the true Sākyamuni reigns on a divine "mountain of vultures surrounded by future Buddhas and imparting to them the true teaching, the true law". Even the true Sākyamuni, according to the teaching of *Saddharma Puṇḍarīka*, though eternal and divine, is not God.

[3] These correspond to *jāti*, *āyu*, and *bhoga* of Patañjali.

ness or a *vītarāga* or an *ānāgāmī* has his lower mind inhibited (though not cleansed, as it reappears on reawakening). The lower mind is held in abeyance in the supernormal way also for a definite period. Even an *Arhat* has to experience the fruits of his earlir *karmas*. Maudgalāyana, for instance, was a great *yogin*, the greatest perhaps among Buddha's disciples, and yet he was tortured and his body cut to pieces by robbers and even the bones were powdered. Buddha explained that this was a retribution of a heinous *karma*, viz patricide committed by him in an earlier life.

How then are we to account for what appears like Mother's body and mind? May they not be due to an act of the Supreme Will playing in its freedom, or to the same Will in response to the cumulative *karmas* of humanity crying out for ages for a Divine Appearance? It comes to this, then Mother's body is no body and Her mind is no mind in the ordinary connotation of terms. They are only apparent and exist for the ignorant who are under *māyā* and unable to see behind the veil. This is a docetic view to be sure, but there seems to be no escape from it. Did we not hear of it in connection with the Buddha's body and also the body of Jesus Christ? Did not Śrī Kṛṣṇa too say that he did not really take any birth and had no *karma* of his own like ordinary men and that his birth and *karma* were both divine in nature?

Mother herself said once as to whether the persistence in consciousness of a body is consistent with the dawn of knowledge:

"For a Self-realized Being neither the world with its pairs of opposites exists, nor does the body. If there is no world there can obviously be no body either!

Who says the body exists? There is no question at all of name and form. To wonder whether a realized Being sees anything outside of himself is also beside the point. Who is there to whom he can say: 'Give, give'? Yet this state of wanting is precisely the reason for one's belief in the reality of the body. Therefore, since there is no world and no body, there can be no action either; this stands to reason. To make it quite clear: after Self-realization there is no body, no world and no action — not even the faintest possibility of these — nor is there such an idea as 'there is not'. To use words is exactly the same as not to speak; to keep silent or not is identical — all is THAT alone." [4]

This is in regard to persons who have awakened to eternal life from the torpor of worldly existence.[5] It is equally applicable certainly with a greater force to those who have never been in that existence.

-IV-

We hear of general complaint that Mother's language is not intelligible. The complaint is unfounded in so far as it relates to the language used by her in ordinary correspondence and conversation. The language of *Mātri Vāni* extracted from letters written to Mother's dictation is, for instance, simple, graceful, straightforward and luminous. The complaint is perhaps true when we consider the language employed for interpreting profound experiences and transcendent truths. But it should be remembered that supramental truths do not easily lend themselves to an expression on the lower or even on the higher mental levels, to which alone our language is adapted. It seems to me that what appears to the average reader with his logical bent of thought-structure as a riddle is a plain truth on a higher level of consciousness and has been recognized as such by eminent philosophers and saints. What looks like contradiction in logic and on the finite plane of mind, is verily a truism when the threshold of consciousness is lifted and we are face to face with the Infinite.

I propose, therefore, to analyze some of Mother's well-known utterances which are apparently meaningless, and try to see if we

---

[4] *Words of Sri Anandamayi Ma*, p. 118.

[5] The context refers to the life of the young queen Chūḍala who realized Self-knowledge through *yoga* and *jñāna* and converted her ignorant husband Sikhidhvaja. It was asked how Chūḍālā could possibly conduct the affairs of the world after her Self-realization, instead of keeping herself as the witness of all that happened in nature's course. Mother said in reply that true knowledge burns out the worldly life and with that the body also.

can discover any great significance in them. Out of a large number of sayings we have chosen a few by way of illustration. This will give an idea of what, for want of a better word, we might call Mother's outlook on life and reality.

(a) Yātā (या'ता'): This expression cannot be easily rendered. The usual rendering would be something like 'It is what it is'. These words are often uttered by Mother when She speaks of the Absolute. It is difficult to say what it exactly stands for. One may equate it with the conception of Pure Being, Non-Being, Self, the Infinite, the Ineffable, the Universal, the Immaculate, the Immutable etc. according to one's point of view. It si the Nameless referred to under different names and the Formless under different forms. She also speaks of it as *Charam Param* (चरम परम) in the sense of Ultimate Reality. As for the implications of this enigmatical expression we may compare the following sayings of Mother Herself:

i) Whether you say it exists or does not exist, or that it is beyond both exisence and non-existence, or even beyond that — as you please.

ii) Whether you call it the One, the Two, or the Infinite, whatever anyone may say, all is well.

iii) When this is possible the wall is not there, although it exists and even if no wall exists, yet it is there.

iv) For the Supreme it is possible to be everything and yet nothing.

v) A state of being exists where it is immaterial whether He assumes a form or not — what is, is He.

vi) In this state of complete poise nothing at all is any longer apart from Him; what is, is the Thing Itself.

This shows that in it there is no difference at all — not even between Being and Non-Being, between Light and Darkness, between Good and Evil, between Motion and Rest and between Personal and Impersonal. All is one — one is all. Even the equation is not possible, for True One is where there is no sense of the one. All this sounds paradoxical, but it is the highest truth. Nāgārjuna says:

शून्यमिति न वक्तव्यमशून्यमिति वा भवेत् ।
उभयं नोमयं चेति प्रज्ञाद्यर्थं तु कथ्यते ॥

It means that it cannot be described as void or non-void, nor even as both void and non-void simultaneously, or as above the two modes of statements. Whatever is expressed in language is only a thought and appeals only to the thought-level of human consciousness.

We have a similar description of the Supreme Reality by Mañju Śrī when he refers to the *dharmakāya* of the Buddha. Thus Mañju Śrī says:

यो नैको नाप्यनेकः स्व-परहित-महासम्पदाधारभूतौ, नैबाभाबो न भावः खमिव समरसो दुर्विभाव्यस्वभावः । निर्लेपं निर्विकारं शिबमसमसमं व्यापिनं निष्प्रपञ्चं, वन्दे प्रत्यात्मवेद्यं तमहमनुपमं धर्म्मकायं जिनानाम् ॥

"The Body of the Truth is neither one nor many, it is the foundation on which the great wealth of individual or universal good is based. It is neither Being nor Non-Being; it is a state of balance like the *Ākāśa*; its nature is beyond man's power of imagination; it does not allow itself to be attached to anything and be soiled by it; it is free from change; it is auspicious; it is equal as well as unequal at one and the same time; it is all-pervading and trascendent."

We have an utterance in a similar strain from the great *yogin* Abhinava Gupta of Kashmir in a still later age. The following lines are addressed by the Guru to the disciple who has attained to Supreme Realization:

भावानां न समुद्भवोस्ति सहजस्त्वद्-भावजा भान्त्ममी
निःसत्यामपि सत्यतामनुभवभ्रान्त्या भजन्ति क्षणम् ।
त्वत् -सङ्कल्पज एव विश्वमहिमा नास्तस्य जन्ममान्यतः
तस्मात् त्वं विभवेन भासि भुवनेष्यकोऽप्यनेकात्मकः ॥
यत् सत्यं यदसत्यमल्पबहुलं नित्यं ह्यनित्यञ्च यन्
मायाभिर्मलिनं यदात्मविमलं चिद्-दर्पणे राजते ।
तत् सर्वं स्वविपर्श-संविदुदयाद् रूपं प्रकाशात्मकं
ज्ञात्वा स्वानुभवाधिरूढ़महिमा विश्वेश्वरस्त्वं स्मर ॥

"Things do not emerge of themselves — they appear only when they are thought out by Thee (projected by Thy imagination). They are unreal and yet for a moment seem to be real due to experience which is only apparent. The glory and grandeur of this creation is the result of Thy will and has its source nowhere else. It is for this reason that Thou, though one, shinest in all these worlds as many by virtue of Thy self-multiplying power.

"Whatever shines in the mirror of consciousness — be it true or false, small or great, eternal or temporary, defiled through *māyā* or pure by itself — all these experienced on the dawn of the Supreme Wisdom is of the nature of *prakāśa* and marked by reflective self-knowledge, Thou, the Lord of the world, realizing Thy greatness through personal intuition, wilt preserve in Thy memory."

The *yogins* speak of two-fold *samādhi*, *viz nīmilana* and *unmilana*. In the former aspect One alone shines in its unity — undifferentiated unity — and one may say that the sense of unity is absent. One is, but it is not aware of itself as one. This means that *Śakti* does not function. In the other aspect *Śakti* is unceasing in its movement, producing in consciousness a sense of one, many-in-one, one-in-many and many. And yet the two aspects are mysteriously one and the same in reality. They are co-eternal, and truly speaking they represent a single truth. The Great *Prakāśa*, infinite in its extension, is wonderful — all contradictions are solved in that Light and it seems as if darkness and light have lost their difference in meaning in that unity.

(b) Kheyāla (ख्याल): It is also very difficult to render correctly and in terms intelligible to the average reader the exact significance of the expression *kheyāla* used often by Mother in Her discourses. Ordinarily it means a sudden and unexpected psychic emergence, be it desire, will, attention, memory or even knowledge, without any adequate causal antecedent behind to account for its origin. There is thus an element of spontaneity in the act. It might thus seem to be analogous to the playful vagaries and caprices of an eccentric and non-purposive mentality. The word is in popular use. Mother has borrowed it and used it in Her own sense, enriching it with Her own associations.

Why one becomes many, why the primal Unity, Being and Power, divides itself into infinite varieties in creation, why the subject itself becomes the object of its own action, or why the Ineffable splits itself up into subject and object is a mystery which no man can dare to unravel. All that we can say is that it is due to an act of the ultimate One, which is named *kheyāla* by Mother and is variously named by various thinkers. By some it is called the Lord's *Svabhāva*, for the One Being free from desires cannot have any desire (*devasyaiva svabhāvo 'yamāpyakāmasya ya spūhā*). By other it is called *krīḍā* (play) (*krīḍato bālasyeva krīḍāṁ tasya niśāmaya*) or *līlā* (*lokavattu līlākaivalyam*). By others still it is called Will (*icchā*) emanating from the overflow of Bliss (*ānanda*) on the white screen of Eternal Consciousness (*cit*) and followed by creative action (*kriyā*). It is called the Divine Word or Logos. It is in fact the Will-to-become where in reality there is neither any will nor any becoming. It is called by different names in different systems of thought. The expression *kheyāla* as used by Mother covers all these senses.

We have spoken of the Supreme Reality, the Ultimate One, as Mother refers to it, and of the expression of its outgoing inner act in the form of what She describes as *kheyāla*. Divine Power is really inscrutable — it is one and yet embraces an infinite range, each being associated with a function appropriate to it.

But we should remember the general truth that behind the outer manifestation each power is within every other as identical with it, so that all powers are latent within each. This is as true in the centre as in every sphere of the manifestation. Still, however, we should confine ourselves, in all schemes of intellectual analysis, to the basic powers of the Divine Reality. The following lines describing the working of some of the central powers may be of some use for a clearer understanding of the empirical side of the Divine Mind. There are, if we may say so, different centres of Being and Consciousness in the Divine Self, and corresponding to these there are different centres in man. So long as man is ego-centric, his actions which follow from his individual will constitute *karma*, the consequences of which in the form of pleasure and pain he has to reap in life. As he believes himself to be the doer of the action independently of Divine initiative, he is affected by its consequences. If he could realize truly that he had no power of his own and that even his will does not really belong to him but forms an expression of the divine Will, he would get rid of moral responsibility. It would be the beginning of Wisdom when a man could see the working of a general Will behind all phenomena in man and nature. Going deeper down along the line he would find that there is no will left in him — no, not even a shadow of it. He then finds no will in the Divine Consciousness as well, for he cannot find in God what he is unable to find in himself. Evidently this refers to a centre in God beyond will — a centre in which will is absent but from which will in the lower centre springs. This centre is the inner Divine Śakti from which Will, Knowledge and Action issue forth in separate streams — it is the centre of *Ānanda* or Divine bliss and love. Behind *Ānanda* is the uncoloured *Cit* or Supernal Light where even Joy transcends itself through self-obliteration. This is the Supreme Divine Power co-related and co-eternal with the Supreme Divine Essence in a sort of undifferentiated oneness. All contradictions and conflicts lose their strength of opposition and become one with the One.

The divine power of action (*kriyā*) is *māyā* controlled by *Īśvara*. The world, as we know it in its lower material aspect, is a product of *māyā* and is under *Īśvara* who, as its moral governor, is responsible for the maintenance of righteousness and justice. The principle of justice called *niyati* as a natural and moral law operates in this world and is inviolable. Man being ignorant and ego-centred sows seeds of *karma*, the fruits of which are awarded by Īśvara in strict conformity to the principle of justice. It is asserted by some that the *karmas* bear their own fruits under the laws of Nature. But these laws are in the ultimate analysis explicable as the dictates of an inscrutable Will in the Divine Centre of that name. For God is law. It was in this sense that *Dharma* used to be identified with the Buddha and *Guru Vākya* is identified with the Guru and the Word of God with God.

The will is of the nature of the general Will and has no special or individual reference. A man who has the insight to see behind his own will has the privilege of discovering in the Divine Will the hidden spring of the Cosmic Laws which regulate individual existence. He sees clearly that like the general Will, special Will also has its place in the centre. Looked at from this view-point God would appear to him as love (*prema*) and compassion (*mahākaruṇā*), which is the fulfilment of Law. If it is true that Law prescribes penalty for its transgression, that any offence is bound to be visited with punishment in proportion to its gravity to meet the demands of justice in nature, it is also true that Love condones, makes amends, forgives and atones. There is no conflict between the two — the special Will or Love when it is exercised simply supplements the general will expressed in Law. Both are forms of *Icchā*. The overflowing qualities of Love and Grace are not in any way incompatible with the evenness of judicial outlook. For does not Śrī Kṛṣṇa say in the *Gīta* that even in the midst of his evenness and impartiality there is a sort of hidden partiality towards those who love him:

समोऽहं सर्वभूतेषु न मे द्वेष्योऽस्ति न प्रियः ।
ये तु भजन्ति मां भक्त्या मयि ते तेषु चाप्यहम् ॥

Between Will and Action is to be found the place of Knowledge, both intuitive and rational. This is judgment, for action follows judgment, which is the function of knowledge as a power.

[6] We all know that some *Vaiṣṇava* philosophers of the mediaeval ages used to distinguish between different aspects of Divine Unity. Thus for instance *Svayaṁ Bhagavān* and *Bhagavān* on one hand and *Bhagavān* and *Paramātmā* on the other are distinguished. There is no functioning of *Māyā* and *Taṭastha Śaktis* (extrinsic and neutral divine powers associated with the manifestation of the soul and with the creation of the world) within the central domain of *Svayaṁ Bhagavān* (God in Himself) or even of *Bhagavān* (God), where the intrinsic Divine Powers consisting of *Sandhinī*, *Saṁvit* and *Hlādinī* as connected with the triple aspects of Supreme Godhead (viz Being, Consciousness and Bliss) alone prevail. But while the latter (*Bhagavān*) represents mainly the Majesty (*aiśvarya*) and Compassion (*karuṇā*) of the Lord, the former (*Svayaṁ Bhagavān*) adds to them His Beauty (*saundarya*) and Love (*prema*). For this reason Goloka, the abode of the former, is distinguished from Vaikuṇṭha, the abode of the latter. Both are

In other words the special Will is in the inmost Centre wherefrom Love and Grace flow out; and general Will functions as the judicial and the executive. With knowledge it is concerned with judgment and with Action it is concerned with its execution. This is how the world administration is being carried on.[6]

Beyond Special Will is the Centre where there is no longer any will at all. The entire creation is there in total abeyance. Creation begins with will and ends with its cessation, both in the individual and in the cosmos. The cessation of will opens out into the centre within the Divine Consciousness, where one enjoys the bliss of communion with the Self, for what the mystics call 'spiritual marriage', generally from the view-point of a basically dualistic Self, is a reflection of the Self-delight of God. This state is free from all outgoing urges and is self-contained. On the background

---

Heavens, but while Vaikuṇṭha is Heaven proper in its highest form, Goloka, though higher than Vaikuṇṭha, is centrally situated and is the most secret region resembling the earth *minus* its defects. Similarly the Lord of Vaikuṇṭha is the Lord proper, being exclusively divine in character, while the Lord of Goloka is human and hides His highest divinity within humanity. Even in Goloka the most secret centre is the Vrindāvana where humanity and love alone have their play. The Lord of Goloka is Śrī Kṛṣṇa as the Divine Man and the Beloved in Vrindāvana is Śrī Kṛṣṇa as man *per excellence.*

In the same way there is a distinction between *Bhagavān* and *Paramātmā*, because *Bhagavān* as such has nothing to do with *māyā* and *taṭastha śaktis*, while *Paramātmā* is the controller of both, as a result of which the worlds and the souls come out into light and begin to function. The Intrinsic Power is there too, for without it the souls or the spiritual monads could not have been manifested and the *Ikṣaṇa* of *Paramātmā* which disturbs the equilibrium of *māyā* could not have been effected. The subsequent history of creation down to the formation of earth and of individual human beings is concerned with the four hypostases of *Paramātmā*, *viz* the four so-called *vyūhas*. The world administration in all its phases including the making and enforcement of Law is entrusted to them. Lower Grace leading to *kaivalya* (freedom from *māyā*) and higher Grace leading to admission into the higher world of Nārāyaṇa (Vaikuṇṭha) or of Śrī Kṛṣṇa (Goloka and Vrindāvana) flow from the respective sources above the *vyūhas*. All these plays are due to the action of *Śakti* or the Divine Power. Brahman, however, in which power is not manifest, stands in its eternity and self-centred aloofness as the silent witness at it were of all these plays. Really it cannot properly be described as the witness also, though it is self-luminous.

of this *Ānanda* there is the all-expansive *Cit*, infinite in extension, continuous, self-revealed, unitary and self-sufficient. These two are expressions of the Divine Power which is always in undivided union with the Godhead.

Now God in His essence is above all activity, but His Power is always bubbling with activities, though it is also true that somewhere in Beyond, God and his Power are absolutely One.

What Mother calls *kheyāla* is really an upsurge of Will in a particular direction which is undoubtedly free and not indicated in the plan of things — it is usually connected with the domain of special Will rather than general Will. No law governs this region and there is no interruption in its freedom of activity. Even predestination which takes into consideration the triple flow of time curren t is not an appropriate word for an urge which knows nothing but the Eternal Present. There is no consideration of an outside factor — *karma* (merits and demerits) or anything of the sort has no meaning there. It is also difficult to say whether it is intellectual or volitional. It has all the freshness of a playful and apparently unpurposive act holding within itself incomprehensible possibilities.

(c) *Jā haye jāy* (जा हये जाय): Literally the expression means the attitude of one's abiding by God's disposal by all means and at all times. It implies an unconditional surrender to the Divine Will which shapes the course of events. Man does not know what lies in store as a possibility in the womb of the future. Ordinarily he has his own likes and dislikes and wishes that the future should be according to his liking. But his life or resignation begins when he is free from these likes and dislikes and is prepared to accept gladly and without murmur whatever turn events may take in the future. This attitude of perfect equanimity under all circumstances makes one really free in spirit, as it does not allow outer forces to disturb the even poise of the mind, but it also makes oneself strong enough to welcome even sorrows as joys. Whatever happens in life or in the world has really the sanction of God's will, and as this will, however it may affect the actual happening, is believed to be not only in consonance with the demands of justice but also truly auspicious, one is able to greet with joy everything that takes place in life or in the world. But the expression also implies an attitude of passive but self-conscious complaisance in Divine Dispensation. As coming from Mother's lips it cannot have the possible sense of forced resignation to the inevitable.

-V-

Mother says that the teachings of all lines and of all teachers, provided they are genuine and proceed from the right sources, are correct and should be followed by those for whom they are meant. They may be opposed to one another, but that does not detract from each its peculiar value as a distinct path leading to the goal set before it. If this path is self-consistent and lies unblocked till the end of the journey it will not mislead, though it may carry the pilgrim to a sectional truth and not the *whole* Truth. But if the pilgrim has within him genuine aspiration for the Supreme Reality, Reality will assert itself and overtake him at any point of the journey. In that case the sectional truth will be either brought into relation with the Whole and make a step in its direction or will be converted into a medium through which the Supreme Truth will reveal itself. The Ultimate Truth is one and the Way to it is also one. An earnest seeker, free from worldly attachments and desires, has no reason for disappointment. What is needed is unfailing patience, grim resolution, persistent endeavour, unflinching faith in Divine Providence and unconditional surrender to the Divine Will, preceded by a life of purity, devotion and self-dedication.

Mother has no line of Her own, no particular teaching or doctrine. She recognizes that though at bottom the Way is unique, it assumes varied forms as the temperaments and capacities of individuals are varied. The true test of real advance in spiritual life lies in the gradual purification, illumination and transformation of the human soul whereby in the end it may be restored to its lost unity with the Divine. She is at times very eloquent on the deprecation of the so-called spiritual favours including revelations, visions, locutions etc. and exhibitions of occult powers. Not that they are always bad or inspired by dark forces, but the point to be remembered is that they have generally a tendency to deflect us from the right path, which consists in a single-minded and all-absorbing attention to the great Aim held in view. She does not, however, actually comment, even in an indirect manner, on anybody's personal experiences. She simply wants that we should be guarded against what Śrī Aurobindo calls "the valley of the false glimmer". Usually these experiences arise from perverted imagination or alien powers, hostile or neutral. Self-deception, She points out, is always possible on the path. In very rare cases these favours are real and welcome and may be helpful on the path. In such cases there is no harm in allowing them to continue, though even then, the *sādhaka* should not actively co-operate with them until he feels strongly fortified against all outer influences. It is very important to bear in mind that the strength of personal will, self-consciousness and power of rational discrimination should not suffer in any way.

It is thus intelligible that Mother is tolerant to all. She sees the bright side of every object and every event and asks all to do the same as far as they can. Everything has its own use and importance. People have different points of view. What one says from his own view-point may be as true as what another says from his own. She speaks to people from their own standpoints so that they may understand Her well, showing that She is familiar with all. This is the secret of Her universal sympathy and compassion. She always makes it clear that different people with different temperaments and intellectual backgrounds have to be led in different ways.

A great World-Teacher said that "there are many mansions in my Father's house". Mother says that there are really infinite mansions and that there are infinite ways leading to each, and yet what She insists on is that we should not forget the fact that the House is one. All the creatures live in the same house and are members of one and the same family. They all have descended from One and are parts of One and verily One and the Same. Differences are in appearance only due to *māyā*, but even this is in reality the play of the One. When we are ourselves again we are bound to realize this. Though She moves about from place to place She is always aware that She is in the same house — movement and rest, many and one are always co-existent in Her consciousness; nay, they are aspects of the self-same Reality, indeed the Reality itself is aspectless.

For the same reason people of different creeds and persuasions find in Her their strongest support, each for reasons best known to himself. *Karma*, *jñāna*, *yoga* and *bhakti*, in fact all the ways of spiritual life, find their best exponent in Her. She knows the value of each, the relation of one with the others and the fact that all are simultaneously operative. She recognizes the different grades of spiritual advancement and yet She is emphatic — of course to those who can appreciate it — that the universal and integral self-revelation of God is always sudden and the question of a Moment does not rise, for it never happens in time. She teaches the law of moral and spiritual causality on the analogy of natural law and yet She stresses the supreme value of Divine Freedom which stands above all laws and restraints. She attaches great importance to Teachers and yet She holds that even Teachers need not be indispensable. She reconciles all conflicts in Her own inimitable way, saying that behind all varieties and diversities one Truth shines in its own glory and adds strength to every position.[7]

There is a deep meaning in Mother's utterances, some of which may seem to be obscure to a casual reader. It should not be thought that Mother is not accustomed to speak in plain language. So far as Her ordinary speeches are concerned, speeches addressed to the people of the world coming to Her in search of blessing or assurance for direction in a state of trouble or embarrassment, they are simple, straight-forward, free from ambiguity and full of wisdom and compassion.

[7] The reader anxious to have some clear ideas of these teachings may consult with profit *Mātri Vāṇī* and *Words of Sri Anandamayi Ma*. The first of these books contains extracts from Mother's letters addressed to people seeking consolation and advice; and the second contains Mother's answers to questions asking for light on great metaphysical problems of a *sādhaka*'s inner life.

From what has been said above one may have a faint idea of what Mother is like and what Her central teachings are, but it would be a futile attempt to try to estimate Mother's position on the strength of what little we know about Her. We must go beyond surmises and grip Reality in its heart. The best thing for us would be to try to love Her deeply and sincerely as Mother, and by loving Her to bring ourselves into closer and closer union with Her true Self. I felt this years ago and feel this even now. I am convinced that as a result of this process Mother will surely reveal Herself to us more and more fully according to the degree of our fitness and receptivity, and that we shall then be in a fortunate position to know *immediately*, and not through our intellect which sees through a veil and perverts what it sees, what Mother truly is. And in so knowing Her we shall be able to know our own selves also. For She is verily one with us. No intellectual approach, however free from predisposition and prejudices, is capable of revealing the heart of truth.

So much of disharmony and opposition in the world today, engendering bitterness and strife, is due to our lack of sympathy and sense of oneness. The root-cause is the lack of self-knowledge. There is but one Self which is Love and Wisdom eternal, and we shall share it if we but know it in a proper way. Discord and hatred are bound to disappear like mist before the light of the sun. It will herald the advent of a New Life in the world, when the central principle of Unity and Love will reign and dominate all its thoughts and activities.

May Mother hasten that glorious day and shower Her blessing on humanity.

Other books of related interest
published by **Indica Books**:

- **A Journey in the World of the Tantras**
  by *Mark S.G. Dyczkowski*

- **The Aphorisms of Siva**
  The Śiva Sūtra with Bhāskara's Commentary, the Vārttika
  tr. with exposition & notes by *Mark S.G. Dyczkowski*

- **The Stanzas of Vibration**
  The Spandakārikā with Four Commentaries
  tr. with introduction and exposition
  by *Mark S.G. Dyczkowski*

- **Abhinavagupta's Commentary on the Bhagavad Gita**
  Sanskrit text with English translation, introduction and notes
  by *Boris Marjanovic*

- **Vijñāna Bhairava**
  The Practice of Centring Awareness
  Sanskrit text, English translation. and commentary by *Swami Lakshman Joo*

- **My Days with Sri Ma Anandamayi**
  by *Bithika Mukerji*

- **Death Must Die**
  Based on the Diaries of Atmananda
  by *Ram Alexander*